LEARNING TO USE

OFFICE 2000

FOR NEW CLAIT & CLAIT PLUS

ANGELA BESSANT

Heinemann Educational Publishers,
Halley Court, Jordan Hill, Oxford OX2 8EJ
A division of Harcourt Education Ltd

Heinemann is a registered trademark of Harcourt Education

OXFORD MELBOURNE AUCKLAND JOHANNESBURG BLANTYRE GABORONE
IBADAN PORTSMOUTH NH (USA) CHICAGO

First published 2002
2006 2005 2004 2003 2002
10 9 8 7 6 5 4 3 2 1

A catalogue record for this book is available from the British Library on request.

ISBN 0 435 45234 7

Designed by Artistix, Thame, Oxon

Typeset by TechType, Abingdon, Oxon

Printed and bound in Great Britain by Thomson Litho Ltd, East Kilbride, Scotland

Please note that the examples of websites suggested in this book were up to date at
the time of writing. It is essential for tutor's to preview each site before using it to
ensure that the URL is still accurate and the content is appropriate. We suggest that
tutors bookmark useful sites and consider enabling students to access them through
the school or college intranet.

Acknowledgements
The author and publishers would like to thank the following people and
organisations for permission to reproduce photographs: Corbis/David H Wells –
page 21; Epson – page 5; Anthony King, Medimage – page 3; Photodisc – page 6.

Screenshots reprinted with permission from Microsoft Corporation.

Tel.: 01865 888058
Website: www.heinemann.co.uk
www.bessant.co.uk

Contents

Introduction

In order to become proficient in using a computer, it is necessary to practise. This book enables you to do that, leading you through Microsoft Office 2000 applications step by step so that you can build up confidence. Currently, Microsoft Office 2000 is the most commonly used suite of applications. It contains word processor (Word), spreadsheet (Excel) and database (Access) applications (amongst other things) that can be used together to produce documents. The documents are created and saved within the particular applications and then sections can be inserted into a final integrated document. This is very useful for generating reports, presentations and longer documents where graphics and sections from spreadsheets and databases need to be combined. Applications in the Microsoft Office suite have many things in common making them user friendly.

This book, which has been endorsed by OCR, covers units for OCR Levels 1 and 2 Certificate for IT Users (New CLAIT* and CLAIT Plus), but it would be equally suitable for anyone wanting to learn Microsoft Office 2000.

Part 1 covers Units 1 (core), 2, 4, 5 and 7 of the OCR syllabus for New CLAIT:
* Unit 1   Using a Computer (Windows 98, Windows Explorer, Word).
* Unit 2   Word Processing (Word).
* Unit 4   Spreadsheets (Excel).
* Unit 7   Graphs and Charts (Excel).
* Unit 5   Databases (Access).

Part 2 covers Units 1 (core), 2, 3 and 9 of the OCR syllabus for CLAIT Plus:
* Unit 1   Create, Manage and Integrate Files (Word).
* Unit 2   Spreadsheets (Excel).
* Unit 9   Graphs and Charts (Excel).
* Unit 3   Databases (Access).

Using this book

With the aid of the quick reference guides at the end of each chapter, and referring back through the sections for points you are unsure of, there is ample practice material for you to attempt, including sample full practice assignments. In this way, you will consolidate your understanding of the methods used. Answers to exercises are provided on the accompanying CD-ROM. The CD-ROM also contains files that you will need as you progress through the practical work. You need to make copies of these files to your own storage medium, eg hard disk to work on (see Appendix for instructions on how to do this). The Appendix contains information that is useful to know but not essential.

There are many ways of performing a task in Windows 98 and Office 2000 applications, for example via the keyboard, using the mouse or using the menus. For simplicity, the practical exercises demonstrated usually show one method. However, there are instructions given for other methods at the end of the chapters or in the Appendix. You will then be able to decide which is the best method for you.

Default settings

Default settings are those that are automatically chosen the first time you use Office 2000. In the main, this book uses default settings. It is easy to change settings to suit your way of working. Instructions of how to change the most common settings are included in the Appendix.

Getting Help

In addition to the quick reference guides at the end of chapters and useful information in the Appendix, there is a Help menu in all Office 2000 applications. Pressing the **F1** key will activate help. There is also the Office Assistant. Throughout the book, I have hidden the Office Assistant so as not to be distracted from the main objectives. More details of the Office Assistant are found in the Appendix.

* CLAIT: Clued up About IT.

Accessing the CD-ROM

The answers to the exercises can be found as PDF files on the accompanying CD-ROM. The answers have been saved by chapter with each chapter being a separate folder.

To access the answers to exercises:

1 Load Acrobat Reader.
2 From the **File** menu, select: **Open.**
3 Select the location from where you want to open the file.
4 With the file selected, click on: **Open.**

To print the answers to exercises:

1 From the **File** menu, select: **Print.**
2 A **Print** dialogue box will appear with a number of different options.
3 Make any changes to the printing options as required.
4 Check that the correct printer is selected and click on: **OK.**

About OCR New CLAIT and CLAIT Plus

The scheme

New CLAIT has been developed from the RSA CLAIT qualification, the most widely recognised basic qualification in practical computing and information technology at Level 1. It is aimed at IT users everywhere of all ages, all abilities and needs. CLAIT Plus has been developed from OCR Level 2 qualifications, including RSA IBT II. Since it builds on the skills and knowledge already learnt in New CLAIT, it is the natural progression.

The syllabus

In order to gain full accreditation for New CLAIT, candidates must achieve the mandatory core unit plus four additional units. This book covers the core unit as well as units for some of the most popular computer applications – word processing, spreadsheets and databases. (It is beneficial to have worked through these units before attempting the CLAIT Plus core unit.) Microsoft Office has established itself as a market leader in these applications. This book covers the knowledge and skills that are necessary to achieve competence in the applications above and also covers the skills necessary to achieve competence in charts and graphs. Possessing skills in these applications enables easy progression to the next stage, OCR CLAIT Plus.

This book is endorsed by OCR. For more details of OCR New CLAIT and CLAIT Plus visit the OCR website at www.ocr.org.uk, or you can contact OCR by phone on 01223 552552 for more details.

PART I
New CLAIT

Using a computer (Unit 1)

1 Getting started

This section introduces the knowledge and understanding associated with Unit 1 that is not fully covered in the practical sections. There is also other background information to help you grasp some of the computer jargon.

1.1 Information and communication technology

Information and communication technology (ICT) is the term commonly used to cover the range of computer and telecommunications technologies involved in the transfer and processing of information.

There has always been a need for accurate up-to-date information, even before the advent of computer technologies, but it used to be a time-consuming process to gather and process relevant information. The advent of very large mainframe computers, relying on specialised staff to operate them, brought a change in the ways that big business handled information. Increasingly over the past decades, as the cost and size of computers have decreased, the mainframes have been replaced by powerful, inexpensive desktop personal computers on a colossal scale. Linking these computers together via the Internet has resulted in an explosion in the amount of data being manipulated every day. Today, almost all businesses rely on information communication technology and this has generated an ever-increasing demand for ICT skills in the workplace.

1.2 The computer system

There are two commonly used personal computers. The most widespread of the two is the computer based on the IBM PC, and all clones of this machine are referred to as *PCs*. The PC is predominant in business and commerce. The other common computer is the Apple Macintosh, also known as the *Mac*. This has a niche in creative fields such as music and design.

The computer system consists of *hardware* and *software*. Computer equipment that you can touch and handle is called *hardware*. It is the name given to all the devices that make up the computer system. These devices include the *input devices* (how we get the information into the computer), such as disk drives and keyboards. It also includes the processor (housed in the *system box*) – the 'brains' of the system that carries out all the instructions received from the operator or the program.

Figure 1.1 A typical computer system

Finally, it includes the *output devices* (how we get the information out of the computer), such as monitors and printers.

Computer systems can be standalone (not connected to any other computer), or they can be linked together to form a network so that information can be exchanged and items such as printers can be shared. Networked computers do not have to be in the same building. Using telecommunications, a computer can be linked to another computer anywhere in the world. Computers that are connected together on a network within an organisation are often referred to as *workstations*.

In order for the hardware to do a useful job, it needs to be instructed what to do. *Software* is the name given to the programs, each made up of a series of instructions that tell the computer what to do. There are different types of software: *operating system* software and *applications* software. The operating system software runs the computer and is used to load and run applications software: MS-DOS (*Microsoft Disk Operating System*), Windows, Mac OS and Linux are examples of operating system software. MS-DOS was a typical early operating system for PCs and it is not very user-friendly because it is necessary to key in commands (that you need to remember or look up) so that the computer can carry out the command.

However, Windows operating systems, developed later, are much more user-friendly. Windows is an example of a popular *graphical user interface* (*GUI* – pronounced 'gooey') operating system. It uses *icons* (small pictures), a *mouse* and *menus* (you will learn how to use these and other GUI components as you progress through the practical tasks). These make it more intuitive to use and reduce the need to remember complicated commands. Another advantage of the GUI is that what you see on the screen is what you will see when a document is printed. This is known as *WYSIWYG* (What You See Is What You Get).

Word processing, *spreadsheet*, *database* and *drawing programs* are all examples of applications software. *Microsoft Office* and *WordPerfect Office* are examples of integrated applications software. They have popular applications bundled together in one *suite*.

Hardware	Computer equipment that you can touch and handle, eg the monitor, keyboard
Software	Programs that allow the computer to do a useful task

Printers

There are two main types of printer commonly in use: *inkjet* and *laser*. Both inkjets and lasers are quiet in operation and print to a high quality. Lasers are generally quicker and produce the highest-quality output. All types have models available to print in black and white and/or colour. Printers come with a recommendation for types of paper, since the quality of paper used has an effect on the quality of output produced. There is sometimes an option of using continuous or single sheet paper. You can choose a specific paper size from the selection available in the software application.

Care of printers

- Do not overload with paper since this could cause a paper jam.
- Ensure that paper is loaded straight so avoiding skewed printouts.
- Avoid spilling drinks and crumbs on the printer by not eating or drinking near it.
- Do not pile things on top of it.

Figure 1.2 Inkjet and laser printers

1.3 Storage of data

Data stored on a computer can be saved to various mediums, eg hard disk, floppy disk and compact disk (CD). These are accessed using alphabetically named *drives*.

Hard disks (usually Drive C)	Most computers have hard disks installed. A hard disk is a fixed disk positioned inside the computer system box that can hold a large number of programs and a large amount of data.
Floppy disks (for use in Drive A or B)	The 3^1/$_2$" floppy disk (Figure 1.3) has become the norm. It is a removable storage medium (it can be taken away and used on another computer). The amount that can be stored on a floppy disk depends on whether it is single or double sided and whether it is single, double or high density. The 3^1/$_2$" disk has a hard plastic case (protecting its floppy interior) with a metal cover which slides back when the disk is placed in the disk drive so that it can be read or written to. Some disks come ready formatted, but if not, the first time you use a new floppy disk, you must *format* it so that it is configured for your particular system (see Appendix for how to do this). On floppy 3^1/$_2$" disks there is a small tab in one corner that slides across to write-protect it so that anything stored on it cannot be deleted or amended.
CD (for use in Drive D)	CD is an acronym for compact disk. A compact disk is a removable storage medium that holds huge quantities of data, eg an entire encyclopaedia. There are different types of CD. A *CD-R* is a recordable CD that can be recorded on once only. A *CD-RW* allows unlimited recordings. A *CD-ROM* is for reading from only. Software such as Microsoft Office is usually distributed on CD-ROM.

Care of removable disks

- Handle disks with care at all times.
- Always store disks carefully.
- Keep the disks away from anything magnetic.
- Keep the disks away from direct heat, eg radiators or sunlight.
- Do not touch the exposed recording surface.

Figure 1.3 Floppy disk

1.4 Backing up

It is always a good idea to produce a *backup* (exact copies) of your files on a regular basis. (See the Appendix for how to produce a backup.) Things can go wrong and, if they do and your files become *corrupted* (damaged) or deleted, you will be able to revert to the safely stored versions. It is best to store the backups in a safe and separate place, away from your computer or office. Backups can be created as often as you want depending on how often you update your files. Generally the more often files are updated, the more often you will need to make backups so that you have a very recent copy to fall back on.

If there is a power cut when you are using your computer, the documents and information that you have not saved to disk will be lost. It is important that you save your work regularly so that you will minimise the amount of effort required to redo the work in such situations. Occasionally the computer may just *crash* (sometimes called *freezing* or *hanging*), ie cease to function, either because there is a program error or a more serious system problem. You may be able to recover your work. If it is a program problem, restart the program. If it is a system problem, restart the computer by pressing the keys **Ctrl**, **Alt** and **Delete** (all at the same time). If this does not have any effect, try the **Reset** button (this does a *warm boot*, ie the power supply is not turned off). As a last resort, turn the computer off and then restart it (a *cold boot*). Specialised disk recovery programs are available for retrieving all or part of the data from damaged files.

1.5 Limiting access

For security reasons, you should be aware of how you can limit access to your computer and files that are confidential or that you do not want changed. Computers can be password protected so that only an authorised user can access the data on them. In some organisations several passwords are needed to access strictly confidential data, giving added extra security. Document files can also be password protected. Screen savers can be useful so that people walking past do not see what is on your screen. These can be password protected too. It is always good practice to use a password that is not easy for anyone to guess and it must not be divulged to anyone. Taking such precautions makes it difficult for *hackers* (unauthorised illegal users) to break into the system to steal or alter confidential information or plant *viruses* (see below).

Computers should be sited in places that:

- are not easily accessible, so that they cannot be stolen (they should be security marked so that they can be easily traced if necessary);
- have fire and smoke alarms;
- are kept clean and dust free; and
- do not flood.

1.6 Viruses

A *computer virus* is a destructive program that is buried within other programs received from disk or e-mail. Viruses are written by people with programming skills who want to cause widespread havoc for computer users. Once an infected program is run, the virus coding is activated and usually attaches copies of itself to other programs. Infected programs then copy the virus to other programs. In this way the virus can spread quickly causing irritating effects (such as displaying messages on screen) to severe damage (destroying complete disk contents) to computers and networks. To protect against viruses, always know the source of your software. When downloading software from the Internet, always save it and virus check it before running it. Also be wary when opening e-mails and attachments. If in doubt, do not open a suspect e-mail but delete it. In May 2000 the *Iloveyou* virus affected 10% of business computer systems in the UK alone and many more throughout the world, costing millions of pounds. It was spread via e-mail. The reason the virus spread so quickly was because people rushed to click on the e-mail attachment; it opened their address book and was then e-mailed to everyone listed.

Antivirus utility programs are available and can alert you to a virus and remove (*disinfect*) it. They are a good 'insurance' investment. They must be updated on a regular basis to cope with any new viruses. If you are unfortunate enough to have a virus on your computer, close down the computer and restart it using a write-protected floppy *boot disk* (a disk that contains the essential elements of the operating system) and then run an antivirus utility. Always remember to backup your files. Then even if the worst has happened and your files have been destroyed, you will be able to replace them with the backup copies.

1.7 Data Protection Act 1998

The UK Data Protection Act was first passed in 1984 and has since been updated (1998) to give full effect to the European Directives on Data Protection. It now not only sets rules for processing personal information on computers but also extends to paper-based records. It gives individuals the right to know about the information held on them. Personal data is kept for many reasons, eg by tax offices, personnel departments, banks and hospitals. Everyone who processes and stores information should register as a data controller with the Data Protection Commissioner. If an individual feels that information is not being properly used, he or she can contact the Data Protection Commissioner who will investigate the claim. There are strict penalties (unlimited fines) for anyone who does not comply with the rules. There are eight principles to ensure that information is handled properly. These are:

Personal data shall be:

- Fairly and lawfully processed.
- Obtained only for one or more specified purposes.
- Adequate, relevant and not excessive.
- Accurate and where necessary kept up to date.
- Not kept for longer than necessary.

- Processed in line with the rights of data subjects.
- Kept secure.
- Not transferred to countries outside the European Economic Area without adequate protection.

1.8 Health and safety

Computing environments must conform to the *Health and Safety at Work* (*HASAW*) legislation. An employer is responsible for providing a safe and comfortable working environment. When you are using a computer it is important that you make yourself comfortable otherwise you may become easily fatigued, ill or injured. *Repetitive strain injury* (*RSI*), an injury arising from making awkward movements or the prolonged use of particular muscles, is a recognised condition. Eyestrain and headaches have also been linked to working with computers. Minimise any risks by being aware of the following:

Positioning of the screen	All screens should be adjustable so that you can set them up for your requirements in order to avoid muscle strain in the neck and shoulders. The screen should be directly in front of you, roughly at arm's length. The top of the screen display should be just above eye level.
Positioning of documents	To prevent visual fatigue and muscle tension and to minimise re-focusing and twisting the neck, these should be near to the screen, at the same height and distance.
Positioning of keyboard	If your keyboard is not comfortable – ie it is placed too near to the edge of the desk so that there is nowhere to rest your wrists – you could put unnecessary strain on your wrists causing RSI. Wrist rests are available.
Using the mouse	Ensure that you are using the mouse correctly. Keep it in a comfortable position and rest your fingers lightly on the buttons. Do not grip it too tightly.
Type of chair	An adjustable chair is essential. Your back should be straight and your feet should rest on the floor. Your forearms should be roughly horizontal when using the keyboard.
Lighting	Screen glare should be avoided by adjusting background lighting and using window blinds or positioning the screen so that it is unaffected. Anti-glare filters are available. Flickering of the screen should be optimised by selecting a high scan rate.
Ventilation	Adequately ventilated working areas should be provided.
Frequent breaks	When working at the computer for prolonged periods, it is important to take frequent breaks every hour to stretch and walk around. Give your eyes a rest so that they do not become tired and sore from staring intently at the small screen area. Focus them in the distance. Consider the possibility that spectacles may be helpful even if you do not normally wear them.
Ensure equipment is safe	It is important to have equipment checked periodically to ensure that it is safe to use. Power cables should be secured so that they cannot be tripped over and power sockets should not be overloaded. Any cable damage should be repaired.
Look after your computer	Do not eat and drink while using your computer. Crumbs can become lodged in the keyboard and spilled drinks can cause quite serious damage. Do not pile things on top of the monitor, system box or printer as this could block air vents. Computers should not be moved when they are in use since this may cause damage to the hard disk.

Working with Windows

This section contains practical exercises to familiarise you with your computer and Windows 98. You will learn how to:

- switch the computer on
- recognise parts of the Windows desktop
- recognise parts of a Window
- shut down the computer
- work with passwords and login to a system
- use the mouse
- access Help

2.1 Switching the computer on

Exercise 1

Switch on the computer.

Method

1. Ensure that the computer is plugged into the electricity socket.
2. Press the button on the computer system box (and on the monitor, if it has a separate button) to switch the power on.
3. The computer will perform its start-up checks and load Windows 98 and accessories (this is sometimes called *powering up* or *booting up*). This can take some time during which there will be whirring noises from the system box and text will scroll across the screen. Eventually you will see the Windows 98 desktop displayed. The items that appear on this screen depend on how your computer is set up. It will look something like Figure 1.4.

Note: The small pictures that Windows 98 uses to represent things, eg programs, documents that you have saved (files) and so on are called *icons*.

 If you are using a password-protected computer, you will need to find out what the procedure is to login and what user name and password you should use. Typically something like the boxes shown below appear on screen.

| New password: | | New password: | xxxxxxxxx |
| Confirm new password: | | Confirm new password: | |

If you choose/change your own password, you should use something that you will remember but, at the same time, something that is not easy for anyone else to guess. Your password may be restricted to a certain number of characters.

When you enter your password, it will appear in a form similar to that shown so that no one can take a sneaky look at it. You will be asked to confirm your password by keying it in again. This ensures that you keyed it in correctly.

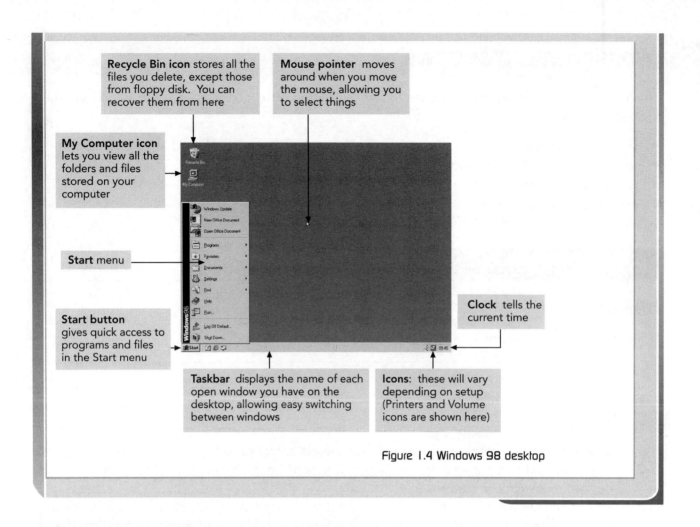

Recycle Bin icon stores all the files you delete, except those from floppy disk. You can recover them from here

Mouse pointer moves around when you move the mouse, allowing you to select things

My Computer icon lets you view all the folders and files stored on your computer

Start menu

Start button gives quick access to programs and files in the Start menu

Clock tells the current time

Taskbar displays the name of each open window you have on the desktop, allowing easy switching between windows

Icons: these will vary depending on setup (Printers and Volume icons are shown here)

Figure 1.4 Windows 98 desktop

2.2 Using the mouse

The mouse lets you select and move items on the screen. When you move the mouse on your desk, the mouse pointer ⍀ moves on the screen in the same direction. You will notice that the mouse pointer changes depending on where it is and what it is doing. A typical mouse has a left and a right button. These can both be used to select and choose options. In Windows 98, the right mouse button is usually used to access alternative context-sensitive pop-up menus. Some mice have a wheel that is very useful for scanning through documents.

Mouse terms

Click: Press and release a mouse button.

Double-click: Quickly press and release a mouse button twice.

Drag and drop: When the mouse pointer is over an object on your screen, press and hold down the left mouse button. Still holding down the button, move to where you want to replace the object. Release the mouse button.

Hover: Place the mouse pointer over an object for a few seconds so that something happens, eg another menu appears, or a *ToolTip*.

Exercise 2

An excellent way of practising mouse skills is to play the game *Solitaire* that comes with Windows 98. Practise now.

1 To start Solitaire follow the directions given in Figure 1.5.

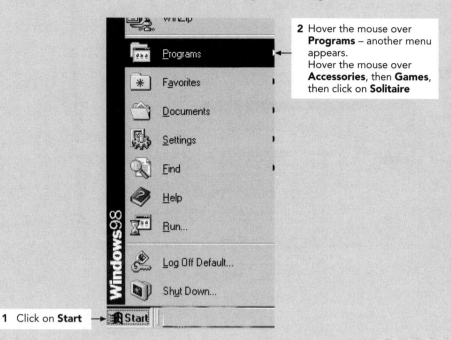

2 Hover the mouse over **Programs** – another menu appears.
Hover the mouse over **Accessories**, then **Games**, then click on **Solitaire**

1 Click on **Start**

Figure 1.5 Starting Solitaire

 If you do not have *Solitaire* on your computer, load any other **Accessories** program and practise some of the skills shown below.

2 The **Solitaire** window appears (Figure 1.6). Notice that the taskbar, at the bottom of your screen, now displays a button for Solitaire.

Minimise button: reduces window from the screen. Redisplay by clicking the left mouse over its button on the title bar

Menu bar   Title bar

Maximise button: window fills screen

Close button: closes the window

Drop-down menu

Mouse pointer

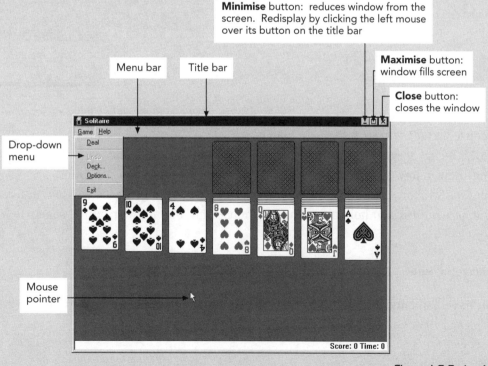

Figure 1.6 Parts of a Window

To play Solitaire:

3   On the **Menu** bar, click on: **Help**; a menu appears.

4   Click on: **Help Topics**; the **Solitaire Help** window appears.

5   Click on: the **Contents** tab, if not already selected (on top of **Index** and **Search** tabs).

6   Click on: **Playing Solitaire** (Figure 1.7).

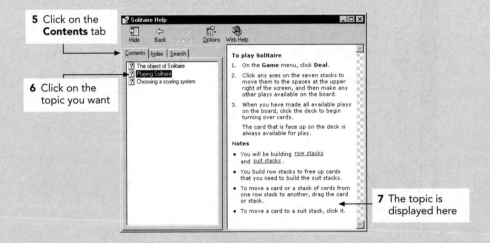

Figure 1.7 Solitaire Help Window

7   The rules of the game are displayed in the right-hand pane.

8   When you have read the rules, click on: the **Close** button of the **Solitaire Help** window (Figure 1.8).

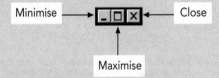

Figure 1.8 The Close button

You are now ready to play Solitaire!

Practise:

● The mouse actions whilst playing the game.
● Using the menus to get Help and choose other options for the game.
● Moving the window by pointing to the Title bar and dragging and dropping.
● Resizing the window by moving the mouse pointer over the edge of the window until a double arrow appears. Press and hold down the left mouse and drag to the required shape. Release the mouse.

Note: To keep the same proportions of the window, drag from a corner.

When you have had enough practising, from the **Game** menu, click on: **Exit** or click on: the **Close** button.

Exercise 3

Practise getting help with any topic from Windows 98 Help, as follows.

Method

1   Click on: the **Start** button, then on: **Help**. The **Windows Help** window appears (Figure 1.9).

a Click on the **Index** tab, if not already selected

b Key in the name of the topic you are looking for. In this exercise, key in **date** (case does not matter)

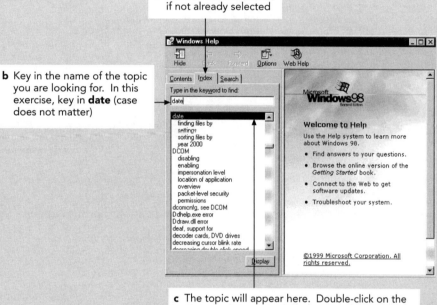

c The topic will appear here. Double-click on the topic or click on the topic and then on **Display**

Figure 1.9 Windows Help

2   The **Topics Found** box appears (Figure 1.10). A list of date-related topics is given.

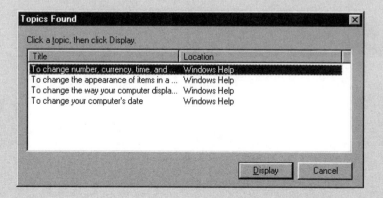

Figure 1.10 Topics Found

3 Choose a topic by double-clicking on it. I have chosen *'To change your computer's date'* and the **Windows Help** appears displaying help in the right-hand pane (Figure 1.11).

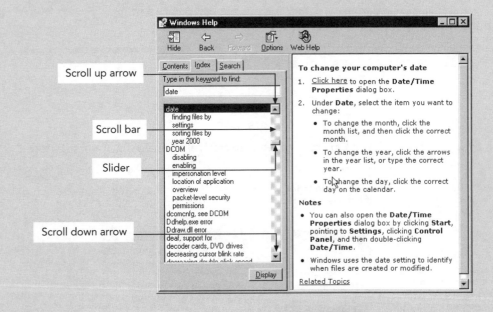

Figure 1.11 Specific windows help is displayed

Scroll bars

When a window is not big enough to display all the information in it, scroll bars appear, vertically and/or horizontally (see Figure 1.11).

Practise:

- Clicking on the scroll bar arrows to move through the index entries.
- Dragging the slider along the scroll bar to move more quickly through the entries.
- Searching for other Help topics.

When you have finished searching for Help topics, close the Help window by clicking on: the **Close** button.

2.4 Shutting down the computer

Exercise 4

Shut down the computer correctly.

1   From the **Start** menu, click on: **Shut Down**. The **Shut Down Windows** dialogue box appears (Figure 1.12).

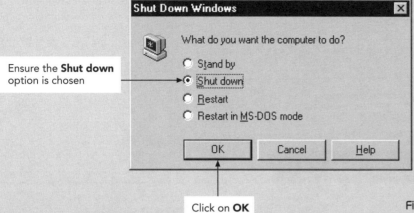

Ensure the **Shut down** option is chosen

Click on **OK**

Figure 1.12 Shutting down Windows

2   A message *'It's now safe to turn off your computer'* is displayed. Your computer may then switch off automatically. If not you can now switch off using the button on the system box.

It is important that you shut down Windows correctly when you have finished your work. If not, files may become corrupted. If you have any work that you have not saved, you will be asked if you want to save it before shutting down. Any work that has not been saved will be lost when the computer is switched off.

It seems odd to use the **Start** menu when you want to stop using the computer. What you are actually doing is 'starting' the shut down process.

Section 2: checklist

Are you familiar with the following?	
Starting the computer	
Using the mouse	
Recognising parts of the desktop and parts of an application window	
Using Help functions	
Reducing/enlarging a window	
Resizing, rescaling and closing a window	
Moving windows on a desktop	
Shutting down the computer	

3 Windows Explorer

This section contains practical exercises to familiarise you with *Windows Explorer*. Windows Explorer allows you to view all the folders and files on your computer. It is useful for disk and file management. You will learn how to:

- start Windows Explorer
- recognise folders and files
- use the Recycle Bin
- close Windows Explorer

3.1 Starting Windows Explorer

Method 1

From the **Start** menu, select: **Programs**, then: **Windows Explorer**.

Method 2

Right-click on: **Start**. Select: **Explore** from the pop-up menu.

The **Exploring** window appears. In the example (Figure 1.13), $3^1/_2$ Floppy (A:) drive is selected in the left (**Folders**) pane and the contents of the disk in Drive A are displayed in the pane on the right. Your window may not look the same since Drive C may be selected. Do not be concerned about this.

Note: If your window has a different layout, you may be in Web Page View. From the **View** menu, select: **as Web Page** so that there is no tick next to it.

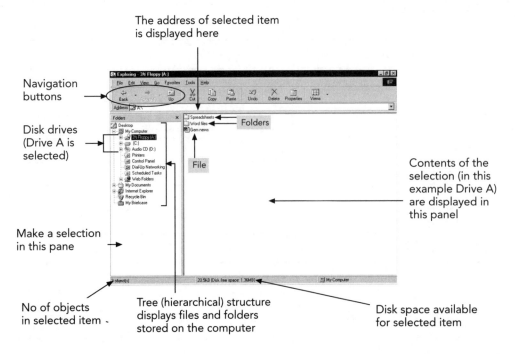

Figure 1.13 Windows Explorer

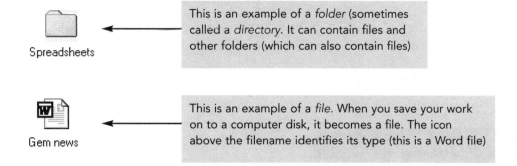

Spreadsheets

This is an example of a *folder* (sometimes called a *directory*. It can contain files and other folders (which can also contain files)

Gem news

This is an example of a *file*. When you save your work on to a computer disk, it becomes a file. The icon above the filename identifies its type (this is a Word file)

Displaying the contents of a folder

Double-click on: the folder.

 It is better to double-click the icon rather than the text as sometimes you will not get the action you expect (if you have not double-clicked properly). Instead a box may appear round the text, waiting for your input. If this happens, press: **Esc** and try again.

Creating a new folder

You can create new folders in which to store related documents. This is always good practice as it makes for easier location at a later date.

Example

To create a new folder on the disk in drive A:

1   In the left-hand (**Folders**) pane, click on: $3^1/_2$ **Floppy (A:)**.

2   The contents of the floppy disk in Drive A are displayed in the right-hand pane.

3   Right-click in: the white space of this pane. A menu appears.

4   Select: **New** and then: **Folder.**

5   Key in the name for the new folder and press: **Enter.**

Deleting a file/folder

Select the file/folder you want to delete by clicking on it. Press: the **Delete** key. You will be asked to confirm file delete. Click on: **Yes.**

Note: When you delete a folder, its contents are also deleted.

You can restore a deleted file (*not one deleted from a floppy disk*) from the **Recycle Bin** by clicking on: the **Recycle Bin,** selecting the file you want to restore and selecting: **Restore** from the **File** menu.

Emptying the Recycle Bin

It is a good idea to remove files from the Recycle Bin from time to time to save cluttering up the hard disk. To do this:

1   Click on: the **Recycle Bin** to select it.

2   From the **File** menu, select: **Empty Recycle Bin.**

3.4 Closing Windows Explorer

From the **File** menu, select: **Close.**

Section 3: checklist

Are you familiar with the following?	
Starting Windows Explorer	
Recognising folders/files	
Understanding file/folder structure	
Closing Windows Explorer	

Inputting data using Word

This section contains practical exercises to familiarise you with the keyboard, more general Windows skills and the application *Word*. Word is a word processing application. You will learn how to:

- load Word
- use the keyboard
- key in text, numbers and symbols
- insert text, numbers and symbols
- delete text, numbers and symbols
- save your work
- close Word

Note: Unit 1 assesses basic text-editing skills. Therefore an application such as *Notepad* or *WordPad* could be alternatives for this unit. Word is covered in more detail in Chapter 2.

4.1 Loading Word

Exercise 1

Load Word.

Method

1   Switch on your computer and wait until the **Windows 98 desktop** screen appears. (*Note:* You may need a password to login.)

2   Hover the mouse pointer over the **Start** button and click the left mouse button – a menu appears (Figure 1.14).

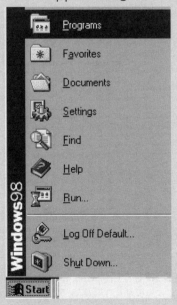

Figure 1.14 Selecting from the Start menu

3   Select: **Programs** by hovering the mouse over it – another menu appears.

4 Select: **Word** by clicking the left mouse on it (Figure 1.15).

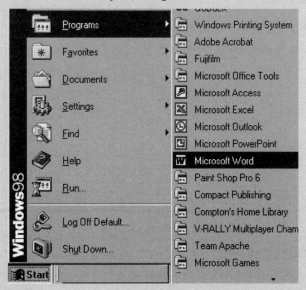

Figure 1.15 Selecting Word

5 The Word window will be displayed on screen looking similar to Figure 1.16.

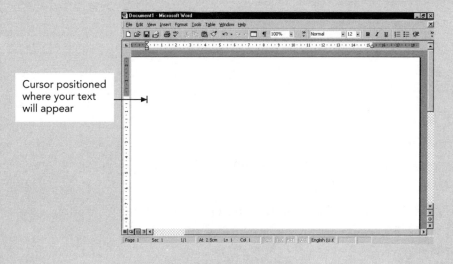

Cursor positioned where your text will appear

Figure 1.16 Word Window

4.2 Examining the keyboard

Exercise 2

Examine the keyboard.

Before keying anything in to Word, take some time to have a close look at the keyboard. Most keyboards are quite similar so it will look something like Figure 1.17. Those who have used typewriters in the past or who can touch type will recognise the standard QWERTY keyboard layout (QWERTY refers to the first six letters on the top row). A computer keyboard has extra keys.

The ones that you need to know about at this stage are labelled in Figure 1.17. They include the following.

Shift key

There are two Shift keys, one at either side of the character keys. They perform the same task so you can use either, whichever is most convenient. Press the Shift key down at the same time as the character key you require to produce an uppercase (capital letter), ie holding down **Shift** and pressing R produces upper case R.

Spacebar   Shift   Enter (or Return)

Figure 1.17 Keyboard layout

Some keys have two characters, eg the number keys above the QWERTY row. For instance the number 1 key also has an exclamation mark !; the number 5 key, a % symbol. To produce the upper part of these keys, hold down the **Shift** key and at the same time press the required key.

Enter (or Return) key

When the text is too long to fit within the space available, it will automatically be carried over to the next line. This is known as *word wrap*. However, if you have not reached the end of a line and you want to move to the next line, you need to press the **Enter** key. If you want to leave a blank line, say after headings or between paragraphs, press the **Enter** key twice.

Space bar

Use the space bar to create a space in between words. Try to be consistent. One space after a comma and one space after a full stop is acceptable, looks neat and is easy to read.

4.3 Keying in text

Exercise 3

Key in the following letters (at this stage do not worry if you make mistakes, you will learn how to correct them later):

qwerty
Leave a space (press the space bar once) and key in:

QWERTY
Move to the next line by pressing: **Enter**.

The keyed in text will look similar to Figure 1.18. Notice how the *cursor* moves with you as you key in.

qwerty QWERTY

Figure 1.18 Text keyed in

Exercise 4

Key in the following text that uses all the letters of the alphabet plus a full stop:

The quick brown fox jumps over the lazy dog.

Exercise 5

Leave a line space by pressing: **Enter** twice and key in your name.

Exercise 6

Leave a line space and key in the following numbers and symbols. Leave a space between each one.

2 ! 4 = 1 / & 3 – 8 # 6 @ 7 : 5 ? £ % * + , 9

Results of your keying in will now look like Figure 1.19.

qwerty QWERTY
The quick brown fox jumps over the lazy dog.

[Your name]

2 ! 4 = 1 / & 3 – 8 # 6 @ 7 : 5 ? £ % * + , 9

Figure 1.19 More keying in

4.4 Moving around

Exercise 7

Now that you have some text keyed in, practise moving around your document.

Here we will learn three methods to move around the document:

1   Using the arrow keys.

2   Using the mouse.

3   Using two keys together, **Ctrl + Home**, and **Ctrl + End**.

1   Moving around your text using the arrow keys

The arrow keys ← ↑ → ↓ (located at the bottom right of the main keyboard) allow you to move the cursor (a flashing black vertical line) in the direction of the arrows. You can move one space forwards or backwards at a time, or you can move up or down one line at a time. If you keep an arrow key pressed down, the cursor will automatically move quickly through the document. Remember to release the arrow key when you reach the required place.

2   Moving around your text using the mouse

As you move the mouse pointer around the screen, you will notice that it turns into an I-beam and moves with you. Move it until you have reached the required position, click the left mouse button once and the cursor will appear where you clicked

3   Using **Ctrl + Home** and **Ctrl + End**

Hold down: the **Ctrl** key at the same time as the **Home** key to move to the start of your document.

Hold down: the **Ctrl** key at the same time as the **End** key to move to the end of your document.

4.5 Inserting text

Exercise 8

Insert the word **cub** between **fox** and **jumps**.

Method

1   Position the cursor at the point where you want to insert text (in this case after the space after the word **fox**), and then key in **cub** and a space (Figure 1.20).

2   Notice how the text to the right of the cursor moves to make room for the new text.

If your text does not move across but overwrites text already there, check that **OVR** is not displayed on the status bar. If it is, press: **Insert** to remove overwrite.

qwerty QWERTY
The quick brown fox cub jumps over the lazy dog.

[Your name]

2!4= 1/&3 − 8#6 @ 7 : 5? £% *+, 9

Figure 1.20 Inserting text

4.6 Deleting text

Exercise 9

Delete the word **quick**. Three methods are shown below. Try each one, reinserting the word **quick** after each deletion in order to delete by another method.

Method 1

Position the cursor to the left of the first character that you want to delete, ie the **q** of **quick** and press: **Delete** until all the letters of **quick** (and the space) have been deleted.

Method 2

Position the cursor to the right of the last character you want to delete and press: ← **Del** (Backspace) key (top right of main keyboard) until all the letters of **quick** (and the space) have been deleted.

Method 3

Double-click on the word **quick** and press: **Delete**.

4.7 Saving

Exercise 10

Save the document using the file name **keyboard**.

The great thing about using a computer is that you can save your work so that you can recall it at a later date to make alterations, update it and so on. Note that the document, when saved, is referred to as a *file*.

1   From the **File** menu, select: **Save As** (Figure 1.21).

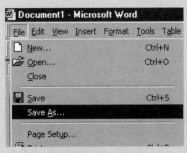

Figure 1.21 Saving a file for the first time using Save As

2   The **Save As** dialogue box is displayed (Figure 1.22).

Click on the down arrow
and then on a location
to store your document

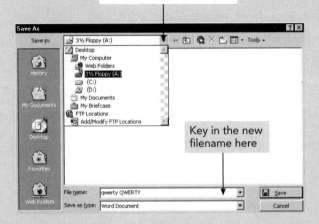

Key in the new
filename here

Figure 1.22 The Save As dialogue box

3   Click on: the down arrow as shown in Figure 1.22 and click on the location where you want to save your document. (If you are saving to a floppy disk, select: **A:** and remember to have your disk inserted in the drive. See INFO box below.)

4   In the **File name** box, double-click on the filename that is already there, ie **qwerty QWERTY**, and delete it by pressing: **Delete**.

5   Key in the filename **keyboard** (case does not matter).

6   Click on: **Save**.

Inserting a floppy disk into the disk drive

Insert the disk metal slider first and with the label side uppermost until it clicks and the eject button pops out.

To eject a disk from a drive

Press: the Eject button on the drive.

Note: Sometimes there are problems when using Drive A because the application program you are using may try to access it when there is no disk in it. If this happens try reinserting the disk into the drive.

Notice that the default filename (**qwerty QWERTY**) has been replaced with the new filename (**keyboard**) on the Title bar.

4.8 Closing the file and exiting Word

Exercise 11

Close the file and exit Word.

Method

Either

From the **File** menu, select: **Close**
From the **File** menu, select: **Exit**

or

Click on: the **Close** button in the top right-hand corner.

> *i* In Word, if you forget to save the document, you will be prompted to do so.

Inputting data practice

Practice 1

1 Load Word.

2 Enter the following leaving line spacing as shown:

Arithmetic/Addition & Subtraction?

6 + 2 – 4 = 4*

***Correct answer!**

Your name and today's date

3 Save the document using the filename **prac1sums**.

4 Close Word.

Practice 2

1 Load Word.

2 Enter the following leaving a line space between each line as shown:

Sales July 01: 25% increase

Profit: £37,000@supplies-2-U

Your name and today's date

3 Save the document using the filename **prac2sales**.

4 Close Word.

In this section you will learn how to:

- open an existing file
- amend an existing document
- resave a previously saved file
- switch on a printer
- load paper
- print a document
- create a new document
- save a document with a different filename

5.1 Opening an existing file

Exercise 1

Load Word and open the file **keyboard** saved in Section 4.

Method

1   Load Word.

2   From the **File** menu, select: **Open** (Figure 1.23).

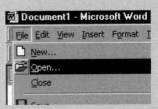

Figure 1.23 Opening a file

3   The **Open** dialogue box appears (Figure 1.24).

Figure 1.24 The Open dialogue box

4   In the **Look in** box, click on the down arrow and then on the location of the file, eg 3$\frac{1}{2}$ Floppy (A:).

5   Click on: the filename, ie **keyboard**.

6   Click on: **Open**.

5.2 Amending

Exercise 2

Using skills learnt in the last section, add the following at the end of the document as shown below, leaving a line space after the existing text:

Learning the keyboard.

Method

1 Move the cursor to the end of the document using one of the methods shown in the previous section.

2 To leave a line space, press: **Enter** twice.

3 Key in the text.

Exercise 3

Delete the symbol @ from the line with the numbers.

Method

Use one of the deletion methods from the previous section. Your document will now look like Figure 1.25. *Note:* Ensure that you still have one space between each character after deletion.

qwerty QWERTY
The brown fox cub jumps over the lazy dog.

[Your name]

2 ! 4 = 1 / & 3 − 8 # 6 7 : 5 ? £ % * + , 9

Learning the keyboard.

Figure 1.25 Document after amendments

It is very important that you pay attention to keying in accurately. Mistakes are easily transferred, eg gas bills for £1,000,000 because someone keyed in too many 0s. There is a computer saying *garbage in garbage out* (GIGO), ie if you key in incorrect information, incorrect information will be stored and printed. Correct any mistakes as you go along.

5.3 Resaving a previously saved file

Exercise 4

Resave the document with the amendments.

 Since you have already saved the first draft of this document, you will now be able to do a quick save instead of using **Save As**. This will overwrite your original with the changes you have made, but still keep the same filename, **keyboard**. If you wanted to keep the original document intact you would need to save the document with a different name using **Save As**. You would then have two files, the original and the amended one.

Method

From the **File** menu, select: **Save**.

5.4 Printing

Note: You will need to ask your tutor or refer to your printer manual for the next exercise.

Exercise 5

Prepare the printer for printing.

Method

1 Locate the printer that is connected to your computer and that is the default printer to be used with Word. (*Note:* There can be more than one printer connected to a computer. The default printer is the one the computer assumes it is printing to unless you tell it otherwise.)
2 Switch the printer on.
3 Load the printer with paper.

Exercise 6

Print the file **keyboard**.

1   From the **File** menu, select: **Print** (Figure 1.26).

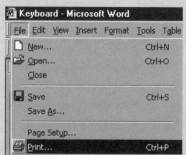

2   The **Print** dialogue box is displayed.
3   Click on: **OK**.

Figure 1.26 Printing

5.5 Creating a new document

Exercise 7

Create the following new document and save with the filename **symbols** and print:

Your name and today's date

I am learning about symbols on the computer keyboard. They are:

* + % = – & £ # / @ ! ? :

I need to be very accurate!

Method

1   With Word loaded, from the **File** menu, select **New** (Figure 1.27).

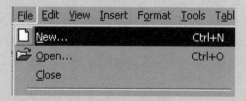

Figure 1.27 Creating a new document

2   The **New** box is displayed.

3   Click on: the **General** tab, then on **Blank Document**, then on **OK**.

Note: Instead of steps 1–3, you could click on: the ☐ **New** button.

4   Create, save and print the document in the normal way.

5.6 Close Word

Editing, saving and printing practice

Practice 3

1 Load Word and open the file **prac1sums** saved in Section 4, Practice 1.

2 Print one copy.

3 On the first line, delete the question mark.

4 Resave the document with the same filename.

5 Print one copy.

6 At the end of the document, leave a line space and on a new line add the following:

10@£3.99

7 Resave the document with the filename **prac3sums**.

8 Print one copy.

9 Close Word.

Practice 4

1 Load Word and open the file **prac2sales** saved in Section 4, Practice 2.

2 Print one copy.

3 On the first line change **July** to **June**.

4 Resave the document with the filename **prac4sales`**.

5 Print one copy.

6 Close Word.

6 Locating and amending files

In this section you will learn how to locate files using file search facilities.

Note: For the exercises in this section you will need to have access to the files **Minutes3**, **Tasks** and **Profits**. These are on the CD-ROM that accompanies this book. In the examples that follow, I have copied the files to a floppy disk.

6.1 Locating files

Exercise 1

Using the operating system's **Find** facility, find the text file **Minutes3**.

Method

1 From the Window's 98 desktop **Start** menu, select: **Find**.

2 From the menu that appears, click on: **Files or Folders** (Figure 1.28).

Figure 1.28 Finding files

3 The **Find: All Files** dialogue box is displayed (Figure 1.29).

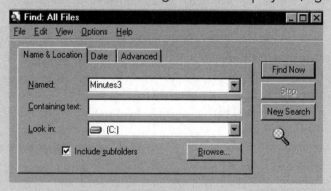

Figure 1.29 Find: All Files dialogue box

4 With the **Name & Location** tab selected (it is positioned in front of the other tabs when selected. If it is not selected, click on it to select it), in the **Named** box, key in: **Minutes3**. (*Note:* Case does not matter but it is important to key in the name correctly.)

5 If you know where it is, eg on a floppy disk, you can select the location by clicking on the down arrow in the **Look in** box and clicking on the location. Otherwise clicking on **My Computer** will ensure that a complete search is made in order to locate it.

6 Click on: **Find Now**.

7 The computer will start to search and when it finds a file with the filename you entered, it will list it in the window below together with the file's location (Figure 1.30). Make a note of the location. (You may need to use the scroll bar to see it in full.)

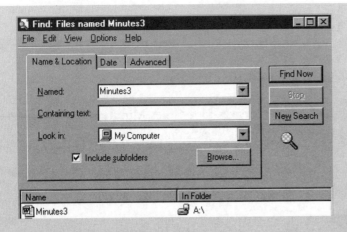

Figure 1.30 File found is listed

8   Double-click on the filename to open the file.

9   It will open in Word.

 In the examples used in this section, files open in Word. If a file does not open in Word but in another application:

    1   Close the application.

    2   Load Word

    3   From the **File** menu, select: **Open**.

    4   The **Open** dialogue box is displayed.

    5   Click on the down arrow in the **Look in** box to access the drive where your file is located.

    6   Click on the appropriate drive so that the files are listed.

    7   Double-click on the file.

If there are still problems opening the file in this way, you will need to discuss it with your tutor.

10   Close the **Find** box by clicking on it (it has minimised) on the taskbar (Figure 1.31), then click on: the ☒ **Close** button.

 Figure 1.31 Find Box – minimised on taskbar

6.2 Amending the file

Exercise 2

Add your name, your centre number and today's date at the end of the document.

Method

Use the methods in the preceding sections to do this.

6.3 Resaving the file with a different filename and print

Exercise 3

Resave the file with the filename **Minutes4**.

Method

Resave and print as in the previous sections.

Locating and amending files practice

Note: For the following exercises you will need access to the files **Tasks** and **Profits** on the CD-ROM.

Practice 5

1 Using the Find facility, find the text file **Tasks**.

2 Using an application that will allow you to read text files (ie Word), open the file **Tasks** in the application.

3 Add your name, your centre number and today's date at the end of the document.

4 Save the document with its original filename **Tasks**.

5 Print the document.

Practice 6

1 Using the Find facility, find the text file **Profits**.

2 Using an application that will allow you to read text files, open the file **Profits** in the application.

3 Add your name, your centre number and today's date at the end of the document.

4 Save the document with its original filename **Profits**.

5 Print the document.

Using a computer quick reference for New CLAIT (Windows Explorer)

Action	Keyboard	Mouse	Right-mouse menu	Menu
Create a new folder	Select where you want the new folder to be			
			New, **Folder**	**File**, **New**, **Folder**
Create a subfolder	Select the folder in which you want the subfolder to be and follow the steps for creating a new folder			
Delete a file/folder	Select the file/folder			
	Delete		**Delete**	**File**, **Delete**
Display contents of folder		Double-click: the folder		
Exit Windows Explorer		Click: the ☒ **Close** button		**File**, **Close**
Format a floppy disk	Select drive			
			Format	
Load Windows Explorer	In Windows 98 desktop			
		Double-click: the **Windows Explorer** shortcut icon		**Start**, **Programs**, **Windows Explorer**

Using a computer quick reference for New CLAIT (Word)

Action	Keyboard	Mouse	Right-mouse menu	Menu
Close a file	**Ctrl + W**	Click: the ☒ **Close** button		**File**, **Close**
Exit Word		Click: the ☒ **Close** button		**File**, **Exit**
Load Word		Double-click: the **Word** shortcut icon		**Start**, **Programs**, **Microsoft Word**
Open a new file	**Ctrl + N**	Click: the ☐ **New** button		**File**, **New**
Open an existing file	**Ctrl + O**	Click: the ☞ **Open** button		**File**, **Open**
	Select the appropriate drive, directory and filename Click: **Open**			
Saving a document for the first time or an existing document with a different filename	Select the appropriate drive and directory and change the filename if relevant			
		Click: the ☐ **Save** button		**File**, **Save As**

Action	Keyboard	Mouse	Right-mouse menu	Menu
Saving an existing document with the same filename	**Ctrl + S**			**File**, **Save**
Printing	**Ctrl + P**	Click: the 🖶 **Print** button		**File**, **Print**

Using a computer quick reference Windows Desktop

Action	Keyboard	Mouse	Right-mouse menu	Menu
Find files/ folders	**Start**, **Find**, **Files or Folders** or in Windows Explorer **File** menu, **Find**			
Login	Enter your user name and password in the appropriate boxes (depending on your system)			
Recycle Bin, restore files	Double-click on the **Recycle Bin** icon Select the file you want to restore			
			Restore	**File**, **Restore**
Recycle Bin, empty			**Empty Recycle Bin**	
Switch on the computer	Ensure that the computer is plugged into the electricity socket. Press the button on the system box to turn the computer on, and on the monitor (if it has one)			
Shut down the computer	**Start**, **Shut Down**			

Hints and tips

- Ensure that you save the documents with the correct filenames.
- Proofread for errors in keyed-in text. In this unit data entry errors are counted per character (max allowed three).
- Can't find a file? Have you keyed it into the **Search** box correctly?
- Password not accepted? Have you keyed it in correctly? Are you using the correct case for each character?

Using a computer: sample full practice assignment

Note: If you want to practise this assignment using a password-protected file you can use **Health1** on the CD-ROM. The password is **Doctor23**. (You must match case when keying in the password.)

For this assignment you will need to use the file **Health** on the CD-ROM. No passwords will be required in this assessment but in an actual assessment they will be. Check that you know how to use them.

Scenario

You are looking to change your role within the large organisation where you work. You have been asked to work through the following tasks to demonstrate that you can use a computer.

Your computer has been set up ready for you to use. You have been given a password to gain access to any files that you need for the tasks. Your tutor will tell you when the password is needed.

1   Switch on the computer and monitor correctly and safely.

2   Wait for the operating system to load fully.

3   Using the operating system's 'find file' or 'search' facility, find the text file **Health**.

4   Using an application that will allow you to read text files, open the file **Health** in the application.

5   Using the mouse and keyboard (or alternatives if available) add your name, your centre number and today's date at the end of the document.

6   Save the document using the original filename, **Health**.

7   Switch on your printer and load a few sheets of paper.

8   Print the document using the default printer settings.

9   Close the **Health** document.

10   Create a new text document using the same software that you used to edit **Health**.

11   Enter the following data as shown, leaving a space between each line:

Computer chairs: Stock Code CC/59#2

@ £95.00–£150 with 10% discount

your name, your centre number and today's date

12   Save this document using the filename **orders**.

13   Print the document using the default printer settings.

14   Close the document **orders**.

15   Exit the application software and shut down the operating system safely.

Chapter 2

Word processing using Word (Unit 2)

 Getting started

In this section you will become familiar with Word and discover the advantages of using a word processor. You will learn how to:

- load Word
- set margins
- enter text
- delete text
- close a file

- understand the parts of the document window
- set text alignment
- insert text
- save a document
- exit Word

Note: Some skills covered in Chapter 1 are repeated here for those who have used an alternative software application for Unit 1. They will act as a refresher for those who have not.

1.1 What is a word processor?

Word processing software applications are the most commonly used computer applications. They allow you to create documents by keying in and manipulating text on screen. The documents can be saved as files and printed. These documents can be stored on disk so that they can be recalled and edited at a later date. Once the basics have been learnt, it is easy to produce professional-looking documents. Microsoft Word is a word processing program. Compared with a text editor (eg *Notepad*), Word has many powerful features, for example formatting text (eg its size, appearance and position), checking spelling, creating indexes and handling graphics. The screen display of the document is usually the same as the printout display. This is known as **WYSIWYG** (What You See Is What You Get). You will learn more about some of these features as you progress through the chapter.

1.2 Loading Word

Exercise 1

Load Word.

Method

1 Switch on your computer and login until the Windows 98 desktop screen appears.

2 Move the mouse cursor over the **Start** button and click the left button – a menu appears.

3 Select: **Programs** by moving the mouse over it – another menu appears.

4 Select: **Microsoft Word** and click the left button (Figure 2.1).

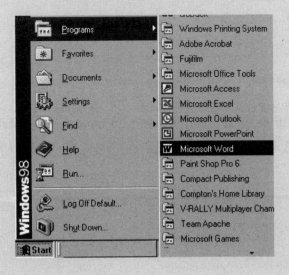

If you have a shortcut icon to Word on your desktop, you can load Word by clicking or double-clicking on: the **W** **Word** icon.

The Word Document window will be displayed on screen (Figure 2.2) showing a new blank document with default values, ie pre-programmed settings such as line spacing, width of margins and font type. These will remain unchanged unless you alter them.

If there is no Document window, click on: the ⬜ **New** button at the top left of the Standard toolbar

Or

Select: **New** from the **File** menu; the **New** window will appear. Click on: **General** tab, **Blank Document** and **OK**.

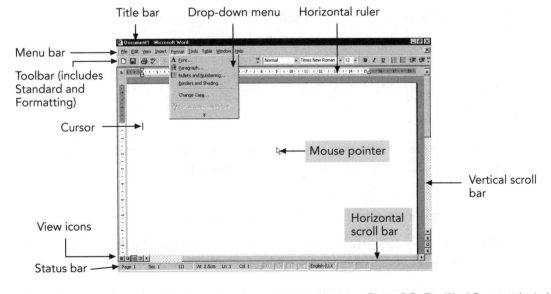

Figure 2.2 The Word Document window

Title bar	This shows the name of the application being used, Microsoft Word, and the current document name, **Document1** (this is the default name).
Menu bar	This has menu names that can be selected using the mouse/keyboard. A *drop-down menu* then gives you further options. This initially displays options used most recently. After a few seconds, the drop-down menu expands to include all available options. These menus will personalise to display your most recently selected options as you progress through your work.
Standard toolbar	This contains shortcut buttons for frequently made actions. For example, to open an existing file, click on: the button shown in Figure 2.3.

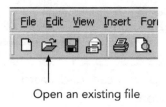

Open an existing file

Figure 2.3 Standard toolbar buttons

To find out quickly what each button on the toolbar does, hover the mouse over the button and wait for a few seconds. A *ToolTip* will appear giving a brief explanation of the button. Try this now.

Formatting toolbar	This allows shortcuts to formatting your document, such as underlining text and centring text.

By default the Standard and Formatting toolbars are displayed together on the same row.

When working towards the New CLAIT qualification it is useful to display both the Standard and Formatting toolbars, in full, on separate rows (the exercises in this book will assume this).

To display the Standard and Formatting toolbars in full on separate rows:

1 From the **View** menu, select: **Toolbars**, then: **Customize**.

2 Click on: the **Options** tab.

3 Click to remove the tick in the **Standard and Formatting toolbars share one row box**.

4 Click on: **Close**.

Note: If you prefer not to alter the toolbars you can still access the remaining options on each toolbar by clicking on: the ⏬ **More Buttons** buttons.

Cursor	The cursor flashes where your text will appear.
Horizontal ruler	This shows the position of text and can be displayed in centimetres or inches. (See the Appendix to change the default.)
Mouse pointer	This will move when you move the mouse – use to select items in the window. The mouse pointer changes shape depending on where it is on the screen.
Scroll bars	You can scroll quickly through your document using the scroll bars.

Status bar	This provides information about the position of the cursor and the text displayed on your screen.
View icons	These allow for different ways of viewing your text. We will be using **Normal View** (the furthest left of the View icons). Click on this now. This view allows fast editing. (See the Appendix for more information on types of View.)

1.4 Setting margins

Margins are the blank space at the top, bottom and sides of text that will be printed on your document. In this exercise you will learn how to set the left and right page margins. You can set margins before or after you have keyed in text. Setting margins before keying in text and making adjustments after keying in text are requirements for New CLAIT.

Exercise 2

Set the left and right page margins to 2 cm.

Method

Note: Before following these instructions, have a look at the horizontal ruler (Figure 2.2). This shows the default width that text entered on the page will be (line length). Make a note of this measurement so that you can see the difference after resetting the margins.

1 From the **File** menu, select: **Page Setup** (Figure 2.4).

Figure 2.4 Selecting Page Setup

2 The **Page Setup** dialogue box is displayed (Figure 2.5). With the **Margins** tab selected, this shows the default margins set by Word, ie **Left** and **Right** margins are 3.17 cm.

Key in the new left margin measurement here

Key in the new right margin measurement here

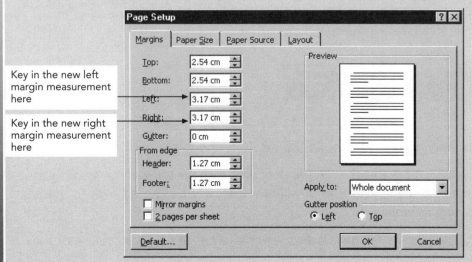

Figure 2.5 Setting margins

3 Click in: the **Left** box, delete 3.17 cm and key in: **2 cm**.

4 Do the same in the **Right** box.

5 Click on: **OK**.

6 You are returned to the document window.

7 Check the horizontal ruler to see the change. The left and right margins are now narrower so the line length is longer.

1.5 Setting alignment

Exercise 3

Set an unjustified right margin and a justified left margin.

There are four types of alignment. They can be accessed via the **Formatting** toolbar (Figure 2.6). Alignment can be set before and after text has been keyed in. When text is fully justified the spacing between words may change slightly to ensure a straight right edge. You do not need to be concerned about this, but should be aware of it.

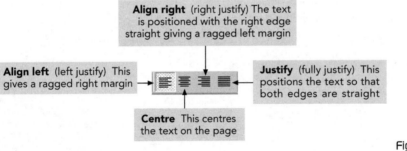

Align right (right justify) The text is positioned with the right edge straight giving a ragged left margin

Align left (left justify) This gives a ragged right margin

Justify (fully justify) This positions the text so that both edges are straight

Centre This centres the text on the page

Figure 2.6 Types of alignment

Method

Click on the appropriate toolbar button. In this case **Align Left** (this is the default so should be already selected).

1.6 Entering text

Before you begin entering text you should be aware of the following:

- You do not need to press **Enter** at the end of each line, because if the text is too long to fit within the space available, it will automatically be carried over to the next line. This is known as *word wrap*.

- To create a space, press: the **space bar** (the wide key at the bottom centre of the keyboard) once.

- You should be consistent with spaces after commas and full stops. One space after a comma and one/two space(s) after a full stop is acceptable, looks neat and is easy to read. You can check that you have been consistent by clicking on: the ¶ **Show/Hide** button. This displays spaces as dots. So one space appears as one dot. To turn Show/Hide off, click on: the **Show/Hide** button again.

- To make documents easier to read, you should leave a blank line after headings and between paragraphs. To do this press: **Enter** twice.

- Organisations have specific *house styles*. These determine how documents should look and when working for an organisation you will need to be aware of their document layout rules.

- To key in capital letters, hold down: **Shift** at the same time as the key for the letter you want to key in.

- If you are keying in a block of capital letters, press: the **Caps Lock** key to start keying in capitals and press: **Caps Lock** again to stop. (See **Change Case** in the quick reference at the end of this chapter.)

- Do not worry if you make mistakes, you can correct them later.

- You may notice that sometimes wiggly lines appear under text that you have keyed in. This is due to the default spellchecking option. To turn this off: from the **Tools** menu, select. **Options**. Click on: the **Spelling and Grammar** tab. In the **Spelling** section, click in: the **Check spelling as you type** box to remove the tick. Click on: **OK**.

For more information on layout, see the Appendix.

Exercise 4

Key in the following text:

Wisdom teeth are so called because they do not appear until the age of 18 to 20 when we are supposed to have become wiser.

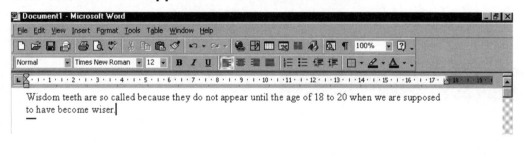

Figure 2.7 The keyed in text will look similar to this

1.7 Moving around your text

Here, we will learn three methods to move around the text:

1   Using the arrow keys.

2   Using the mouse.

3   Using two keys together, Ctrl + Home, and Ctrl + End.

1 Moving around your text using the arrow keys

The arrow keys ← ↑ → ↓ (located at the bottom right of the main keyboard) allow you to move the cursor (a flashing black vertical line) in the direction of the arrows.

You can move one space forwards or backwards at a time, or you can move up or down one line at a time. If you keep an arrow key pressed down, the cursor will move quickly through the document. Remember to release the arrow key when you reach the required place.

2 Moving around your text using the mouse

As you move the mouse around the screen, you will notice that the I-beam moves with you. Move it until you have reached the required position, click the left mouse button once and the cursor will appear where you have clicked.

3 Using **Ctrl** + **Home** and **Ctrl** + **End**

Hold down: the **Ctrl** key at the same time as the **Home** key to move to the top of your text.

Hold down: the **Ctrl** key at the same time as the **End** key to move to the bottom of your text.

 There are other ways to move around the document and these are included in the quick reference at the end of this chapter.

1.8 Inserting text

Exercise 5

Insert the word **usually** between the words **not** and **appear**.

Method

Position the cursor at the point where you want to insert text (in this case immediately before the letter **a** of the word **appear**), and then key in **usually** and a space (Figure 2.8).

> Wisdom teeth are so called because they do not usually |appear until the age of 18 to 20 when we are supposed to have become wiser.

Figure 2.8 Inserting text

Notice how the text to the right of the cursor moves to make room for the new text and some text at the end of the line has automatically moved to the next line.

 If your text does not move across but overwrites text already there, check that **OVR** is not displayed on the Status bar. If it is, press: **Insert** to remove overwrite.

1.9 Deleting text

Exercise 6

Delete the word **of**.

There are three methods:

Method 1

Position the cursor to the left of the first character that you want to delete, ie the **o** of **of** and press: **Delete** until the letters **of** (and the space) have been deleted.

Method 2

Position the cursor to the right of the last character you want to delete and press: **Del ←** (Backspace) key (top right of the main keyboard) until the letters **of** (and the space) have been deleted.

Method 3

Double-click on the word **of** to select it and press: **Delete**.

Try each method. Reinsert the word **of** after each method by clicking on: the ↶ **Undo** button.

Exercise 7

Now try keying in a longer piece of text. Set the left and right margins to 3 cm. Use a justified left margin and an unjustified right margin.

Method

1   Click on: the 🗋 **New** button.
2   Set the margins as specified.
3   Set the alignment as specified.

4 Key in the following text:

(This should not be in bold lettering and the line endings will not necessarily be in the same place.)

Better Travel & Co Information

The cathedral of Pisa in Tuscany, Italy, has a bell tower known as the leaning tower of Pisa. It is a big attraction to visitors to the area.

Why does it lean? Work started on the tower in 1173. When the building was half finished the sandy soil under one half of the circular structure began to subside and the tower tipped. Work was discontinued for a century.

Architects devised a plan to counteract the 5.5% tilt. They decided that two storeys should be built slightly askew so as to alter the tower's centre of gravity. When the bell tower section was added at the top, the extra weight increased the tilting even more!

Ten years ago the tower was on the brink of collapse and closed to visitors. The tower underwent major restoration work at a cost of £3 million. Thirty tonnes of subsoil were removed from underneath it. This allowed the tower to settle under its own weight in a more stable but still leaning position. The tower reopened in June 2000.

1.10 Saving documents

Exercise 8

Save the document.

Method

 Note that the text will now be referred to as a file.

1 From the **File** menu, select: **Save As** (Figure 2.9).

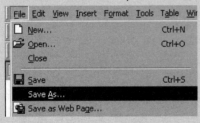

Figure 2.9 Saving a file for the first time using Save As

2 The **Save As** dialogue box is displayed (Figure 2.10).

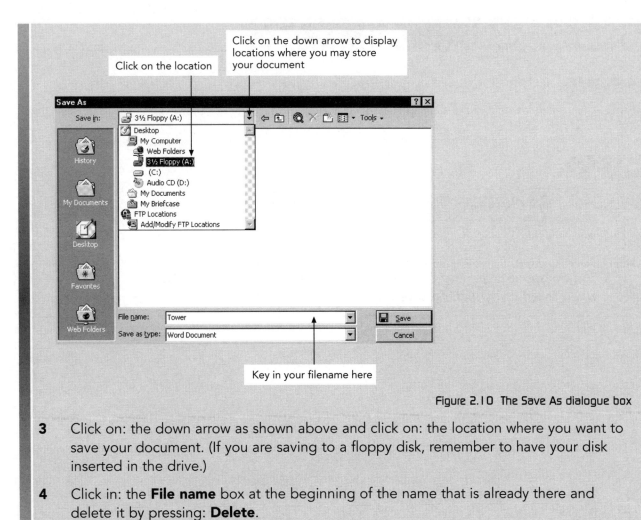

Click on the location

Click on the down arrow to display locations where you may store your document

Key in your filename here

Figure 2.10 The Save As dialogue box

3   Click on: the down arrow as shown above and click on: the location where you want to save your document. (If you are saving to a floppy disk, remember to have your disk inserted in the drive.)

4   Click in: the **File name** box at the beginning of the name that is already there and delete it by pressing: **Delete**.

5   Key in the filename **Tower** (case does not matter).

6   Click on: **Save**.

> Notice that the default filename (**Documentx**) has been replaced with the new filename (**Tower**) on the **Title** bar.

1.11 Closing a file

Exercise 9

Close the file **Tower**.

Method

From the **File** menu, select: **Close**.

1.12 Exiting Word

Exercise 10

Exit Word.

Method

Click on: the **Close** button in the top right-hand corner.

> *i* You do not need to save the one-sentence practice file. Click on: **No** when asked if you want to save.

Word processing practice

Practice 1

1 Create a new word processing document.

2 Set the left and right margins to 2 cm.

3 Enter the following text with an unjustified right margin and a justified left margin:

Electronic Mail Etiquette

It is believed that 87% of Internet users use e-mail. Some businesses cite that they make savings of at least £5,000 per year by communicating in this way.

You should not expect an immediate response to your e-mails. If you require an immediate response, use the telephone. E-mail is there for the user's convenience and not to cause inconvenience!

There has been much debate about e-mail etiquette. There are unwritten rules of business behaviour. These include being polite, being brief and not shouting. Shouting in e-mail terms means using capital letters to make a point stand out. Using too much punctuation, such as repeated exclamation marks to add emphasis is also bad form. Try to express what you want to say in your text.

When using abbreviations, try to stick to the more common ones, such as BTW, meaning by the way, and FYI, meaning for your information. If you received a message would you understand what ROTFL meant? What would be your response?

4 Save your document with the filename **P1 sec1 email**.

Practice 2

1 Create a new word processing document.

2 Set the left and right margins to 2.5 cm.

3 Enter the following text fully justified:

Computer Passwords

It is most important at ABC Financial Services that passwords are used routinely when creating documents that are of a sensitive nature. These include all internal reports, personal letters to customers and to other financial institutions.

All computer systems within this department have recently been upgraded at a cost of £150,000. We estimate that this will be of benefit to 90% of ABC's computer users. This upgrade includes new security access.

Typing in of passwords is now required to access individual workstations. It is very important that you choose your password so that others cannot easily guess it. For example, your boyfriend's name is not a good idea or, indeed, your birth date.

Passwords can be a mixture of letters and numbers to a maximum of fifteen. They are case sensitive. When typing in passwords the characters appear as asterisks on the screen. However, ensure that nobody can see what you are typing in. Always remain vigilant.

4 Save your document with the filename **P2 sec1 passwords**.

2 Editing, formatting and printing I

In this section you will practise and learn how to:

- reload a saved file
- spellcheck
- print preview and print
- change font size
- insert a block of text
- save document with a new filename

- proofread and correct errors
- resave a previously saved file
- change font
- emphasise text – embolden, italicise, underline
- move text
- insert a paragraph break

2.1 Reloading a saved file

Exercise 1

Load Word and open the file **Tower** saved in Section 1.

Method

1   Click on: the 📂 **Open** button.

2   The **Open** dialogue box appears (Figure 2.11).

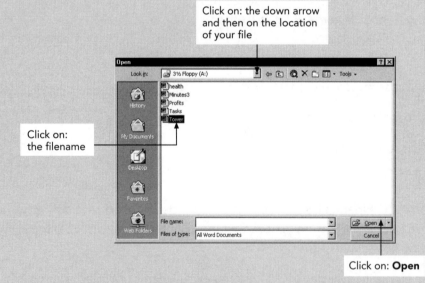

Click on: the down arrow and then on the location of your file

Click on: the filename

Click on: **Open**

Figure 2.11 Opening a file

3   In the **Look in** box, click on: the down arrow and then on the location of your file.

4   Click on: the filename.

5   Click on: **Open**.

It is important to proofread your work carefully against the hard copy. Correct any errors in the text using the methods described in Section 1.

2.3 Spellchecking

It is always useful to run the spellchecker through a document before you print as it will pick up most misspelt words and provide you with the chance to correct them. It will also pick up repeated words, eg the the, so that you can delete one of them. Word provides an option to check spelling and grammar together, or check spelling and grammar as you type, but at this stage it is more straightforward to check spelling only and I have set this option in the examples (see the Appendix for changing the default).

Note: There are limitations to the spellchecker's abilities and it may not pick up wrong usage of words (eg where and were, stair and stare). Although these words are spelt correctly it may be that they are being used in the wrong context.

Always check that you are using the English (UK) spellchecker. From the **Tools** menu, select: **Language**, **Set Language**, **English (UK)**.

Note: Using the spellchecker is advisable, but is not a requirement for New CLAIT.

Exercise 2

Run the spellchecker through the document.

Method

1   Position the cursor at the start of the document by pressing: **Ctrl + Home**.

2   Click on: the 📝 **Spelling and Grammar** button.

3   The **Spelling and Grammar** dialogue box is displayed (Figure 2.12).

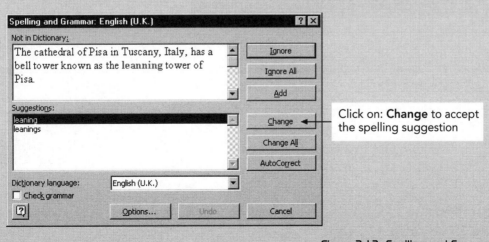

Click on: **Change** to accept the spelling suggestion

Figure 2.12 Spelling and Grammar dialogue box

The spellchecker will go through your text and match it with the words in its dictionary. It will highlight unrecognisable words and offer suggestions. (You may not have made any spelling errors!) In the example above, the spellchecker has highlighted the word **leanning** and it is offering its preferred replacement, **leaning**, also highlighted in the lower box. In this case accept the suggestion by clicking on: **Change**.

If you do not want to accept a suggestion that the spellchecker has made, click on: **Ignore**.

If you want to accept one of the other suggestions, click it to select it and then click on: **Change**.

The spellchecker will repeat this process until it has finished checking all the text. It will then display a message telling you that the spellcheck is complete.

2.4 Resaving a previously saved file

Exercise 3

Resave the file **Tower**.

 As you have already saved the first draft of this document, you will now be able to do a quick save instead of using **Save As**. This will overwrite your original with the changes you have made, but still keep the same filename, **Tower**.

Method

To resave

Click on: the 💾 **Save** toolbar button.

2.5 Print Preview

Exercise 4

Print Preview your document.

Method

If you want to see how your document is going to look on the page before printing it, you can use Word's **Print Preview** facility.

1   Click on: the 🔍 **Print Preview** button. The **Print Preview** screen appears (Figure 2.13).

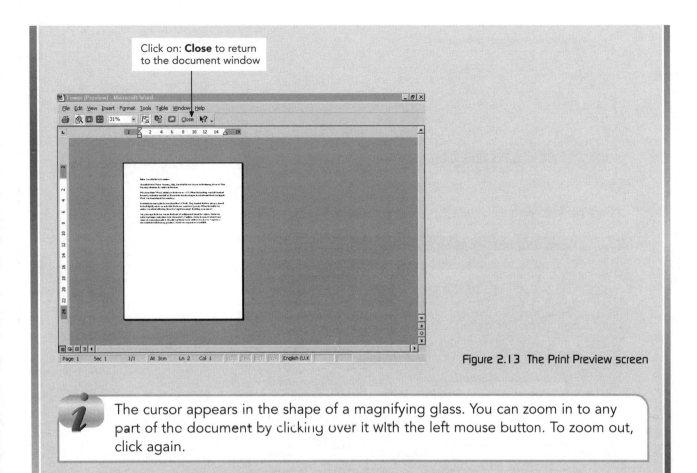

Click on: **Close** to return to the document window

Figure 2.13 The Print Preview screen

> *The cursor appears in the shape of a magnifying glass. You can zoom in to any part of the document by clicking over it with the left mouse button. To zoom out, click again.*

2 Press: **Esc** or click on: **Close** to return to the document window.

2.6 Printing a document

Exercise 5

Key in your name and the date a few lines below the end of the text. Resave the document using the **Save** toolbar button. Print one copy of the document.

Method

1 Move to the end of the document using one of the methods you have learnt.

2 Leave a few line spaces by pressing: **Enter** for each line space.

3 Key in your name and press: **Enter**.

4 Key in the date and press: **Enter**.

5 Resave the file.

Printing

1 From the **File** menu, select: **Print** (Figure 2.14).

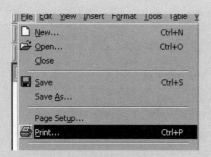

Figure 2.14 File menu, Print

2   The **Print** dialogue box is displayed (Figure 2.15).

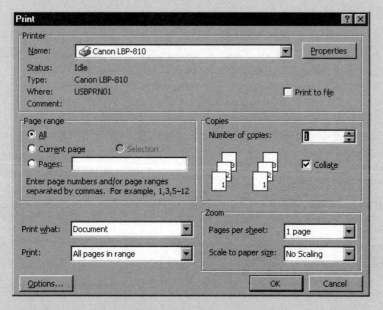

Figure 2.15 Print dialogue box

3   Check that the printer is turned on, ready and loaded with paper.

4   There are several default control options concerning printing, such as number of copies and page range (shown in the **Print** dialogue box). At this stage, you should not need to change any settings, so just click on: **OK**.

Quick method to print

On the toolbar, click on: the 🖨 **Print** button.

Use this if you know that you do not need to alter anything in the Print dialogue box.

2.7 Changing font and font size

Exercise 6

Change the font of the main heading to **Arial** and the size to **16 pt**, ie so that it is larger than the rest of the text.

Changing font type

The term *font* refers to the design of the characters in the character set. In Word there are numerous fonts to choose from. The default font is *Times New Roman*. This is a **serif** font. Serifs are small lines that stem from the upper and lower ends of characters. Serif fonts have such lines. *Sans serif* fonts do not have these lines. Examples:

Times New Roman is a serif font
Arial is a sans serif font

The vertical height of fonts is measured in *points* (*pt*). The default point size is 12 so when asked for a font size larger than the rest of the text, 14 pt or 16 pt would be good choices. Below are some example point sizes:

6 pt
10 pt
12 pt
18 pt
28 pt
36 pt
44 pt

1 Select the heading **Better Travel & Co Information** so that it is highlighted. To do this:

a Position the cursor at the beginning of the text to select – in this case the **B** of **Better**.

b Hold down the left mouse button and drag the I-beam pointer across the heading so that it is highlighted.

c Release the mouse.

There are many ways to select text. These are given in the quick reference at the end of this chapter. There is no right or wrong way. Experiment to find your own preferred method.

2 Click on the down arrow in the **Font** box (where *Times New Roman* is displayed, shown in Figure 2.16) to display fonts that are available on your computer.

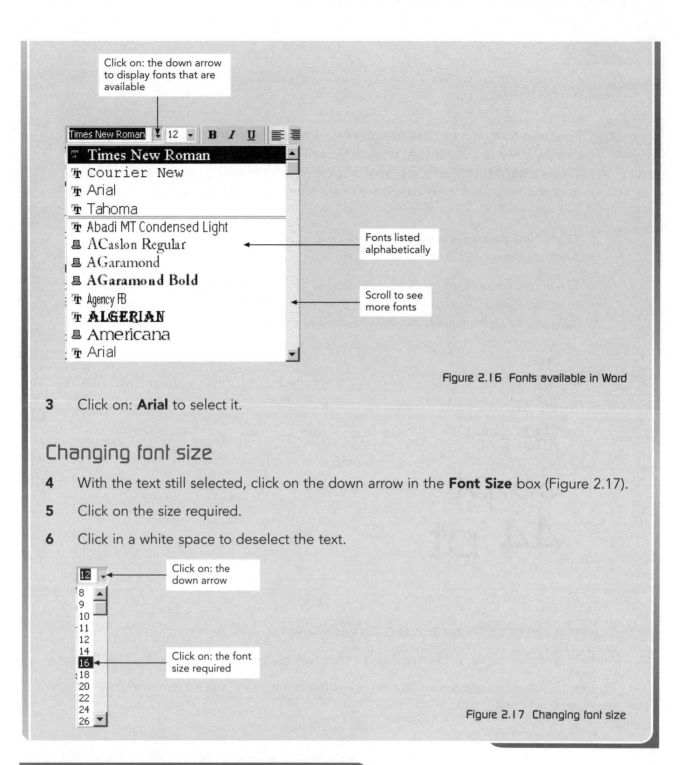

Figure 2.16 Fonts available in Word

3 Click on: **Arial** to select it.

Changing font size

4 With the text still selected, click on the down arrow in the **Font Size** box (Figure 2.17).

5 Click on the size required.

6 Click in a white space to deselect the text.

Figure 2.17 Changing font size

 Emboldening, italicising or underlining text is a way of giving emphasis to the text.

Emboldening text

Exercise 7

Embolden the heading **Better Travel and Co Information**.

Italicising text

Exercise 8

Italicise the word **Tuscany** in the first paragraph.

Method

Follow the method shown above except at step 2 click on: the *I* **Italic** button.

Underlining text

Exercise 9

In the second sentence of the final paragraph underline **£3 million**.

Method

Follow the method shown above except at step 2 click on: the **U** **Underline** button.

When underlining, do not extend the underline before or beyond the words to be underlined as shown in the examples below:

<u>Your name</u> is correct

<u>Your name </u>is incorrect.

2.9 Inserting a block of text

Exercise 10

Using the instructions for inserting text in Section 1.8 and below, insert the new text (shown below) at the end of the first paragraph ending **... attraction to visitors to the area.**

Many people visit Pisa just so that they can have their photograph taken beside the leaning tower. How many visitors would want to see the upright tower of Pisa?

1   Position the cursor after the full stop after the word **area**.

2   Create a space between the sentences by pressing the space bar once/twice (depending on your preferences).

3   Key in the text.

 Remember: When you insert or delete text, check that the spacing between words, sentences and paragraphs is still consistent. Use the **¶ Show/Hide** button to check this.

2.10 Moving text

Exercise 11

Move the first sentence of the third paragraph: **Why does it lean?** so that it then becomes the final sentence of the second paragraph.

Method

1   Select the sentence by dragging the mouse over it as in Section 2.7.

2   Click on: the ✂ **Cut** button. The text will be saved on to a clipboard (you will not see or be told this).

3   Position the cursor where you want the text to reappear, click on: the 📋 **Paste** button.

 Remember to check that spacing is still consistent. Delete any extra spaces by positioning the cursor in front of them and pressing: **Delete**. Insert spaces as necessary by positioning the cursor where you want the space to appear and pressing the **space bar**.

Note: You can also use the above method for copying. In this case, at step 2, click on: the **Copy** button.

If you have good control of the mouse you can use the *drag and drop* method to move text. To do this:

1   Select the text as above.

2   Hold down the left mouse button over the selected text and drag the block of text to the required position.

3   Release the mouse button.

4   Check for spacing consistency.

This is quite difficult to master! Use the **Undo** button if you have problems.

2.11 Inserting a paragraph break

Exercise 12

Insert a paragraph break and clear line space in the first paragraph after the text **... to the area.**

Method

1   Position the cursor immediately in front of the word **Many**.
2   Press: **Enter** twice.
3   Check for consistency of spacing.

2.12 Saving the document

Exercise 13

Save the document with the filename **Tower1** (as shown in Section 1.10) and print one copy.

 By saving your file as **Tower1**, you will ensure that the original file is not overwritten. This is important when working through New CLAIT assignments because you will then be able to go back and correct any errors should this be necessary.

2.13 Exiting Word

Exercise 14

Close the file and exit Word.

Editing, formatting and printing practice 1

Practice 3

1   Reload the file **P1 sec1 email**, saved in Practice 1, Section 1.

2   Enter your name, centre number and today's date a few lines below the end of the text.

3   Format the heading so that it is larger than the rest of the text.

4   Save the document with the filename **P3 sec2 email** and print one copy.

5   Insert a paragraph break and clear line space in the third paragraph after the words **...point stand out.**

6   Insert the following text as the last sentence of the last paragraph after the text **...be your response?**

   For your information, ROTFL means rolling on the floor laughing.

7   Change only the heading to a different font.

8   Embolden the words **at least** in the second sentence of the first paragraph.

9   In the paragraph beginning **You should not**..., move the last sentence beginning **E-mail is there...** so that it is the first sentence of this paragraph.

10   Save the document with the filename **email step 10** and print one copy.

Practice 4

1   Reload the file **P2 sec1 passwords**, saved in Section 1.

2   Enter your name, centre number and today's date a few lines below the end of the text.

3   Format the heading so that it is larger than the rest of the text.

4   Save the document with the filename **P4 sec2 passwords** and print one copy.

5   Insert a paragraph break and clear line space in the final paragraph after the words **...case sensitive.**

6   Insert the following paragraph after the first paragraph:

   Accessing unauthorised information is a serious matter. Passwords should not be divulged to anyone. They should be changed on a regular basis.

7   Change only the heading to a different font.

8   Underline the word **most** in the first sentence of the first paragraph.

9   In the final paragraph move the sentence **Always remain vigilant** so that it is the second sentence of the first paragraph.

10   Save the document with the filename **passwords step 10** and print one copy.

In this section you will practise and learn how to:

- delete blocks of text
- amend margins
- realign text

- replace specified text
- change line spacing

3.1 Reload the file Tower1 saved in section 2

3.2 Deleting blocks of text

We have already learnt how to delete text using the **Delete** or ← Del (Backspace) key. However, this is not the quickest method to delete whole sentences or longer portions of text. To do this we need to select the text to be deleted.

Exercise 1

In the last paragraph, delete the sentence beginning: **Thirty tonnes of...**.

Method

1 Move the cursor to the beginning of the text you want to delete – in this case the **T** of **Thirty** (Figure 2.18).

> t a cost of £3 million. Thirty tonnes of subsoil were
> lowed the tower to settle under its own weight in a

Figure 2.18 Positioning the cursor

2 Hold down the left mouse button and drag the I-beam pointer across the sentence (Figure 2.19).

> underwent major restoration work at a cost of £3 million. Thirty tonnes of subsoil were removed from underneath it. This allowed the tower to settle under its own weight in a

Figure 2.19 Selecting text

3 Release the mouse button. The highlighting shows the text that is selected. If you need to cancel the selection, click anywhere on the screen or press any arrow key.

4 Press: **Delete**.

5 Check for consistency of spacing.

 If you want to undo the last action(s), click on: the ↰ **Undo** button on the toolbar. This button is very useful and can be used at any time.

There is no need for you to scan through text manually to replace it because Word can automatically find and replace text. It is thorough in its searching and saves time.

Exercise 2

The word **visitors** appears three times in the text. Replace the word **visitors** with the word **tourists** each time it appears.

Method

1   Move your cursor to the top of the document (**Ctrl + Home**).

2   From the **Edit** menu, select: **Replace** (Figure 2.20).

Figure 2.20 Edit menu, Replace

3   The **Find and Replace** dialogue box is displayed.

4   Click on: the **Replace** tab (if not already selected).

5   Click in: the **Find what** box; key in the word **visitors**. *NB*: Do not press enter yet.

6   Click in: the **Replace with** box; key in the word **tourists** (lower case).

7   Click on: **Replace All** (Figure 2.21).

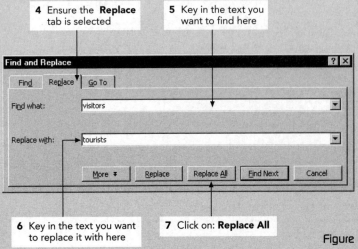

4 Ensure the **Replace** tab is selected

5 Key in the text you want to find here

6 Key in the text you want to replace it with here

7 Click on: **Replace All**

Figure 2.21 The Find and Replace dialogue box

8   A box appears telling you how many replacements have been made (Figure 2.22).

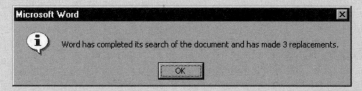

Figure 2.22 You are advised how many replacements have been made

9   Click on: **OK**.

10 Click on: **Close**.

 There are options available within Find and Replace. The commonly used option is **Match Case**. Use this if you are replacing a word consisting of capital letters. If you do not use it, the replacement word will also have capital letters (it will not have matched the case you have keyed in). To set Match Case, in the **Find and Replace** dialogue box, click on: **More**, click on: **Match Case** and proceed as before.

3.4 Changing line spacing

Exercise 3

Change the whole document to double line spacing.

 Word lets you apply a variety of line space settings (the distance between individual lines of text). Examples are:

Single line spacing   this is the default.
Double line spacing   one blank line is left between the lines of text.

This is an example of single line spacing. The default setting is single line spacing. If the specification for a document is single line spacing, then usually you need do nothing.

This is an example of double line spacing. There is one blank line left between lines of

text. It is often used when a section needs extra emphasis.

Method

1   Select all the text using the quick method (press: **Ctrl + A**).

2   From the **Format** menu, select: **Paragraph**. The Paragraph dialogue box is displayed (Figure 2.23).

3   Ensure the **Indents and Spacing** tab is selected.

4   In the **Spacing** section, **Line spacing** box, click on the down arrow and click on: **Double**.

5 Click on: **OK**.

6 Click in a white space to remove highlighting.

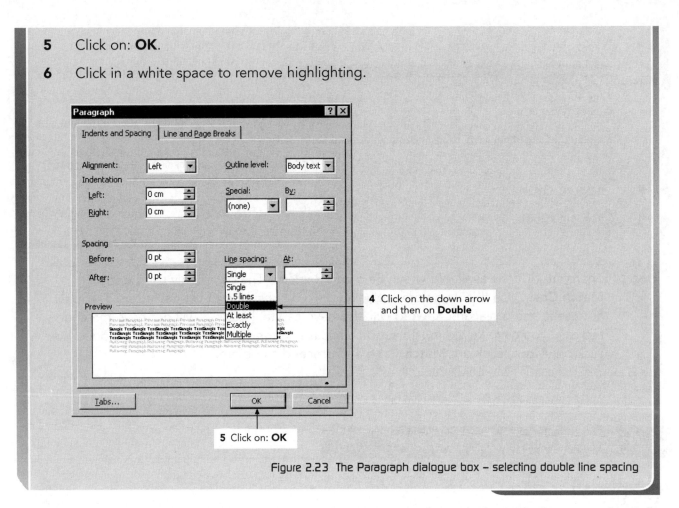

Figure 2.23 The Paragraph dialogue box – selecting double line spacing

 In double line spacing there are usually three lines between paragraphs. If you look on the Status bar you may notice that your document now takes up 2 pages (depending on how many line spaces you have left between the main text and your name) since 1/2 is displayed. When you scroll through your document you will see a dotted line across the page indicating that Word has inserted a page break.

3.5 Amending margins

Exercise 4

Change the left and right margins from 3 cm to 2 cm.

Method

Follow the method in Section 1.4.

3.6 Realigning text

Exercise 5

Centre the heading.

Method

1 Select the text to be centred or click on the line to centre.
2 Click on: the ≡ **Centre** button.

Exercise 6

Fully justify only the fourth paragraph beginning **Architects devised…**.

Method

1 Select the paragraph to justify.
2 Click on: the ≡ **Justify** button.

3.7 Save the file with the name Tower2 and print one copy

3.8 Close the file and exit Word

Editing, formatting and printing practice 2

Practice 5

1   Reload the file **email step 10**, saved in Practice 3, Section 2.

2   In the third paragraph, which begins **There has been...**, delete the sentence:

    These include being polite, being brief and not shouting.

3   Replace all occurrences of the word **response** with the word **reply** (three times in all).

4   Centre the heading **Electronic Mail Etiquette**.

5   Fully justify all except the heading.

6   Set the final paragraph in double line spacing.

7   Change the left and right margins from 2 cm to 3 cm.

8   Save the document with the filename **P5 sec3 email**.

9   Print a final copy.

10 Close the document and exit the application securely.

Practice 6

1   Reload the file **passwords step 10**, saved in Practice 3, Section 2.

2   In the third paragraph, which begins **All computer systems...**, delete the sentence:

    We estimate that this will be of benefit to 90% of ABC's computer users.

3   Replace all occurrences of the word **typing** with the word **keying** (three times in all).

4   Centre and embolden the heading **Computer Passwords**.

5   Left justify the first paragraph only.

6   Set the heading and first two paragraphs in double line spacing.

7   Change the left and right margins from 2.5 cm to 1.5 cm.

8   Save the document with the filename **P6 sec3 passwords**.

9   Print a final copy.

10 Close the document and exit the application securely.

Action	Keyboard	Mouse	Right-mouse menu	Menu
Bold text	Select text to embolden			
	Ctrl + B	Click: the **B** **Bold** button	Font	**Format, Font**
			Select: **Bold** from the **Font style:** menu	
Capitals (blocked)	Caps Lock Key in the text **Caps Lock** again to remove			Select text to be changed to capitals: **Format, Change Case, UPPERCASE**
Centre text	Select the text to centre			
	Ctrl + E	Click: the ≡ **Center** button	**Paragraph**	**Format, Paragraph**
			Select: **Centered** from the **Alignment:** drop-down menu	
Change case	Select the text to be changed From the **Format** menu, select: **Change Case** Select the appropriate case			
Close a file	**Ctrl + W**	Click: the ✗ **Close**		**File, Close**
Cut text	Select the text to be cut			
	Ctrl + X	Click: the ✂ **Cut** button	**Cut**	**Edit, Cut**
Delete a character	Press **Delete** to delete the character to the right of the cursor Press ← (Backspace) to delete the character to the left of the cursor			
Delete a word	Double-click: the word to select it. Press: **Delete**			
Delete/cut a block of text	Select the text you want to delete			
	Delete or **Ctrl + X**	Click: the ✂ **Cut** button	**Cut**	**Edit, Cut**
Exit Word		Click: the ✗ **Close** button		**File, Exit**
Font size	Select the text you want to change			
		Click: the ▼ down arrow next to the **Font Size** box Select: the font size you require	**Font**	**Format, Font**
			Select: the required size from the **Size:** menu	
Font	Select the text you want to change			
		Click: the ▼ down arrow next to the **Font** box Select: the font you require	**Font**	**Format, Font**
			Select: the required font from the **Font:** menu	
Help	F1			**Help, Microsoft Word Help**
	Shift + F1			**Help, What's This?**
Insert text	Position the cursor where you want the text to appear Key in the text			

Action	Keyboard	Mouse	Right-mouse menu	Menu
Italics	Select text to italicise			
	Ctrl + I	Click: the *I* **Italic** button	Font	F**ormat**, **Font**
			Select: **Italic** from the **Font style**: menu	
Justified margins	Select the text you want to change			
	Ctrl + J	Click: the ▤ **Justify** icon	**Paragraph**	F**ormat**, **Paragraph**
			Select **Justified** from the **Alignment**: drop-down menu	
Line spacing			**Paragraph**	F**ormat**, **Paragraph**, **Indents and Spacing**
			In the **Spacing** section, select the options you require	
Load Word	In Windows 98 desktop			
		Double-click: the **Word** shortcut icon		**Start**, **Programs**, **Microsoft Word**
Margins				**File**, **Page Setup**, **Margins**
Move a block of text	Select: the text to be moved Cut and paste the text where you want it or Select: the text to be moved Click and drag: the text to the correct position Release the mouse button			
Moving around the document	Use the cursor keys (see separate table for more)	Click: in the required position		
New file, creating	**Ctrl + N**	Click: the ▯ **New** button		**File**, **New**
Open an existing file	**Ctrl + O**	Click: the 🗁 **Open** button		**File**, **Open**
	Select the appropriate directory and filename Click: **Open**			
Page display	Click: the appropriate ▤|▣|▤|▤ **View** button (at the bottom of the Word window)			**View**
Page Setup				**File**, **Page Setup** (Choose from **Margins**, **Paper Size**, **Paper Source**, **Layout**)
Paper size	(See Page Setup)			
Paragraphs – splitting/joining	*Splitting*: Move the cursor to the first letter of the new paragraph Press: **Enter** twice *Joining*: Move the cursor to the first character of the second paragraph Press ← (Backspace) twice (Press the space bar to insert a space after a full stop)			

Action	Keyboard	Mouse	Right-mouse menu	Menu
Print file	**Ctrl + P** Select the options you need Press: **Enter**	Click: the 🖨 **Print** button		**File**, **Print** Select the options you need and click **OK**
Print Preview		Click: the 🔍 **Print Preview** button		**File**, **Print Preview**
Ragged right margin	**Ctrl + L**	Click: the ≣ **Align Left** button	**Paragraph**	**Format**, **Paragraph**
				Select **Left** from the **Alignment:** drop-down menu
Remove text emphasis	Select text to be changed			
	Ctrl + B (remove bold) **Ctrl + I** (remove italics) **Ctrl + U** (remove underline)	Click: the appropriate button: **B** **I** **U**	**Font**	**Format**, **Font**
				Select **Regular** from the **Font Style:** menu
Replace text	**Ctrl + H**			**Edit**, **Replace**
Save	**Ctrl + S**	Click: the 💾 **Save** button		**File**, **Save**
	If you have not already saved the file you will be prompted to specify the directory and to name the file If you have already done this, then Word will automatically save it			
Save using a different name or to a different directory	Select the appropriate drive and change the filename if relevant Click: **Save**			**File**, **Save As**
Save file in a different file format	Save as above, select from **Save as type**			
Spellcheck	**F7**	Click: the ✓ **Spelling** button		**Tools**, **Spelling and Grammar**
Toolbar, modify				**View**, **Toolbars**, **Customize**
Underline	Select text to underline			
	Ctrl + U	Click: the **U** **Underline** button	**Font**	**Format**, **Font**
				Select: **Underline** from the **Font style:** menu
Undo	**Ctrl + Z**	Click: the ↺ **Undo** button		**Edit**, **Undo Typing**
Zoom	Click: the 100% ▾ **Zoom** button			**View**, **Zoom**

MOVING AROUND THE DOCUMENT	
Move	**Keyboard action**
To top of document	**Ctrl + Home**
To end of document	**Ctrl + End**
Left word by word	**Ctrl + ←**
Right word by word	**Ctrl + →**
To end of line	**End**
To start of line	**Home**

SELECTING TEXT	
Selecting what	**Action**
Whole document	**Ctrl + A**
One word	Double-click on word
One paragraph	Double-click in selection border (ie to the side of the text)
Any block of text	Click cursor at start of text, press: Shift. Click cursor at end of text and click.
Deselect text	Click in any white space

See the Appendix for keyboard shortcuts.

Hints and tips

Common errors made when completing New CLAIT assignments:

- Not proofreading well enough – missing out words or longer portions of text. Omitting exclamation/question marks.
- Not using capital letters for the heading and centring it (where appropriate).
- Inconsistency of spacing – between words, between paragraphs.
- Not printing when instructed, resulting in too few printouts.

Check your work carefully. Have you done everything asked?

Word processing: sample full practice assignment

Scenario

You work as a Project Assistant for a travel company. Your job is to create and format reports as requested by the Department Manager.

Your Department Manager has asked you to create a report based on a recent survey.

1 Create a new word processing document.

2 Set the left and right margins to 3 cm.

3 Enter the following text with an unjustified right margin and a justified left margin:

CITY TRAVELLERS

City Travellers is a small company that specialises in short breaks to cities in the UK. It has an annual turnover in excess of £250,000. Last year City Travellers arranged city breaks for several thousand people.

During the month of September, representatives of City Travellers conducted a survey. A sample of five hundred people was taken. This was deemed sufficient to gain an overall picture of the number of people who would be likely to consider a short city break in the coming year.

An analysis of the results has revealed some interesting facts. Preferred destinations included Bristol, Leeds, London and Edinburgh. Most people preferred to take their own transport, 72%, and of the rest, 12%, favoured train travel. Only 10% opted for travel by coach.

Most of those questioned thought that hotel accommodation would be preferable to Bed and Breakfast, especially in the winter months. Half of those questioned said that they would consider a short break if the price was right.

4 Enter your name, centre number and today's date a few lines below the end of the text.

5 Format the heading so that it is larger than the rest of the text.

6 Save the report with the filename **City** and print one copy.

Your Department Manager has asked for amendments to be made to the report.

7 Insert a paragraph break and clear line space in the third paragraph, after the words, **London and Edinburgh**.

8 Insert the following text as the second sentence of the first paragraph, after the text **...cities in the UK**:

It currently employs one hundred staff.

9 Move the last sentence of the first paragraph:

Last year City Travellers arranged city breaks for several thousand people.
to become the first sentence of the first (ie same) paragraph:

10 In the second paragraph beginning **During the month...**, delete the sentence:

A sample of five hundred people was taken.

11 Replace all occurrences of the word **short** with the word **weekend** (three times in all).

12 Change only the heading **CITY TRAVELLERS** to a different font.

13 Italicise and centre the heading **CITY TRAVELLERS**. Make sure that the rest of the text is not italicised.

14 Fully justify all text except the heading.

15 Set the second paragraph only in double line spacing.

16 Change the left and right margins from 3 cm to 2 cm.

17 Save the report with the new filename **City2**.

18 Print a final copy of the report.

19 Close the document and exit the application securely.

Spreadsheets using Excel (Unit 4)

1 Getting started

In this section you will become familiar with spreadsheet terminology and Excel. You will discover the advantages of using a spreadsheet application. You will learn how to:

- load Excel
- enter text and numeric data
- enter simple formulae
- print the spreadsheet
- close the spreadsheet file

- understand the parts of the Excel window
- change column width
- save the spreadsheet
- print the spreadsheet showing formulae
- exit Excel

1.1 What is a spreadsheet application?

A spreadsheet has some aspects of a filing system and some of a calculator. It consists of a large area, or grid, in which you enter data and text and in which calculations are carried out. The application performs calculations as instructed by you. You can edit spreadsheets and, when changes are made, new values are recalculated automatically. Spreadsheets are very fast, accurate and flexible. You can print them or parts of them and save them to disk to edit later. Spreadsheets are used for various tasks, including accounting to produce budgets, balance sheets and payrolls, and in scientific analysis and 'What if' scenarios. Microsoft Excel is a spreadsheet application. You will learn about and appreciate the advantages of spreadsheet applications as you progress through this chapter.

1.2 Loading Excel

Exercise 1

Load Excel.

Method

Load Excel in the same way as other Office 2000 applications, this time selecting:

 Microsoft Excel   from the **Programs** menu

or

Click on: the ![Excel icon] **Excel** shortcut icon (if you have one).

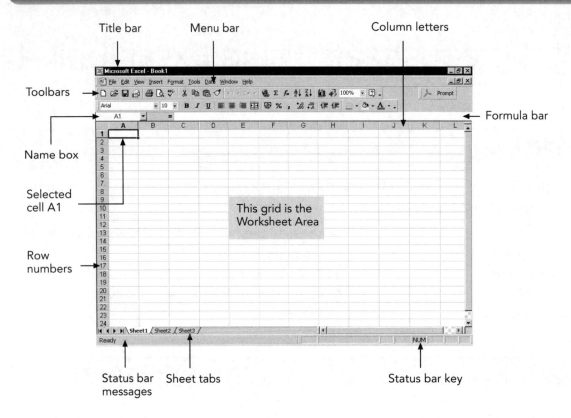

Figure 3.1 The application window

The **Title bar** and **Menu bar** are at the top of the application window.

The **Menu bar** has a set of *drop-down* menus that provide access to all of Excel's features.

The **Toolbar** is a row of buttons and selection boxes that, in most cases, provide shortcuts to the menu options or quick ways of entering values. (In Figure 3.1 the *Standard* and *Formatting* toolbars are shown.)

The **Formula bar** displays the data you enter into your worksheet.

The **Name box** displays the active cell reference.

The **Sheet tabs** allow you to move from one sheet to the next. (You can have more than one spreadsheet in an Excel document. Together these sheets are known as a *Workbook*.)

The **Status bar**, located at the bottom of the window, displays messages about current events as you work on the spreadsheet.

The **Status bar key** shows NUM (by default). This denotes that the **Num Lock** key on your keyboard is on, enabling you to use the number keys 0 to 9 (at the right of the keyboard) to enter numbers more quickly. If you want to use the movement keys instead, press: the **Num Lock** key to turn **Num Lock** off.

The Worksheet Area

This is the area between the Formula bar and the Status bar where your document (spreadsheet) is displayed. It consists of cells, each with their own cell reference, eg A1, B7, F9.

- Rows go across and are labelled 1, 2, 3, 4 ...
- Columns go down and are labelled A, B, C, D ...

Figure 3.2 shows the position of cell C6.

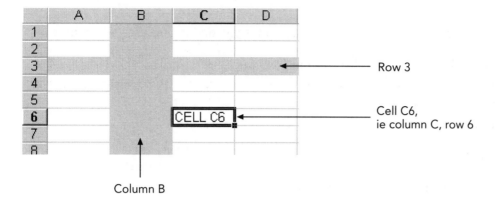

Figure 3.2 Cell references

Practise:

Moving around the spreadsheet:

1   Moving around your document using the scroll bars (Figure 3.3).

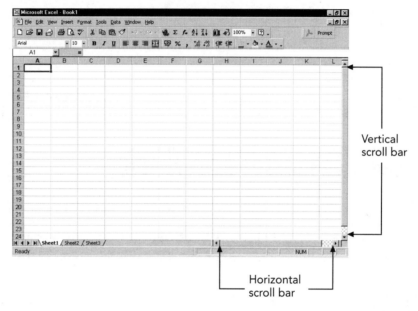

Figure 3.3 Scroll bars

2   Using navigation keys, **Page Up** and **Page Down,** to move up and down a page at a time.

3   Moving the cell selector with the arrow keys.

4   Using the **Go To** command in the **Edit** menu. Enter the cell address, eg C5 in the **Reference** box and click on: **OK.**

5   Point to a cell with the mouse and click.

6   Pressing: **Ctrl + Home** takes you to the top of your spreadsheet. **Ctrl + End** will take you to the last cell with data entered on your spreadsheet (when you have entered data).

1.4 Spreadsheet contents

You can enter:

● text   ● numeric data   ● formulae.

Text entries are used for titles, headings and any notes. They are entries that you do not want to manipulate arithmetically.

Numeric data consists of numbers you want to add, subtract, multiply, divide and use in formulae.

Formulae are used to calculate the value of a cell from the contents of other cells. For instance, formulae may be used to calculate totals or averages. *Formulae always start with an = sign*. A typical formula could look like the examples below:

   =A1+A2   =SUM(A1:A6)   =B6-B4   =C2*C7   =A2/B9

   =A2*B6+A4 =C2/D2-F8

The following operators (symbols) are used in formulae:

   +(ADD)   -(SUBTRACT)   *(MULTIPLY)   /(DIVIDE)

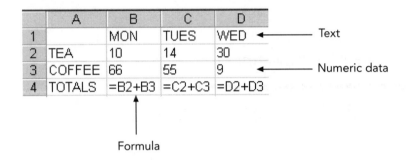

Figure 3.4 Types of spreadsheet entry

1.5 Inserting text and numeric data

Exercise 2

The spreadsheet below (Figure 3.5) shows the sales figures for three different cosmetic companies over a four-month period. Enter the data into the spreadsheet.

	A	B	C	D
1	MONTH	ESSENZ	LIVENUP	STARS
2	JAN	490	210	130
3	FEB	608	419	400
4	MAR	309	318	534
5	APR	600	521	470

Figure 3.5 Spreadsheet data

Method

1   Move to cell A1 and key in **MONTH**.

2   Move to cell B1 and key in **ESSENZ**.

3   Move to cell C1 and key in **LIVENUP**.

4   Complete the spreadsheet in this way until it looks like Figure 3.5.

Sometimes you need to enter data that is too long to display in full in the cell. (The default is about nine numeric characters.) You can adjust the column width to display cell entries in full. All entries must be displayed in full for New CLAIT.

To widen a column

1 Position the cursor at the column border (see below); a double arrow appears.

2 Drag the right-hand edge of the column border (next to the column letter) to the right.

or

Double-click on the column border to fit the widest entry.

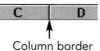

Column border

This topic is covered in more detail in Section 3.

1.6 Entering simple formulae

Exercise 3

Enter simple formulae to add up cell contents.

Remember: Formulae must always begin with the = sign.

Method

1 Move to cell A6 and key in **TOTAL**.

2 We want to add up the sales figures for ESSENZ. These are displayed in cells B2, B3, B4 and B5. Move to cell B6 (where you want the answer to appear).

Notice as you key in that the formula appears on the Formula bar. It may be too long to fit the cell but you can ignore this. Cell references can be in upper or lower case.

Key in: **=B2+B3+B4+B5** and press: **Enter**. The answer 2007 appears in cell B6.

3 Add up the sales figures for LIVENUP in the same way by keying in: **=C2+C3+C4+C5** and press: **Enter**. The answer 1468 appears in cell C6.

In the early stages of learning how to construct formulae it is worth checking that the answer is as expected by working out the result for yourself. Of course once you are confident, let the spreadsheet application do things for you! However, it is still worth having a rough idea of what the answer should be, just in case you have mis-keyed an entry.

Your spreadsheet will now look like Figure 3.6.

	A	B	C	D
1	MONTH	ESSENZ	LIVENUP	STARS
2	JAN	490	210	130
3	FEB	608	419	400
4	MAR	309	318	534
5	APR	600	521	470
6	TOTAL	2007	1468	

Figure 3.6 Totalling column B and column C

Using the built-in SUM function

On a large business spreadsheet, you might need to add a huge number of cell contents and specifying each cell reference would not be practical. A quicker way to add up figures is by using one of Excel's built-in *functions*, SUM, to work out the formula as follows:

To produce a TOTAL for STARS:

1   Move to cell D6 (where you want the answer to appear).

2   Key in =SUM(D2:D5) and press: **Enter.**

> The colon between the cell references in the formula above means 'to include all the cells in between D2 and D5'. To speed things up, Excel has many functions including SUM (used for adding) and AVERAGE (used to calculate the average value for a range of cells), ie instead of keying in, for example
>
> **=A1+B1+C1+D1/4** you can use **=AVERAGE(A1:D1)**
>
> *Note:* You do not need to use SUM in the formula when subtracting, multiplying or dividing. For instance, the formula for subtracting the contents of cell A6 from those in cell D4 would be **=D4-A6**.

Your spreadsheet will now look like Figure 3.7.

	A	B	C	D
1	MONTH	ESSENZ	LIVENUP	STARS
2	JAN	490	210	130
3	FEB	608	419	400
4	MAR	309	318	534
5	APR	600	521	470
6	TOTAL	2007	1468	1534

Figure 3.7 Totalling column D

Practise using the SUM function:

1   Delete the Totals of ESSENZ (cell B6) and LIVENUP (cell C6) by selecting them and pressing: **Delete.**

2   Add the Totals again, this time using the SUM function, in cell B6 **=SUM(B2:B5)** and in cell C6 **=SUM(C2:C5).**

Using the AutoSum button

There is an even quicker way to add cell values using the toolbar button **AutoSum.**

To practise this, let's add up the totals for the three cosmetic companies for each month.

1   Move to cell E1 and key in **SALES.**

2   Move to cell E2, the cell where you want the total sales for JAN to appear.

3   Click on: the **Σ** AutoSum button. You will notice that a dotted line has appeared around cells B2 to D2.

In this example, Excel has automatically chosen the correct cells to add. Sometimes it chooses the wrong ones. If this happens you will need to select the cells you want. Click on the cell you want to start with, holding down the left mouse and dragging the dotted line across the correct cells. Be careful that you don't drag too far and include the cell where you want the answer to appear by mistake. The answer cell cannot be included in the formula. If you try to include the cell reference where you want the answer to appear in a formula, an error message will be displayed. Follow the instructions given in the error message.

4   Press: **Enter.**

5   The answer 830 appears in cell E2.

6   Use this method to calculate the sales totals for FEB, MAR and APR.

When adding sales for MAR, you will notice that Excel has mistakenly decided that you now want to add the figures from above the cell and has placed the dotted line around cells E2 and E3. Move the highlight by clicking the first cell you want to add (B4) and dragging across to D4. Watch out for this.

If you have done everything correctly, the totals will be as in Figure 3.8.

FEB   in cell E3   Total = 1427
MAR   in cell E4   Total = 1161
APR   in cell E5   Total = 1591

	A	B	C	D	E
1	MONTH	ESSENZ	LIVENUP	STARS	SALES
2	JAN	490	210	130	830
3	FEB	608	419	400	1427
4	MAR	309	318	534	1161
5	APR	600	521	470	1591
6	TOTAL	2007	1468	1534	

Figure 3.8 Sales figures for JAN, FEB, MAR and APR

1.7 Saving the spreadsheet

Exercise 4

Save the spreadsheet.

Method

1   From the **File** menu, select: **Save As**. The **Save As** dialogue box appears (Figure 3.9).

2   Select the location where you want to save your file and key in **Sales** in the **File name** box.

3   Click on: **Save**.

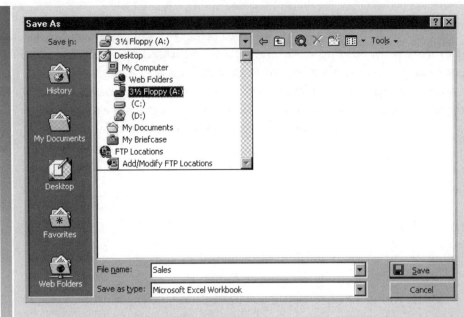

Figure 3.9 The Save As dialogue box

Exercise 5

Print the spreadsheet.

Method

Note: If you are working in a shared printer situation, it is a good idea to add your initials in a cell a few rows below the bottom row of cell entries (so that you will recognise your printout).

Previewing a spreadsheet before printing

It is always wise to preview your spreadsheet before printing so you are sure that it will print exactly what you want. This will save paper as well as effort.

1   Click on: the **Print Preview** button.

2   Click on: the **Zoom** option to see your spreadsheet contents. Click on: **Zoom** again to return to default view.

3   If you are happy with the **Print Preview**, click on: **Print**. (You can change default options here if necessary.)

4   Click on: **OK**.

Should you need to exit Print Preview at step 3, press: **Esc** *or* click on: **Close** to return to the spreadsheet.

Always examine your printout very carefully to check that all data is showing in full; you may have overlooked something, or your default printer may be set up so that you need to leave additional space on your spreadsheet.

Printing in landscape

By default the spreadsheet will print a portrait display (the narrow edge at the top of the page). If you prefer, or if your spreadsheet does not fit across the page, you can change the display to landscape.

Note: Dotted lines appear on the spreadsheet to denote a page break.

Portrait

Landscape

To do this from **Print Preview**, click on: **Setup**:

1   Click on: the **Page** tab, then on: the **Landscape** option button.

2   Click on: **OK**.

If not using Print Preview:

1   From the **File** menu, select: **Page Setup**.

2   Click on: the **Page** tab, then on: the **Landscape** option button.

3   Click on: **Print**.

1.9 Printing formulae

Exercise 6

Print a copy of the spreadsheet showing the formulae used.

It is useful to have a printout of the formulae used on your spreadsheet so you can cross-reference for accuracy. This is required for the CLAIT assessment.

Method

To show formulae on your spreadsheet

1   With your spreadsheet on screen, from the **Tools** menu, select: **Options**.

2   Click on: the **View** tab (if not already selected); the **Options** dialogue box appears. Click on: the **Formulas** check box so that a tick appears in this box. Click on: **OK** (Figure 3.10).

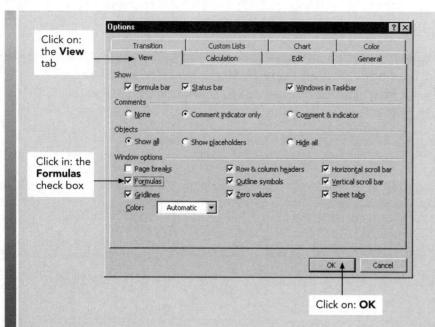

Figure 3.10 Showing formulae

3 Notice that the columns have widened to accommodate the formulae.

> Do not reduce the column widths because when you take the 'show formulas' off the cell widths will need altering again. For a quicker way to show formulae, press: **Ctrl** + ` (to the left of the number one key).

4 Check that the spreadsheet will fit on one page by using **Print Preview** (as above).

5 If it fits, print as before.

6 If it does not fit, check that it is in landscape by following the instructions above.

7 Check that all the formulae are displayed in full. If they are not, you will need to widen the cells as appropriate and reprint.

> In **Page Setup** in the **Scaling** section, there is also an option **Fit to page**. This ensures that the whole spreadsheet (although reduced in size) will fit on one page. *Note:* You will still need to widen cells that are not displaying their entire contents.

Exercise 7

Change the spreadsheet so that numbers are displayed instead of formulae.

Removing showing formulae

Method

1 From the **Tools** menu, select: **Options**.

2 Click on: the **View** tab (if not already selected); click in: the **Formulas** check box so that the tick is removed. Click on: **OK**.

A quick way to change back to values display – press: **Ctrl** +`.

1.10 Closing a spreadsheet file

Exercise 8

Close the spreadsheet file.

Method

From the **File** menu, select: **Close**. *Note:* You may be asked if you want to save changes, click on: **Yes**.

1.11 Exiting Excel

Exercise 9

Exit Excel.

Method

Click on: the ☒ **Close** button in the top right-hand corner.

Spreadsheets practice 1

In the following exercises, some of the numeric data has decimal places, ie figures after the decimal point (the decimal point is entered using the full stop key (but no spaces after it)). When there is one number to the right of the decimal point, the number has one decimal place. When there are two numbers after the decimal point, the number has two decimal places. If there is no decimal point, the number is a whole number (also known as an *integer*). You will be working with formatting decimal places in Section 3.

Note: When entering numbers with decimal places and trailing zeros, eg 12.30, this may appear on the spreadsheet as 12.3 (the trailing 0 is missing). You need not be concerned about this at this stage.

Practice 1

1 Create a new spreadsheet.

2 Enter the following data, leaving the **TOTAL** column blank.

DEPT SALES						
DEPT	OVERHEADS	MARK UP	MON	TUE	WED	TOTAL
FRUIT	6	0.17	44	68	22	
VEG	4	0.15	55	88	21	
FISH	10	0.12	52.5	16	28	
CHILLED	7	0.1	12	72	14	
DAIRY	6	0.13	65	32	43	
DRINKS	2.5	0.25	19	31	41.5	

3 Enter your name, centre number and today's date a few lines below the data.

4 The TOTAL for each department is calculated by adding the figures for **MON**, **TUE** and **WED**.

Insert a formula to calculate the **TOTAL** for **FRUIT**.

5 Save your spreadsheet report with the filename **P1 sec1shop** and print one copy. Make sure that all the data is displayed in full.

6 Print a copy showing the formula used. Make sure the formula is displayed in full.

7 Close the spreadsheet file and exit Excel.

Practice 2

1 Create a new spreadsheet.

2 Enter the following data, leaving the **TOTAL** column blank.

GOODS						
PRODUCT	WEEK1	WEEK2	WEEK3	COST	CARRIAGE	TOTAL
BACKPACK	328	627	321	32.5	22.5	
HOLDALL	198	562	1211	45.2	25.25	
WHEELBAG	231	125	324	17.99	35.5	
BRIEFCASE	362	321	375	40	15.55	
PILOT	732	268	432	39.75	50	
ATTACHE	120	112	39	12.99	32.5	
BINDER	560	270	110	6	9.5	

3 Enter your name, centre number and today's date a few lines below the data.

4 The **TOTAL** for each product is calculated by adding the figures for **WEEK1**, **WEEK2** and **WEEK3**.

   Insert a formula to calculate the **TOTAL** for **BACKPACK**.

5 Save your spreadsheet report with the filename **P2 sec1 travel** and print one copy. Make sure that all the data is displayed in full.

6 Print a copy showing the formula used. Make sure the formula is displayed in full.

7 Close the spreadsheet file and exit Excel.

2 Editing and manipulating

In this section you will learn how to:

- reload a saved file
- change entries made to your spreadsheet
- delete a row or column
- copy or replicate entries and formulae
- insert a new row or column
- recalculate data
- save the spreadsheet using a new filename

2.1 Reloading a saved file

Exercise 1

Reload the spreadsheet **Sales** saved in Section 1.

Method

1 With Excel loaded, click on: the 📂 **Open** button; the **Open** dialogue box appears (Figure 3.11).

2 Select the location where your file is stored by clicking on: the down arrow.

3 Click on: the filename **Sales**.

4 Click on: **Open**.

Figure 3.11 Opening a saved file

2.2 Changing entries made to your spreadsheet

Exercise 2

Some of the original data in the spreadsheet **Sales** has been found to be incorrect:

The Sales figures for ESSENZ should be **520** in **JAN** and **250** in **MAR**.

We need to change these entries.

Method

1   Move to cell B2 and key in: **520** and press: **Enter**.

2   Move to cell B4 and key in: **250** and press: **Enter**.

> Notice that the original figures are overwritten. Look what has happened to the Total for ESSENZ. You will see that the formula has been recalculated to give a new Total. The Sales figures for JAN and MAR in column E have also been updated to reflect the changes made. This will usually happen. When you change cell contents within a spreadsheet, all the formulae referring to that cell will be recalculated automatically.

Your spreadsheet will now look like Figure 3.12.

	A	B	C	D	E
1	MONTH	ESSENZ	LIVENUP	STARS	SALES
2	JAN	520	210	130	860
3	FEB	608	419	400	1427
4	MAR	250	318	534	1102
5	APR	600	521	470	1591
6	TOTAL	1978	1468	1534	

Figure 3.12 Updated spreadsheet

2.3 Deleting a row or column

Exercise 3

It has been decided that the figures for FEB are not required. Delete this row. Close up space, do not leave a blank row.

Method

1   Click on: the box to the left of the row to be deleted, ie row 3. Row 3 is highlighted (Figure 3.13).

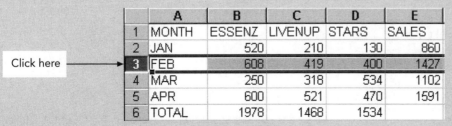

Figure 3.13 Selecting a row

2   Right-click on: the selected row; a pop-up menu appears (Figure 3.14).

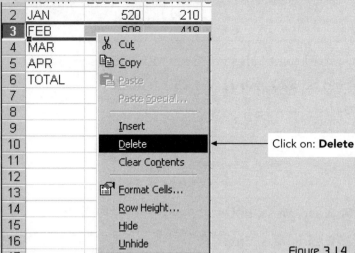

Click on: **Delete**

Figure 3.14 Right-clicking displays a pop-up menu

3   Click on: **Delete**. The spreadsheet contents move up to occupy the empty space and the figures are recalculated to reflect the change (Figure 3.15).

	A	B	C	D	E
1	MONTH	ESSENZ	LIVENUP	STARS	SALES
2	JAN	520	210	130	860
3	MAR	250	318	534	1102
4	APR	600	521	470	1591
5	TOTAL	1370	1049	1134	

Figure 3.15 Spreadsheet after deletion of the FEB row

When you are asked to delete rows or columns, it is necessary to delete the whole row/column as shown in the method above. Do not just clear the contents by pressing (thus leaving an empty row/column). If you are familiar with Excel, do not use Excel's **Hide** facility. This simply hides, ie it does not delete, the row or column.

Exercise 4

The figures for LIVENUP are no longer required. Delete this column.

Method

1   Click in: the box at the top of the column to be deleted, ie C; column C is highlighted.

2   Right-click on: the selection; a pop-up menu appears.

3   Click on: **Delete**.

The spreadsheet now looks like Figure 3.16.

	A	B	C	D
1	MONTH	ESSENZ	STARS	SALES
2	JAN	520	130	650
3	MAR	250	534	784
4	APR	600	470	1070
5	TOTAL	1370	1134	

Figure 3.16 Spreadsheet after deletion of the LIVENUP column

2.4 Copying/replicating entries and formulae

Exercise 5

Replicate the formula used to calculate the TOTAL for STARS so that the TOTAL for SALES is also calculated.

Method

1 Move to the cell in which the formula you want to copy is stored. In this case C5.

2 Point the mouse at the bottom right of this cell until a black cross + appears then, holding down the left mouse, drag across cell D5 (where you want the formula copied to). Release the mouse.

The spreadsheet now looks like Figure 3.17.

	A	B	C	D
1	MONTH	ESSENZ	STARS	SALES
2	JAN	520	130	650
3	MAR	250	534	784
4	APR	600	470	1070
5	TOTAL	1370	1134	2504

Figure 3.17 Spreadsheet after replication of formula

If you make an error performing this procedure, Click on: the **Undo** button and try again. You can not only replicate formulae in this way but also copy other spreadsheet entries.

Relative and absolute cell references

When replicating formulae, the cell references change to reflect their new position. (You can check this by looking at the formula that you have just replicated.) A relative cell reference will change relatively to its position on the spreadsheet. By contrast, a cell reference can be made absolute. This means that it will not change even if it is replicated or moved to another part of the spreadsheet. You can copy entries that do not contain formulae using the method above. This results in exact copies of the initial cell entry into the destination cells.

2.5 Adding a new column and a new row

Exercise 6

Adding a new column

Insert a new column headed JUST4U after ESSENZ and before STARS. Enter the following information:

JAN, 720.15   **MAR, 630.25**   **APR, 938.5**

1 Click in: the box at the top of the column after where the new column is to appear, ie column C; column C is highlighted (Figure 3.18).

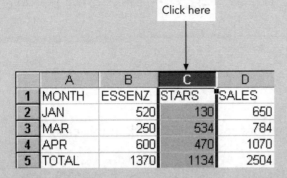

Figure 3.18 Selecting a column

2 Right-click on: the selection; a pop-up menu appears. Click on: **Insert** (Figure 3.19). An empty column appears.

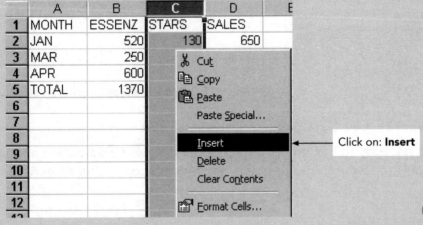

Figure 3.19 Inserting a column

3 Enter the new text and data shown above.

The spreadsheet now looks like Figure 3.20.

	A	B	C	D	E
1	MONTH	ESSENZ	JUST4U	STARS	SALES
2	JAN	520	720.15	130	1370.15
3	MAR	250	630.25	534	1414.25
4	APR	600	938.5	470	2008.5
5	TOTAL	1370		1134	4792.9

Figure 3.20 Spreadsheet after addition of JUST4U column and data

Calculate the Total for JUST4U, using one of the quicker methods you have learnt. The Total is 2288.9.

Exercise 7

Adding a new row

It has been decided to re-insert the figures for FEB. Insert a new row for FEB with the following information: **ESSENZ 608, JUST4U 99.60, STARS 400**.

1 Click in: the box to the left of the row below where you want the new row to appear, ie row 3. Row 3 is highlighted (Figure 3.21).

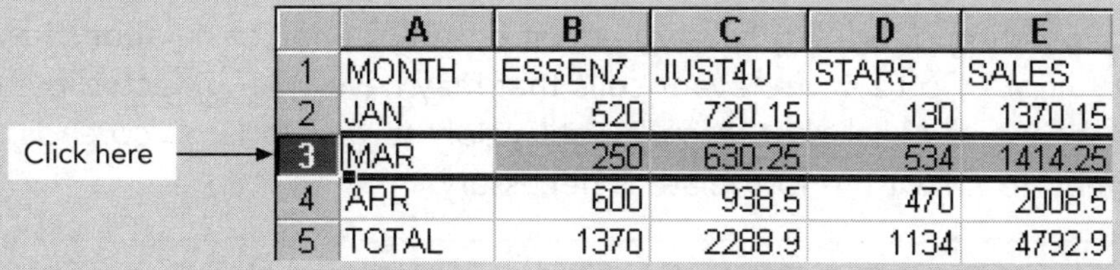

	A	B	C	D	E
1	MONTH	ESSENZ	JUST4U	STARS	SALES
2	JAN	520	720.15	130	1370.15
3	MAR	250	630.25	534	1414.25
4	APR	600	938.5	470	2008.5
5	TOTAL	1370	2288.9	1134	4792.9

Click here →

Figure 3.21 Adding a new row

2 Right-click on: the highlighted row; a pop-up menu appears (Figure 3.22). Click on: **Insert**. An empty row appears.

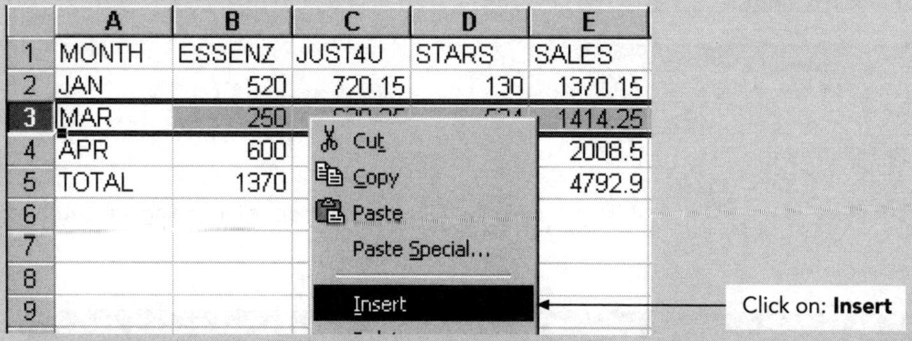

	A	B	C	D	E
1	MONTH	ESSENZ	JUST4U	STARS	SALES
2	JAN	520	720.15	130	1370.15
3	MAR	250			1414.25
4	APR	600			2008.5
5	TOTAL	1370			4792.9
6					
7					
8					
9					

✂ Cut
📋 Copy
📋 Paste
Paste Special...
Insert ← Click on: **Insert**

Figure 3.22 Inserting a row

3 Enter the new text and data shown above.

Replicate the formula from cell E2 to produce a Total in cell E3 for FEB SALES. The total is 1107.6.

2.6 Adding a new column or row to create new values

Exercise 8

Insert a new column for LOOKS after STARS and before the SALES column (see above Section 2.5).

Enter the following data:

JAN, 654.43   FEB, 821.12   MAR, 500.3   APR, 320.55

Replicate the formula from D6 to give a Total value in cell E6 for LOOKS.

Note: In Excel 2000, these figures (although at the end of the existing SUM cell range) are automatically included in the Sales column figures. This did not happen in earlier versions of Excel. Look out for this as you may not always want Excel to include new data in formulae.

When adding, deleting or editing cells you must ensure that all calculations have been updated accordingly. Go to any relevant cells that may have been affected by a change to the spreadsheet and check that formulae still apply to the updated spreadsheet. If not you will need to adjust the formulae as necessary.

Method

Follow the method in Section 2.5.

The spreadsheet now looks like Figure 3.23.

	A	B	C	D	E	F
1	MONTH	ESSENZ	JUST4U	STARS	LOOKS	SALES
2	JAN	520	720.15	130	654.43	2024.58
3	FEB	608	99.6	400	821.12	1928.72
4	MAR	250	630.25	534	500.3	1914.55
5	APR	600	938.5	470	320.55	2329.05
6	TOTAL	1978	2388.5	1534	2296.4	8196.9

Figure 3.23 Spreadsheet after adding the LOOKS column

2.7 Save your spreadsheet as Sales 1

 Saving your spreadsheet with a new filename will ensure that the original version is not overwritten. You will now have two spreadsheets, **Sales** (the original) and **Sales1** (the updated spreadsheet).

2.8 Print one copy of your spreadsheet, Sales 1

2.9 Close the file and exit Excel

Spreadsheets practice 2

Practice 3

1 Load Excel.

2 Reload the spreadsheet **P1 sec1 shop** saved in Section 1.

3 In the **TOTAL** column, replicate the formula in the **FRUIT** row to show totals for all departments.

4 Resave using the original filename and print one copy of the spreadsheet.

5 Insert a new column entitled **PROFIT** between the columns **DEPT** and **OVERHEADS**.

6 **PROFIT** is calculated by multiplying the **TOTAL** figure by the **MARK UP** and subtracting the **OVERHEADS**.

Insert a formula to calculate the **PROFIT** for **FRUIT**. Replicate this formula to show the **PROFIT** for each department.

Some changes need to be made to the spreadsheet.

7 Delete the entire row for **DIARY**.

8 Make the following amendments to the spreadsheet:

    a The **MARK UP** for **FISH** should be **0.10**.
    b The **OVERHEADS** for **VEG** should be **2.5**.
    c The **WED** sales for **VEG** should be **36**.
    d **CHILLED** should be **FROZEN**.

Make sure the **TOTAL** and **PROFIT** have updated as a result of these changes.

9 Save the spreadsheet as **P3 sec2 shop**.

10 Print one copy showing the data and one copy showing the formulae used.

Ensure all data and formulae are showing in full on the printouts.

11 Close the spreadsheet file and exit Excel.

Practice 4

1 Load Excel.

2 Reload the spreadsheet **P2 sec1 travel** saved in Section 1.

3 In the **TOTAL** column, replicate the formula in the **BACKPACK** row to show totals for all departments.

4 Resave using the original filename and print one copy of the spreadsheet.

5 Insert a new column entitled **TOTAL COST** between the columns **WEEK3** and **COST**.

6 **TOTAL COST** is calculated by multiplying the **TOTAL** figure by the **COST** and adding the **CARRIAGE**.

Insert a formula to calculate the **TOTAL COST** for **BACKPACK**.

7 Replicate this formula to show the **TOTAL COST** for each item.

Some changes need to be made to the spreadsheet.

8 Delete the entire row for **PILOT**.

9 Make the following amendments to the spreadsheet:

a The **COST** for **HOLDALL** should be **32.5**.
b The **CARRIAGE** for **BINDER** should be **6.5**.
c The **WEEK3** orders for **BRIEFCASE** should be **430**.
d **WHEELBAG** should be **TROLLEY**.

10 Make sure the **TOTAL COST** and **TOTAL** have updated as a result of these changes.

11 Save the spreadsheet as **P4 sec2 travel**.

12 Print one copy showing the data and one copy showing the formulae used. Ensure all data and formulae are showing in full on the printouts.

13 Close the spreadsheet file and exit Excel.

Using display features

In this section you will learn how to:

- left and right align text and numeric data
- use integer format and decimal format to display numbers
- display in currency format

Reload the spreadsheet **Sales1** saved at the end of Section 2.

3.1 Left and right justifying text

 When data is first entered, text is placed on the left of the cell and numbers line up on the right. Three toolbar buttons can be used to apply a new alignment to a selected range.

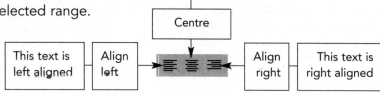

To align cell contents

1 Select the cells to be realigned.
2 Click on: the appropriate toolbar button.

Exercise 1

Display the headings: **MONTH, ESSENZ, JUST4U, STARS, LOOKS** and **SALES** so that **MONTH** is left justified and **ESSENZ, JUST4U, STARS, LOOKS** and **SALES** are right justified.

Method

The heading **MONTH** is already left justified. To right justify the other headings:

1 Select cells **B1** to **F1** (Figure 3.24).

	A	B	C	D	E	F
1	MONTH	ESSENZ	JUST4U	STARS	LOOKS	SALES
2	JAN	520	720.15	130	654.43	2024.58
3	FEB	608	99.6	400	821.12	1928.72

Figure 3.24 Cells selected to right justify

2 Click on: the **Align Right** toolbar button.

3.2 Changing column width

Exercise 2

Change the heading **SALES** so that it becomes **MONTHLY SALES**.

1   Move to cell F1.

2   Click the cursor in front of the **S** of **SALES** (Figure 3.25) on the formula bar and key in:
MONTHLY and a space. Press: **Enter**.

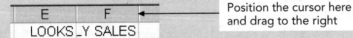

	A	B	C	D	E	F
1	MONTH	ESSENZ	JUST4U	STARS	LOOKS	SALES
2	JAN	520	720.15	130	654.43	2024.58

Figure 3.25 Positioning the cursor to alter a heading

3   The entry is now too long to fit the cell. There are several ways to widen the column:

> Click on: the **Undo** toolbar button after trying each method so that you can
> practise.

a   Position the cursor at the column border; a double arrow appears. Drag the right-
hand edge of the column border (next to the column letter) to the right (Figure 3.26).

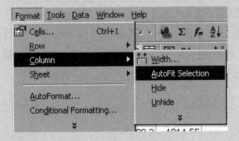

E	F
LOOKS	_Y SALES

Position the cursor here
and drag to the right

Figure 3.26 Changing column width

b   Position the cursor as above and double-click the mouse (this action widens to fit
the longest entry exactly).

c   With the cell selected, from the **Format** menu, select: **Column**, **Width**. Key in a
new width (ie the number of characters in the cell).

d   With the cell selected, from the **Format** menu, select: **Column, AutoFit Selection**
(Figure 3.27).

Format Tools Data Window Help

Cells...	Ctrl+1
Row	▶
Column	▶
Sheet	▶
AutoFormat...	
Conditional Formatting...	

Width...
AutoFit Selection
Hide
Unhide

Figure 3.27 Widening a column using the menus

> If a cell is filled with ####### characters, the column is not wide enough to display the
> numeric value held in that cell. Widen the cell, as above, to display the cell contents.

Exercise 3

Enter a column headed **AVERAGE SALES** after the MONTHLY SALES column. Right justify this heading and widen the cell to display this heading in full.

In cell G2, enter a formula to work out the AVERAGE SALES for JAN, ie MONTHLY SALES divided by 4 (as there are 4 companies). The formula is: =F2/4.

Replicate this formula to cells G3, G4, G5 and G6.

The spreadsheet will now look like Figure 3.28.

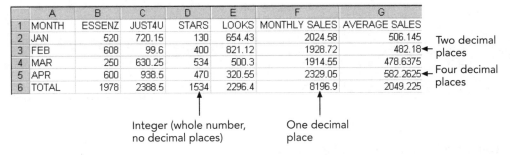

	A	B	C	D	E	F	G	
1	MONTH	ESSENZ	JUST4U	STARS	LOOKS	MONTHLY SALES	AVERAGE SALES	
2	JAN	520	720.15	130	654.43	2024.58	506.145	Two decimal
3	FEB	608	99.6	400	821.12	1928.72	482.18 ← places
4	MAR	250	630.25	534	500.3	1914.55	478.6375	Four decimal
5	APR	600	938.5	470	320.55	2329.05	582.2625 ← places
6	TOTAL	1978	2388.5	1534	2296.4	8196.9	2049.225	

Integer (whole number, no decimal places)

One decimal place

Figure 3.28 Spreadsheet with the Average Sales column added

Exercise 4

Display the numeric data in the AVERAGE SALES column as integers (no decimal places).

Method

1 Select the column entries, ie cells G2 to G6.

2 Right-click: the highlighted area; a pop-up menu appears (Figure 3.29).

Figure 3.29 Formatting cells

3 From the menu, select: **Format Cells**; the **Format Cells** dialogue box is displayed (Figure 3.30).

4 Click on: the **Number** tab.

5 In the **Category** box, click on: **Number**.

6 In the **Decimal places** box, use the down arrow to set to zero (0).

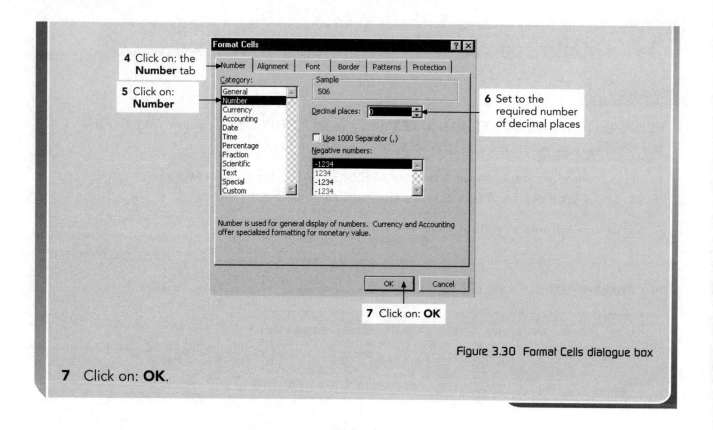

4 Click on: the **Number** tab

5 Click on: **Number**

6 Set to the required number of decimal places

7 Click on: **OK**

Figure 3.30 Format Cells dialogue box

7 Click on: **OK**.

The AVERAGE SALES column will now look like Figure 3.31.

G
AVERAGE SALES
506
482
479
582
2049

Figure 3.31 Average Sales figures displayed as integers

Notice that the figure for MAR, which was 478.6375, is now 479. Excel will display figures rounded up to the nearest whole number when the number after the decimal point is 5 or greater than 5. Although it displays as a whole number, when performing calculations Excel works on the original entry. Therefore if you were to work out the result on a calculator using the displayed figures, there would be a slight difference in the answer (ie Excel would be more accurate).

Note: With the cells selected, you can also use the toolbar buttons **Increase Decimal/Decrease Decimal** to change the number of decimal places.

Follow the instructions above to display the numeric data in the **LOOKS** column to two decimal places, ie two 2 places after the decimal point.

The LOOKS column should now look like Figure 3.32.

E
LOOKS
654.43
821.12
500.30
320.55
2296.40

Figure 3.32 LOOKS figures displayed with 2 decimal places

3.4 Displaying in currency format

Exercise 5

Display the numeric data in the TOTAL row in currency format (displaying a £ sign) to two decimal places.

Method

1. Select: the row entries, ie cells B6 to G6.

2. Right-click: the highlighted area; a pop-up menu appears.

3. From the menu, select: **Format Cells**; the **Format Cells** dialogue box is displayed.

4. Click on: the **Number** tab.

5. In the **Category** box, click on: **Currency**.

6. In the **Decimal places** box, use the down arrow to set to **2**.

7. In the **Symbol** box, use the down arrow to select the **£** sign. *Note:* You should not add the £ sign manually.

Although it is normal to show currency with two decimal places, ie £13.57 to indicate 13 pounds and 57 pence, when working with spreadsheets none, one or more than two decimal places can also be displayed. Set this in the **Decimal places** box.

When you want to format currency to two decimal places and a £ sign, you can also use the ☐ **Currency** button.

3.5 Save spreadsheet

Save the spreadsheet as **Sales2**, print a copy showing the data and another showing the formulae.

3.6 Close spreadsheet file and exit Excel

Spreadsheet practice 3

Practice 5

1   Load Excel.

2   Reload the spreadsheet **P3 sec2 shop** saved in Practice 3, Section 2.

3   Apply alignment as follows:

    a The column heading **DEPT SALES** and all row labels (eg **FRUIT**, **VEG**, etc) should be left-aligned.

    b The other column headings (eg **PROFIT**, **OVERHEADS**, **MARK UP**, etc) should be right-aligned.

    c All numeric values should be right-aligned.

4   Format the data as follows:

    a The figures for **MON**, **TUE** and **WED** should be displayed in integer format (to zero decimal places).

    b The figures for **OVERHEADS**, **MARK UP** and **TOTAL** should be displayed to two decimal places.

    c The **PROFIT** data only should be displayed with a £ sign and to two decimal places.

5   Save your spreadsheet using the filename **P5 sec3 shop**.

6   Print one copy showing figures, not formulae. Make sure that all data is displayed in full.

7   Print the spreadsheet with all the formulae showing. Make sure that all formulae are displayed in full.

8   Close the spreadsheet file and exit Excel.

Practice 6

1   Load Excel.

2   Reload the spreadsheet **P4 sec2 travel** saved in Practice 4, Section 2.

3   Apply alignment as follows:

    a The column heading **GOODS** and all row labels (eg **BACKPACK**, **HOLDALL**, etc) should be right-aligned.

    b The other column headings (eg **WEEK1**, **WEEK2**, etc) should be left-aligned.

    c All numeric values should be right-aligned.

4   Format the data as follows:

    a The figures for **CARRIAGE** and **TOTAL** should be displayed in integer format (to zero decimal places).

    b The figures for **COST** should be displayed to two decimal places.

    c The **TOTAL COST** data only should be displayed with a £ sign and to one decimal place.

5   Save your spreadsheet using the filename **P6 sec3 travel**.

6   Print one copy showing figures, not formulae. Make sure that all data is displayed in full.

7   Print the spreadsheet with all the formulae showing. Make sure that all formulae are displayed in full.

8   Close the spreadsheet file and exit Excel.

Spreadsheets quick reference for New CLAIT (Excel)

Action	Keyboard	Mouse	Right-mouse menu	Menu
Align cell entries	Select cells to align			
		Click: the relevant button: ▤ ▤ ▤	**Format Cells**	**Format**, **Cells**
			Select the **Alignment** tab Select from the **Horizontal**: drop-down menu as appropriate	
Capitals (blocked)	**Caps Lock** (press again to remove)			
Close a file	**Ctrl + W**	Click: the ✕ **Close** button		**File**, **Close**
Columns, changing width of		Drag the column border ▦ C ✛ D ▦ to fit the widest entry	Select the column(s) by clicking (and dragging) on the column ref box (at top of column)	
			Column Width Key in the width you want	**Format**, **Column**, **Width** Key in the width you want *or* **Format**, **Column**, **AutoFit Selection**
Columns, deleting	Select the column you want to delete by clicking on the column ref box (at top of column)			
	Delete		**Delete**	**Edit**, **Delete**
Columns, inserting	Select the column following the one where you want the new column to appear – by clicking on the column ref box (at top of column)			
			Insert	**Insert**, **Columns**
Copy (replicate) formulae	Select cell with formula to be copied Drag the mouse from bottom right corner of cell over cells to copy to, release mouse			
Currency symbols		Click: the 🏦 **Currency** button for UK currency		**Format**, **Cells**, **Number**, **Category**, **Currency**. Select number of decimal places
Decimal places		Click: the ⁘ **Increase Decimal** button to increase the number of decimal places Click: the ⁙ **Decrease Decimal** button to decrease the number of decimal places	**Format Cells** Select the **Number** tab Click: **Number** in the **Category**: menu Select the number of decimal places you need	**Format**, **Cells**
Enter formulae	Click: in the cell where you want text to appear Key in: = followed by the formula Press: **Enter**			
Enter numeric data	Click: in the cell where you want text to appear Key in: the data Press: **Enter**			
Enter text	Click: in the cell where you want text to appear Key in: the text Press: **Enter**			

Action	Keyboard	Mouse	Right-mouse menu	Menu
Exit Excel		Click: the ✕ **Close** button		**F**ile, E**x**it
Fit to page				**F**ile, **Page Setup**, **F**it to (1) **Page(s) wide**
Formulae, functions	Click on the cell where the result is required Use: =**SUM(cell ref:cell ref)** for adding a range of cells or Click: Σ **AutoSum** button Click and drag over the cell range Press: **Enter**			
Formulae, operators	+ add - subtract * multiply / divide			
Formulae, showing	**Ctrl + `**			**T**ools, **O**ptions, View Under **Window options**, select **Formulas** so that a tick appears
Formulae, printing	Ensure the formulae are showing			
				File, **Page Setup**, **Page tab**, **Landscape** or **File**, **Page Setup**, **Page tab** Under **Scaling**, select **Fit to 1 page wide by 1 page tall**
Help	**F1**			**Help** **Microsoft Excel Help**
	Shift + F1			**Help, What's This?**
Integers (whole numbers)		Click: the ⁺⁰⁰ **Decrease Decimal** button until you have reduced the number of decimal places to zero	**Format Cells** Select the **Number** tab Click: **Number** in the **Category** menu Change the number of decimal places to zero	**Fo**rmat, C**e**lls
Loading Excel	In Windows 98 desktop			
		Double-click: the **Excel** shortcut icon		**Start, Programs, Microsoft Excel**
Moving around	Use the cursor keys	Click where you want to move to		
Move to top of document	**Ctrl + Home**			
Move to end of document	**Ctrl + End**			
New file	**Ctrl + N**	Click: the ☐ **New** button		**F**ile, **N**ew
Open an existing file	**Ctrl + O**	Click: the 📂 **Open** button		**F**ile, **O**pen
	Select: the drive required Select: the filename Click: **Open**			
Page Setup	From the **File** menu, select: **Page Setup** Choose from **Margins, Paper Size, Paper Source, Layout**			

Action	Keyboard	Mouse	Right-mouse menu	Menu
Print file	**Ctrl + P** Select the options you need Press: **Enter**	Click: the 🖨 **Print** button		**File**, **Print** Select the options you need and click: **OK**
Printing in Landscape	From the **File** menu, select: **Page Setup** Click: the **Page** tab Select: **Landscape** Click: **OK**			
Print Preview		Click: the 🔍 **Print Preview** button		**File**, **Print Preview**
Replicate (copy) formulae	Select: the cell with the formula to be copied Drag the mouse from the bottom right corner of the cell over the cells to copy to Release mouse			
Restore deleted input	**Ctrl + Z**	Click: the ↺ **Undo** button		**Edit**, **Undo**
Rows, adding	Select the row by clicking in the row ref box (at side of row) below the one where you want the new row to appear			
			Insert	**Insert**, **Rows**
Rows, deleting	Select the row by clicking in the row ref box (at side of row) below the one that you want to delete			
			Delete	**Edit**, **Delete**
Save	**Ctrl + S**	Click: the 💾 **Save** button		**File**, **Save**
	If you have not already saved the file you will be prompted to specify the directory and to name the file. If you have already done this, then Excel will automatically save it.			
Save using a different name or to a different directory				**File**, **Save As**
	Select the appropriate drive and change the filename if relevant. Click: **Save**			
Selecting cells	Click and drag across cells			
Removing selection	Click in any white space			
Undo	**Ctrl + Z**	Click: the ↺ **Undo** button		**Edit**, **Undo**
Zoom		Click: the `100%` ▾ **Zoom** button		**View**, **Zoom**

Using AutoFill

If the cell contains a number, date or time period that can extend in a series, by dragging the fill handle of a cell you can copy that cell to other cells in the same row or column. The values are incremented. For example, if the cell contains MONDAY, you can quickly fill in other cells in a row or column with TUESDAY, WEDNESDAY and so on.

1 Key in and enter the first label or if numeric key in and enter the first two numbers.

2 Select the cell(s) containing the label or numbers you entered.

3 Move the mouse over the bottom right corner of the selected cell(s).

4 Press and hold down the left mouse and drag over the cells you want to include in the series.

5 Release the mouse.

You must not have a cell active whilst trying to format it.

When deleting columns/rows, you should not delete contents only, ie you should not leave a blank row after a deletion.

Do you have the correct number of printouts? Is the data showing in full as requested? On the printout showing formula, check that the formulae are displayed in full.

Check that any amendments have changed calculations accordingly.

Check your work carefully. All numeric data must be 100% correct in spreadsheet assignments.

Spreadsheets: sample full practice assignment

Scenario

You are working as an Administrative Assistant for a car rental company. Your job is to produce routine customer invoices.

Produce a spreadsheet report showing the three-day rental costs including costs for surplus mileage for different classes of vehicles.

1 Create a new spreadsheet.

2 Enter the following data, leaving the **SURPLUS** column blank.

RENTAL COSTS						
CAR	COST	RATE	DAY1	DAY2	DAY3	SURPLUS
MINI	100	0.2	12	4	18	
ECONOMY	120	0.25	22	0	6	
COMPACT	140	0.27	10	12	45	
STANDARD	176	0.3	6.5	12	21	
PREMIUM	276	0.42	14	60	53	
LUXURY	316	0.62	10	23	0	
SPECIAL	356	0.79	8	1	5	

3 Enter your name, centre number and today's date a few lines below the data.

4 The **SURPLUS** for each car is calculated by adding the figures for **DAY1**, **DAY2** and **DAY3**.

    a Insert a formula to calculate the **SURPLUS** for **MINI**.
    b Replicate this formula to show the **SURPLUS** for each car.

5 Save your spreadsheet report with the filename **rentals** and print one copy, showing the figures not the formula. Make sure that all the data is displayed in full.

6 Insert a new column entitled **TOTAL COST** between the columns **COST** and **RATE**.

7 **TOTAL COST** is calculated by multiplying the **SURPLUS** figure by the **RATE** and then adding the **COST**.

    a Insert a formula to calculate the **TOTAL COST** for **MINI**.
    b Replicate this formula to show the **TOTAL COST** for all cars.

8   Your Team Leader would like you to align as follows:

    a The column heading **CAR** and all row labels (eg **MINI**, **COMPACT**, etc) should be left-aligned.

    b The other column headings (**COST, TOTAL COST** etc) should be right-aligned.

    c All numeric values should be right-aligned.

9   Format the data as follows:

    a The surplus mileage figures for **DAY1**, **DAY2** and **DAY3** should be displayed in integer format (to zero decimal places).

    b The figures for **COST**, **RATE** and **SURPLUS** should be displayed to two decimal places.

    c The **TOTAL COST** figures data only should be displayed with a £ sign and to two decimal places.

Your Team Leader has noticed that there were some errors in the original data so you will need to make changes to the report.

10   Currently there are no cars in the **COMPACT** class. Delete this entire row.

11   Make the following amendments to the spreadsheet:

    a The **RATE** for **STANDARD** should be **0.4**.

    b The **COST** for **LUXURY** should be **330**.

    c The mileage figure for **PREMIUM** for **DAY2** should be **49**.

    d **SPECIAL** should read **SPORTS SPECIAL**.

Make sure that the **SURPLUS** and **TOTAL COST** have updated as a result of these changes.

12   Save the spreadsheet using the filename **car invoices**. Print one copy showing figures, not formulae. Make sure that all data is displayed in full.

13   Print the spreadsheet with all formulae showing. Make sure that all formulae are displayed in full.

14   Close the spreadsheet and exit the software securely.

Graphs and charts using Excel (Unit 7)

Types of graphical representation

In this section you will learn about different ways of representing data using graphs and charts.

In this chapter we will be using the spreadsheet application Excel to produce graphs and charts. When you have created a spreadsheet, there are many different ways of graphically displaying its data. You will need to be aware of four of these: pie charts, bar charts, line graphs and comparative charts. The charts and graphs can display all the spreadsheet data or selected parts only. If data is changed in the spreadsheet, the graphs and charts will update accordingly to reflect the new data.

 Excel uses the word *chart* and not *graph* for all its graphical displays. In the UK we tend to differentiate between charts and graphs. Throughout this chapter the word chart, ie pie chart, column chart and bar chart, is used except when working with lines when the word graph is used, ie line graph.

1.1 Pie chart

A pie chart consists of a circle divided into a number of segments. In the example below (Figure 4.1), there are three segments, representing eye colours blue, brown and green in Tutor Group A. The largest segment is brown and it tells us that 44% of Tutor Group A have brown eyes, the next largest is green with 30%, and the smallest is blue with 26%. There is a legend (key) to show us which colour or shade represents which eye colour.

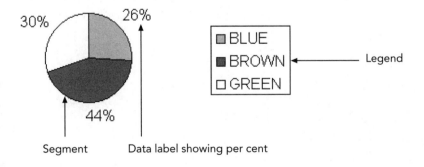

Figure 4.1 Pie chart

Chart title   The chart title should be descriptive and clear.

Data labels   On a pie chart you can show percentage values or actual values. You can show the legend labels next to the segments instead of a legend.

Legend   A legend is a key showing the different colours/shades that correspond to the data
                represented in the pie chart.

Segment   The pie chart is made up of segments that represent different data types.

1.2 Bar chart

A bar chart uses bars to represent values. These can be vertical columns (as shown in Figure 4.2) or horizontal bars. (*Note:* For CLAIT assignments use vertical columns, known as a **Column** chart, not a **Bar** chart as in Excel.) The chart has two axes, the x (horizontal) axis and the y (vertical) axis. The x axis usually represents data that does not change, such as days of the week. The y axis usually represents values that fluctuate, such as monetary values or temperatures. This type of chart is useful for showing comparisons.

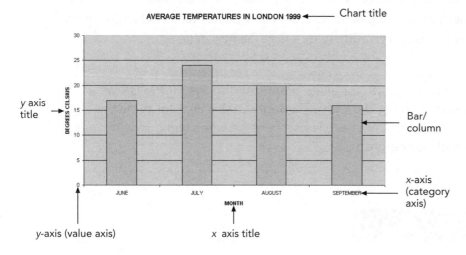

Figure 4.2 Bar chart

The bar chart (Figure 4.2) shows the comparison of average temperatures in London. The tallest bar, July, shows the overall hottest average temperature. The shortest bar, September, shows that this was the coolest month of those shown.

1.3 Line graph

A line graph shows trends in data at equal intervals. Points on the graph are joined together to form a continuous line. Line graphs have properties in common with bar charts, such as x and y axes and axes titles.

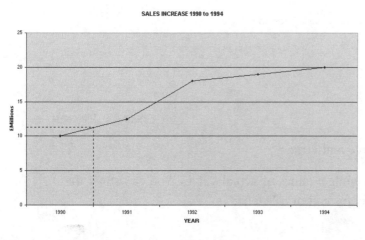

Figure 4.3 Line graph

The line graph (Figure 4.3) shows that the trend is up as the line is going up and not down. Sales have been increasing steadily since 1990. I have drawn a line from the *x* axis, at the end of 1990, to the plotted line, and then drawn a line to the *y* axis. Where this line joins the *y* axis, the value can be read, just over £11 million. This was the value of sales at the end of 1990.

1.4 Comparative chart/graph

A comparative chart is used to compare sets of data. The display shows two or more columns (if a comparative bar chart, Figure 4.4) or two or more lines (if a comparative line graph, Figure 4.5) of the same item.

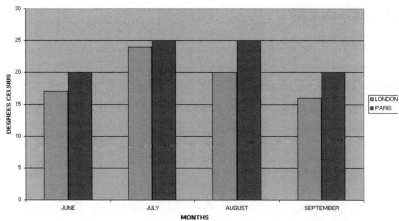

Figure 4.4 Comparative bar chart

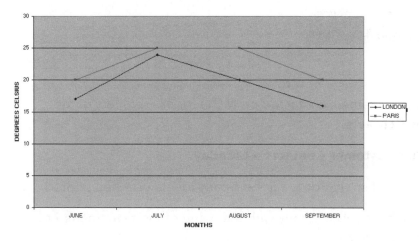

Figure 4.5 Comparative line graph

Section 1: checklist

Explain the following:

1 pie chart
2 bar chart
3 line graph
4 comparative graph/chart
5 legend
6 *x* axis
7 *y* axis.

Creating pie charts

In this section you will practise and learn how to:

- select a single data set
- save a chart
- close a chart
- create a pie chart
- print a chart

Note: The exercises in this section use the Excel datafile **Customers** on the CD-ROM. It is advisable to copy this file to your own storage medium before you begin (details of how to do this are given in the Appendix).

2.1 Accessing the data to chart

Exercise 1

Load Excel and the datafile **Customers**. (This file contains data on the number of existing customers that have been contacted by each member of a telesales team during one week.)

Method

Follow the methods in Chapter 3.

2.2 Creating a pie chart

Exercise 2

Produce a pie chart displaying the customers contacted on **MON** for all members of the telesales team. Save the chart as **Contacts**.

1   Give the chart the title: **Team Customer Contacts – Monday**.

2   Ensure that each sector is shaded so that data can be clearly identified when printed.

3   Each sector of the chart must be labelled clearly with the name of the team member and the number or percentage of customers.

Method

1   Examine the spreadsheet and select the range of cells (the *single data set*) that make up this data, ie A2 to B6 (Figure 4.6).

	A	B	C	D	E	F	G
1	Operator	Mon	Tue	Wed	Thu	Fri	Sat
2	Greg	15	16	12	10	4	27
3	Polly	12	22	10	3	12	30
4	Adjoa	21	17	14	10	19	22
5	Aidan	12	23	29	27	26	34
6	Jack	20	10	12	21	30	31

Figure 4.6 Data selected for charting

2 Click on: the **Chart Wizard** button.

3 **Step 1 of 4 Chart Wizard** dialogue box appears: **Chart Type** (Figure 4.7).

   a The **Standard Types** tab is selected. In the **Chart type** box, click on: **Pie**.

   b In the **Chart sub-type** box, click on: the top left pie type as shown. This is usually already selected as the default setting.

   c Click on: **Next**.

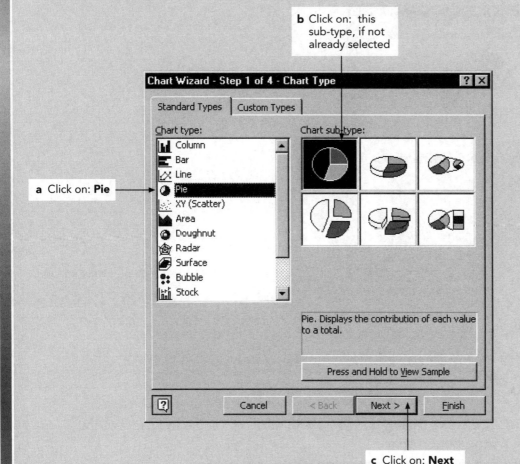

b Click on: this sub-type, if not already selected

a Click on: **Pie**

c Click on: **Next**

Figure 4.7 Step 1 of Chart Wizard

There are many different types of pie charts that you can choose. For the purposes of New CLAIT, the simple pie type (chosen here in Figure 4.7) is a good choice. If you are not printing to a colour printer you may need to choose a pie chart that displays in black and white. The following methods ensure that the sectors of the pie chart are shaded so that they are easily identified. Always check that this is the case. To do this, click on: the **Custom Types** tab and then on **B&W Pie** (black and white pie chart). However, you can create a colour chart and then later select **B&W** for the printout.

To view other pie chart samples, with the **Standard Types** tab selected, click and hold the mouse on: **Press and hold to view sample**. Try experimenting with the different types.

4   Step 2 Chart Wizard dialogue box appears: **Chart Source Data** (Figure 4.8).

There is a preview of the pie chart together with a legend (key representing the different segments of the pie). With the **Data Range** tab selected, the data range selected is shown as:

=Sheet1$A$2:$B$6

Ignoring the $ signs, this represents Sheet1, cells A2 to B6.

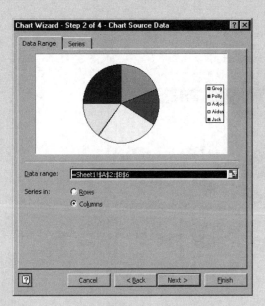

If you have made an error in selecting the data range to chart, *either*:

change the data range by clicking in: the **Data range** box and keying in the correct range

or

click on: the **Collapse Dialog** button, reselect the cell range and click on: the **Collapse Dialog** button again.

> =Sheet1!$A$2:$B$6

Collapse Dialog
button

In this example we have the data series in columns. You will need to click in the **Rows** option button if the data series is in rows.
Should you need to go back a Step, after Step 1 of Chart Wizard, click on: **Back**.

In some circumstances, Excel will automatically make assumptions about what is a data range and will try to include, for example, years (ie 1993, 1994, 1995), since they are numerical. In such cases you will need to carry out steps (a) and (b) (above) to overwrite Excel's assumptions. Then click on: the **Series** tab. In the **Category (X) axis labels**, click on: the **Collapse Dialog** button and select the cell range for year labels. Click on: the **Collapse Dialog** button again. You can also overcome this problem by setting the years as text entries. To do this, *either*:

Select the cells containing the years. Then from the **Format** menu, select: **Cells**. The **Format Cells** box is displayed. With the **Number** tab selected, select: **Text**. Click on: **OK**.

or

Key in an apostrophe before keying in the first date in the range, ie '1993.

5 Click on: **Next**.

6 **Step 3 Chart Wizard** dialogue box appears: **Chart Options** (Figure 4.9).

    a With the **Titles** tab selected, click in: the **Chart title** box and key in: **Team Customer Contacts – Monday**.

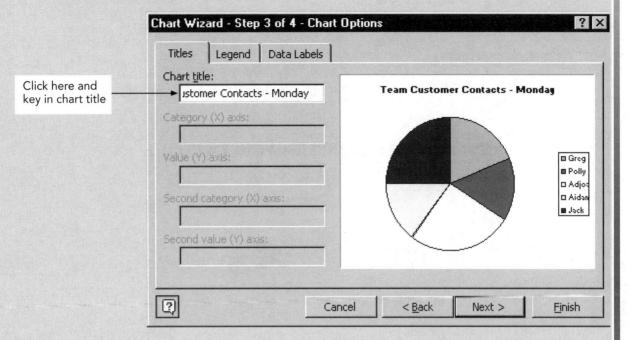

Click here and key in chart title

Figure 4.9 Step 3 of Chart Wizard

 In some cases you may not be able to see all the title as it will scroll out of the visible section. In such cases, do not press **Enter** as this will result in moving to the next step of Chart Wizard. If you do, press: **Enter**, click on: **Back**.

    b Click on: the **Legend** tab.

    c Click in: the **Show legend** tick box to remove the tick.

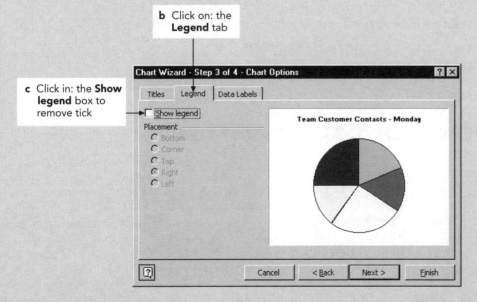

b Click on: the **Legend** tab

c Click in: the **Show legend** box to remove tick

Figure 4.10 Removing a legend

You have been asked to show labels for each of the segments, together with a number or percentage, not a legend. Having segment data labels and a legend duplicates information and will make the chart appear cluttered.

d Click on: the **Data Labels** tab.

e Click in: the **Show label and percent** option button.

f Click on: **Next**.

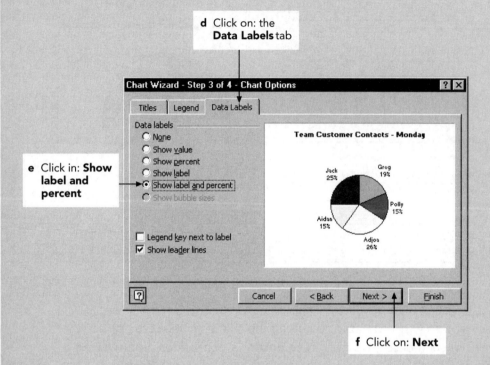

d Click on: the **Data Labels** tab

e Click in: **Show label and percent**

f Click on: **Next**

Figure 4.11 Showing labels

 You will notice that labels and choices appear on the chart preview as you work. If you make an error, carry out the instruction again. Notice other data labelling options.

7 **Step 4 Chart Wizard** dialogue box appears: **Chart Location** (Figure 4.12).

a Click in: the **As new sheet** option button.

b In the adjacent box, key in the name **Contacts**.

c Click on: **Finish**.

b Key in chart name

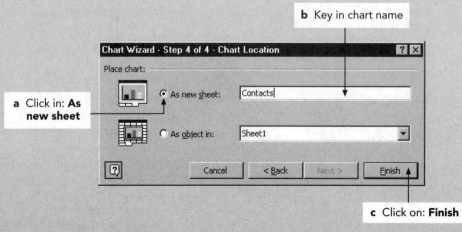

a Click in: **As new sheet**

c Click on: **Finish**

Figure 4.12 Step 4 of Chart Wizard

The chart will be located with the spreadsheet file whichever option you choose. Saving **As new sheet** is a good idea when you have a series of charts to plot from the same data. The sheet tabs and navigation arrows (shown below), at the bottom left of the Excel window, allow navigation between the sheets containing charts and the data spreadsheets. Click on the relevant sheet tab to view it.

The completed pie chart is displayed as shown in Figure 4.13.

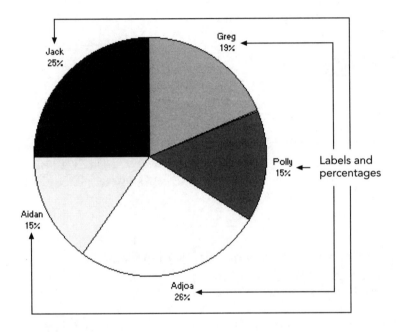

Figure 4.13 Completed pie chart

Should you need to make any changes, with the chart displayed on screen, right-click in the chart area to bring up the menu shown. You will notice that the menu items in the second section, ie below **Format Chart Area**, correspond to the dialogue boxes of **Chart Wizard**. Choose from these options:

Exercise 3

Save the datafile with its existing filename **Customers**.

Method

Click on: the **Save** button.

You can use this quick saving method since the original datafile **Customers** (an Excel spreadsheet file) already exists. When you save the spreadsheet file the chart is saved with it. When you want to keep the original datafile intact, you need to save using the **File** menu, **Save As** and give the file a new name.

2.4 Printing the chart

Exercise 4

Print one copy of the pie chart.

Method

Note: Steps 1 to 4 ensure that the segments of the pie chart are clearly identifiable when printed. If you have chosen a B&W pie when proceeding through Chart Wizard, you can skip these steps and, instead, before step 5, from the **File** menu, select: **Print**.

1   With the chart displayed on screen, from the **File** menu, select: **Page Setup**. The **Page Setup** dialogue box appears (Figure 4.14).

2   Click on: the **Chart** tab.

Click on: the **Chart** tab

Click in: **Print in black and white** box so that a tick is displayed

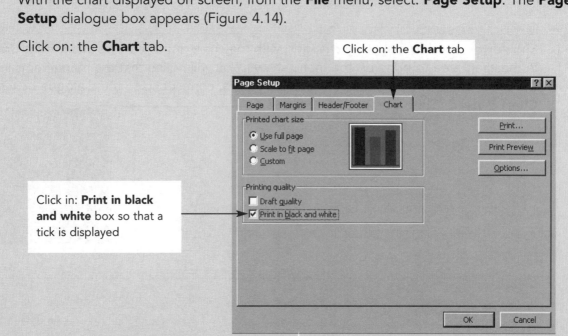

Figure 4.14 Page Setup dialogue box

3 Click in: the **Print in black and white** box so that a tick appears.

4 Click on: **Print**.

5 The **Print** dialogue box appears (Figure 4.15).

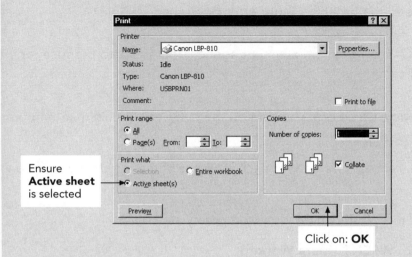

Ensure
Active sheet
is selected

Click on: **OK**

Figure 4.15 Print dialogue box

6 In the **Print what** section, ensure that the **Active sheet** option button is selected.

7 Click on: **OK**.

 By default the chart will print in landscape format.

2.5 Closing the datafile

Exercise 5

Close the datafile.

Method

From the **File** menu, select: **Close**.

 You can close with the display on either the chart or the spreadsheet containing the data. *Remember:* The chart and the data sheet will be saved together with the same filename.

Graphs and charts practice I

Practice I

Note: For this practice you will need the Excel file **Temp agency** on the CD-ROM.

You work as an Administrative Assistant for an employment agency. Your job is to produce reports on temporary staff for the Team Leader.

1   Open the datafile **Temp agency**, which contains data on the number of hours that temporary employees worked over a 5-week period.

   The first report will compare the hours worked for each member of the temporary staff during **WEEK1**, using a pie chart.

2   Create a pie chart to display the **WEEK1** data for all temporary staff.

   a Give the chart the heading: **WEEK1 Hours Worked**.
   b Ensure that each sector is shaded in such a way that the data can be clearly identified when printed.
   c Each sector of the chart must be labelled clearly with the name of the team member and percentage of hours worked.

3   Save the file using the name **hours**.

4   Print one copy of the pie chart.

5   Close the datafile.

Practice 2

Note: For this practice you will need the Excel file **books** on the CD-ROM.

You work as an Administrative Assistant for a bookstore. Your job is to produce reports on book sales for the Store Manager.

1   Open the datafile **books**, which contains data on the number of books sold in the past 6 days.

2   The first report will compare the books sold for each type on **MON**, using a pie chart.

3   Create a pie chart to display the **MON** data for all types of book.

   a Give the chart the heading: **Monday Sales**.
   b Ensure that each sector is shaded in such a way that the data can be clearly identified when printed.
   c Each sector of the chart must be labelled clearly with the number of books sold.
   d A legend should be shown to indicate the book types.

4   Save the file using the name **book sales**.

5   Print one copy of the pie chart.

6   Close the datafile.

3 Creating bar charts

In this section you will practise and learn how to:

- select a subset of a single data set
- create a bar chart
- set upper and lower limits for axes

3.1 Creating a bar chart

Exercise 1

Produce a bar chart showing the data for **Greg** from **Mon** to **Thu**.

1 Display the days along the x axis.

2 Give the bar chart the heading: **Greg Contacts Mon to Thu**.

3 Give the x axis the title **Day**.

4 Give the y axis the title **Contacts**.

Method

1 Load Excel and the datafile **Customers** saved in Section 2.

2 Ensure that the spreadsheet data is displayed. If not, click on the appropriate sheet tab, ie **Sheet1**, at the bottom of the screen.

3 Select the relevant data to chart (this is a *subset* of the data for **Greg** since it does not include all the data for **Greg**), ie **B1 to E2** (Figure 4.16).

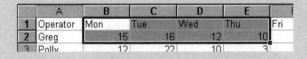

Figure 4.16 Selecting a subset of data

4 Click on: the **Chart Wizard** button. **Step 1 of 4 Chart Wizard** dialogue box appears: **Chart Type**.

a With the **Standard Types** tab selected, click on: **Column**. (This is the default.)

> Notice that in Excel **bar** charts have horizontal bars. We are therefore choosing **Column** instead of **Bar** as the column option is the more common way that bar charts are represented, ie with the bars vertical rather than horizontal.

b In the **Chart sub-type** box, click on: the top left chart. (This is the default so may already be selected.)

c Click on: **Next**.

Practise experimenting with the different chart types.

5 **Step 2 Chart Wizard** dialogue box appears: **Chart Source Data**.

6 Click on: **Next**.

7 **Step 3 Chart Wizard** dialogue box appears: **Chart Options**.

    a Select the **Titles** tab (if not already selected), click in: the **Chart title** box and key in: **Greg Contacts Mon to Thu**.

    b Click in the **Category (x) axis** box and key in: **Day**.

    c Click in the **Value (y) axis** box and key in: **Contacts**.

    d Click on: the **Legend** tab.

    e Click in: the **Show legend** tick box to remove the tick.

    f Click on: **Next**.

8 **Step 4 Chart Wizard** dialogue box appears: **Chart Location**.

    a Click on: **As new sheet** option button and key in the name **Greg**.

    b Click on: **Finish**.

The completed bar chart is displayed as shown (Figure 4.17).

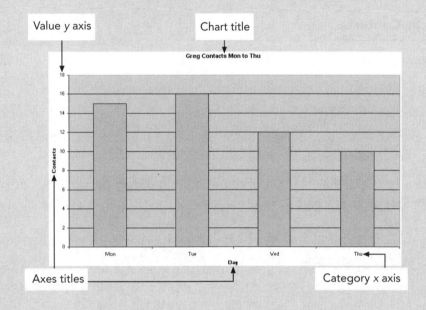

Figure 4.17 Bar chart

3.2 Setting upper and lower limits for axes

Exercise 2

Set the y axis to display the range 2 to 22.

Method

Referring back to Figure 4.17, you will see that the y axis is displaying 0 to 18. To alter this:

1 With the chart displayed, double-click on the **Value Axis** (the y axis).

2 The **Format Axis** dialogue box is displayed (Figure 4.18).

3 Click on: the **Scale** tab.

4 Click in: the **Minimum** box and key in: **2**.

5 Click in: the **Maximum** box and key in: **22**.

6 Click on: **OK**.

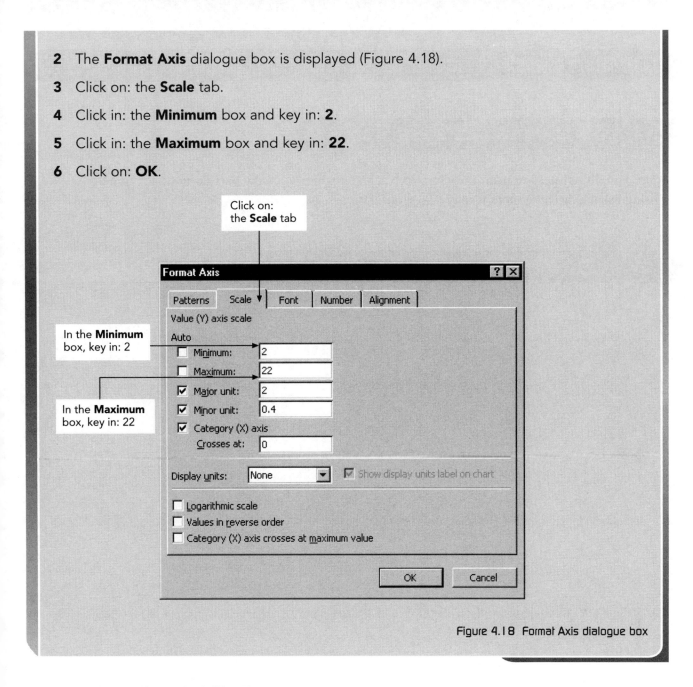

Figure 4.18 Format Axis dialogue box

The bar chart will now look like Figure 4.19.

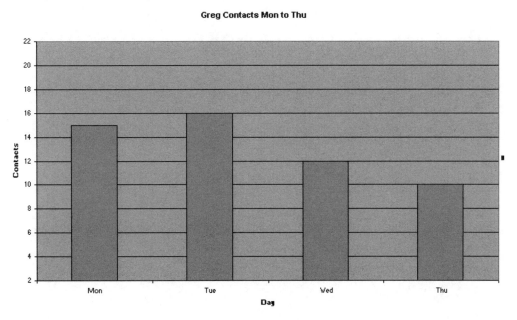

Fig 4.19 Chart with *y* axis set as specified

3.3 Save the chart named Greg within the datafile Customers

3.4 Print the chart as in Section 2.4

Note: You do not need to print this chart in black and white since the bars do not need to be distinguishable because there is only one set of data.

3.5 Close the datafile as in Section 2.5

Practice 3

The Team Leader has asked you to produce a bar chart showing the data for **Kym** from **WEEK1** to **WEEK4**.

1 Load the datafile **hours** saved in Practice 1, Section 2.

2 Produce a bar chart showing the data for **KYM** from **WEEK1** to **WEEK4**.

   a Display the weeks along the x axis.
   b Set the y axis to display the range **5** to **25**.
   c Give the bar chart the heading **Kym Hours – Week1 to Week4**.
   d Give the x axis the title **Weeks**.
   e Give the y axis the title **No of hours**.

3 Save the chart with the name **Kym** and the file with the name **Kym hours**.

4 Print one copy of the bar chart.

5 Close the datafile.

Practice 4

The Store Manager has asked you to produce a bar chart showing the data for the **Classics** genre from **Monday** to **Thursday**.

1 Load the datafile **book sales** saved in Practice 2, Section 2.

2 Produce a bar chart showing the data for **CLASSICS** from **MON** to **THU**.

   a Display the days along the x axis.
   b Set the y axis to display the range **25** to **225**.
   c Give the bar chart the heading: **Sales of Classics – Mon to Thu**.
   d Give the x axis the title **Day**.
   e Give the y axis the title **Number Sold**.

3 Save the file using the name **classics**.

4 Print one copy of the bar chart.

5 Close the datafile.

4 Creating line graphs

In this section you will practise and learn how to create line graphs.

4.1 Creating a line graph

Produce a line graph showing the customer contacts on **Mon** for all the team *except* **Jack**.

1   Display the names of the team members along the *x* axis.

2   Give the line graph the heading: **CUSTOMER CONTACTS (EXCEPT JACK) – MON**.

3   Give the *x* axis the title **Team Members**.

4   Give the *y* axis the title **Contacts**.

Method

1   Load Excel and the datafile **Customers**.

2   Ensure that the spreadsheet data is displayed.

3   Select the relevant data to chart, ie A2 to B5.

4   Click on: the [icon] **Chart Wizard** button.

5   **Step 1 of 4 Chart Wizard** dialogue box appears: **Chart type**.

    a   With the **Standard Types** tab selected, click on: **Line**.
    b   In the **Chart sub-type** box, click on: the top left chart.
    c   Click on: **Next**.

6   **Step 2 Chart Wizard** dialogue box appears: **Chart Source Data**. Click on: **Next**.

7   **Step 3 Chart Wizard** dialogue box appears: **Chart Options**.

    a   Select the **Titles** tab, click in: the **Chart title** box and key in: **CUSTOMER CONTACTS (EXCEPT JACK) – MON**.
    b   Click in: the **Category (x) axis** box and key in: **Team Members**.
    c   Click in: the **Value (y) axis** box and key in: **Contacts**.
    d   Click on: the **Legend** tab.
    e   Click in: the **Show legend** tick box to remove the tick.
    f   Click on: **Next**.

8   **Step 4 Chart Wizard** dialogue box appears: **Chart Location**.

    a   Click on: **As new sheet** option button and key in the name **Excluding Jack**.
    b   Click on: **Finish**.

The completed line graph is displayed as shown in Figure 4.20.

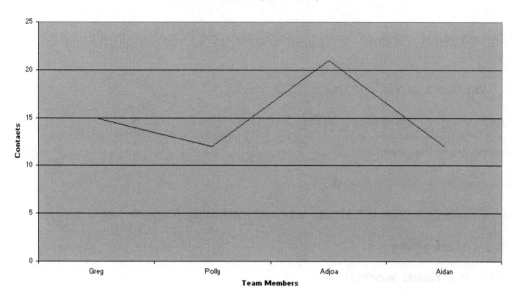

Figure 4.20 Completed line graph

4.2 Set upper and lower limits for axes

Exercise 2

Set the y axis to display the range 5 to 30.

Method

Follow the instructions in Section 3.2.

4.3 Save graph

Save the graph within the datafile with the original filename **Customers**, as in Section 2.3.

4.4 Print the graph as in Section 2.4

4.5 Close the datafile as in Section 2.5

Graphs and charts practice 3

Practice 5

The Team Leader has asked you to produce a line graph showing hours worked in WEEK1 for all the employees except KARL.

1   Load the datafile **Kym hours** saved in Practice 3, Section 3.

2   Produce a line graph showing the data for **WEEK1** all employees *except* **Karl**.

   a Display the weeks along the x axis.

   b Set the y axis to display the range **5** to **40**.

   c Give the graph the heading: **Week 1 Hours worked excluding Karl**.

   d Give the x axis the title **Employees**.

   e Give the y axis the title **Hours worked**.

3   Save the file using the name **Employees**.

4   Print one copy of the line graph.

5   Close the datafile.

Practice 6

The Store Manager has asked you to produce a line graph showing all book types sales on Monday.

1   Load the datafile **classics** saved in Practice 4, Section 3.

2   Produce a line graph showing the data for **MON** for all book types.

   a Display the book types along the x axis.

   b Set the y axis to display the range **40** to **220**.

   c Give the graph the heading: **Monday Sales**.

   d Give the x axis the title **Book Types**.

   e Give the y axis the title **Number of Sales**.

3   Save the file using the name **Monday sales**.

4   Print one copy of the bar chart.

5   Close the datafile.

5 Creating comparative graphs

In this section you will practise and learn how to create comparative graphs and charts.

5.1 Creating a comparative bar chart

Exercise 1

Using the datafile **Customers**, produce a comparative bar chart comparing the data for **Greg** and **Polly** from **Mon** to **Sat**.

1 Display the days along the x axis.

2 Set the y axis to display the range **5** to **30**.

3 Give the chart the heading: **Greg and Polly Customer Contacts**.

4 Give the x axis the title **Day**.

5 Give the y axis the title **Contacts**.

6 Use a legend to identify the bars. Make sure that the bars are distinctive and can be identified when printed.

Method

1 Load the datafile **Customers**.

2 Display the spreadsheet data.

3 Select the relevant data to chart, ie A1 to G3.

   Note: In this case we need to include the data range in row 1 in the selection so that the x axis labels (days) are automatically displayed on the chart.

4 Click on: the **Chart Wizard** button.

5 **Step 1 Chart Wizard**

   a With the **Standard Types** tab selected, click on: **Column**.
   b In the **Chart sub-type** box, click on: the first chart at the top left.
   c Click on: **Next**.

6 **Step 2 Chart Wizard**. Click on: **Next**.

7 **Step 3 Chart Wizard**

   a Select the **Titles** tab, click in: the **Chart title** box and key in: **Greg and Polly Customer Contacts**.
   b Click in: the **Category (x) axis** box and key in: **Day**.
   c Click in the **Value (y) axis** box and key in: **Contacts**.
   d Click on: **Next**.

8 **Step 4 Chart Wizard**

   a Click on: the **As new sheet** option button and key in **Greg and Polly Comparison**.
   b Click on: **Finish**.

9 Set the y axis display as requested.

The completed comparative chart is displayed as shown in Figure 4.21.

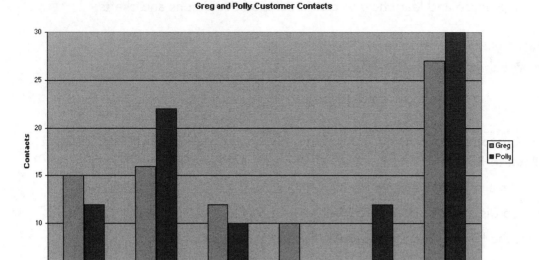

Figure 4.21 Completed comparative graph

 In this example, we need to show a legend to indicate which colour bars represent Greg and Polly. If you are printing in black and white, check that the bars and legend are displaying so that they are distinguishable. When necessary, use the **File** menu, **Page Setup** to select black and white printout.

5.2 Save the chart within the datafile as in Section 2.3

5.3 Print the chart as in Section 2.4

5.4 Creating a comparative line graph

Exercise 2

Produce a line graph comparing the data for Greg and Polly from Mon to Sat (as in Exercise 1).

1 Display the days along the x axis.

2 Set the y axis to display the range **0** to **30**.

3 Give the chart the heading: **Greg and Polly Customer Contacts**.

4 Give the x axis the title **Day**.

5 Give the y axis the title **Contacts**.

6 Use a legend to identify each line. Make sure that the lines and/or data points are distinctive and can be identified when printed.

Use the method as for Exercise 1, except at step 5 select: **Line**. In the **Chart sub-type** box select: the chart on the left of the second row, ie **Line with markers displayed at each data value**.

 If you are printing a comparative line graph to a black and white printer, be careful to choose a chart type that displays different shapes on the lines to distinguish them. The type chosen above is suitable.

The chart will look like Figure 4.22.

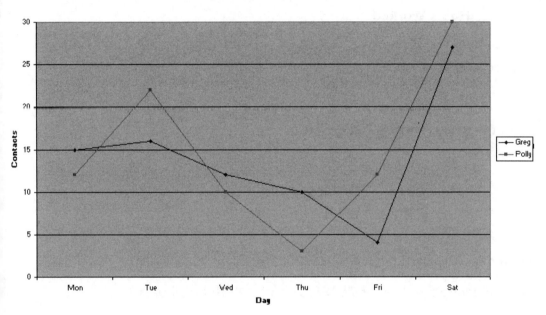

Figure 4.22 Comparative line graph

5.5 Save the chart within the datafile as in Section 2.3

5.6 Print the chart as in Section 2.4

5.7 Close the datafile and exit Excel

Practice 7

The Team Leader has asked you to produce a line graph comparing Danny's hours with Kym's.

1   Load the datafile **Employees** saved in Practice 5, Section 4.

2   Produce a line graph comparing the data for **KYM** and **DANNY** for all weeks.

    a   Display the weeks along the x axis.

    b   Set the y axis to display the range **5** to **50**.

    c   Give the graph the heading: **Comparison of Hours for Kym and Danny**.

    d   Give the x axis the title **Week**.

    e   Give the y axis the title **Hours Worked**.

    f   Use a legend to identify each line. Make sure that the lines and/data points are distinctive and can be identified when printed.

3   Print one copy of the line graph.

4   Save the datafile with the name **Practice 7 compline**.

Practice 8

The Store Manager has asked you to produce a bar chart comparing crime and classics book types sales from Monday to Saturday.

1   Load the datafile **Monday sales** saved in Practice 6, Section 4.

2   Produce a bar chart comparing the data for **CLASSICS** and **CRIME** for all days.

    a   Display the days along the x axis.

    b   Set the y axis to display the range **0** to **300**.

    c   Give the graph the heading: **Classics and Crime Genres**.

    d   Give the x axis the title **Day**.

    e   Give the y axis the title **Number of Sales**.

    f   Use a legend to identify each bar. Make sure that the bars are distinctive and can be identified when printed.

3   Print one copy of the bar chart.

4   Save the datafile with the name **Practice 8 compbar**.

Graphs and charts quick reference for New CLAIT (Excel)

Action	Keyboard	Mouse	Right-mouse menu	Menu
Create a chart	Select the data to chart			
		Click: the ▥ **Chart Wizard button**		**Insert**, **Chart**
	STEP 1 Select: the chart type Click: **Next** **STEP 2** Check that the source data is correct, if not change it Click: **Next** **STEP 3** Select: the **Titles** tab Key in the **Chart** title, the **Category (x) axis** title and the **Category (y) axis** title Select: the **Legend** tab Click: in the **Show legend** box to add/remove tick as appropriate (*For pie charts only*) Select: the **Data Labels** tab Click: **Show label** if appropriate Click: **Next** **STEP 4** Click: **As new sheet** or **As object in** Key in: the chart name Click: **Finish**			
Edit a chart	Select the chart by clicking on it			
			Right-click on the chart. Select from options	
Print a chart	With the chart displayed on screen			
	Ctrl + P Ensure **Active sheet** is selected Click: **OK**	Click: the 🖨 **Print** button (This will automatically print the sheet)		**File**, **Print** Ensure **Active sheet** is selected Click: **OK**
Save a chart	**Ctrl + S**	Click: the 💾 **Save** button		**File**, **Save**
Set upper and lower limits on the y axis	*To set upper and lower limits for y (vertical) axis:* With the graph on screen Double-click: the **Value Axis** In the **Format Axis** dialogue box: Click: the **Scale** tab Key in: the new values in the **Maximum** and **Minimum** boxes Click: **OK**			

Hints and tips

- Reloading a saved chart – reload the spreadsheet from which the chart was produced. Click on: the **chartname** tab at the bottom of the sheet.
- When you change data in the spreadsheet, the data on the corresponding chart will change automatically to incorporate the amended data.
- Ensure that you create the type of chart requested.
- Have you labelled the charts as requested?
- Do you have the correct number of printouts?

- Ensure that you do not have any unwanted labels.
- Ensure that you do not have blank slices on the pie chart that do not relate to any data.
- Ensure that the printouts have easily distinguishable components where appropriate (eg on pie charts and comparative data charts and graphs) so that the chart is meaningful.

Graphs and charts: sample full practice assignment

Note: For this assignment you will need the datafile **Deliveries** on the CD-ROM.

Scenario

You are working as an Administrative Assistant for a company that makes musical instruments. Your job is to produce various reports on deliveries made to different towns in the West of England region.

Your Manager has asked you to produce a set of reports in graph format showing deliveries made over the past six months.

1 Open the datafile **Deliveries** that contains data on the number of deliveries to West of England towns from July to December.

The first report will compare the number of deliveries to each town in July, using a pie chart.

2 Create a pie chart to display the **JUL** data for all towns.

   a Give the chart the heading: **July Deliveries**.
   b Ensure that each sector is shaded in such a way that the data can be clearly identified when printed.
   c Each sector of the chart must be clearly labelled with the name of the town and the **number** or **percentage** of deliveries.

3 Save the file using the name **towns**.

4 Print one copy of the pie chart.

Your manager would like to check the deliveries to Bristol until the end of October.

5 Produce a bar chart showing the data for **BRISTOL** from **JUL** to **OCT**.

   a Display the months along the x axis.
   b Set the y axis to display the range **5** to **55**.
   c Give the bar chart the heading: **Deliveries to Bristol**.
   d Give the x axis the title **Month**.
   e Give the y axis the title **No of Deliveries**.

6 Save the file keeping the name **towns**.

7 Print one copy of the bar chart.

Your manager would like to compare the deliveries to Bristol with those to Yeovil.

8 Produce a line graph comparing the data for **BRISTOL** and **YEOVIL** from **JUL** to **DEC**.

   a Display the months along the x axis.
   b Set the y axis to display the range **5** to **65**.
   c Give the graph the heading: **Comparison Bristol and Yeovil**.
   d Give the x axis the title **Month**.
   e Give the y axis the title **No of Deliveries**.
   f Use a legend to identify each line. Make sure that the lines and/or data points are distinctive, and can be identified when printed.

9 Save the file keeping the name **towns**.

10 Print one copy of the line graph.

11 Close the document and exit the software securely.

Databases using Access (Unit 5)

Getting started

In this section you will practise and learn how to:

- understand database applications basics
- understand the parts of the document window
- enter new records
- amend data
- print data in table format
- close the database file

- load Access
- open an existing database
- delete records
- replace specified data
- save the database data
- exit Access

Note: The exercises in this section use the Access datafiles **Fitness**, **Car sales** and **Holidays** on the CD-ROM. It is advisable to copy these files to your own storage medium before you begin (details of how to do this are given in the Appendix).

1.1 Understanding database applications basics

A database application allows you to store data in an organised record format. It is sometimes known as an 'electronic filing system' and is structured so that it can be used to retrieve, sort and search for data quickly and in many different ways. Database files can be saved to disk and printed. Computerised databases have vast storage capacity to store records such as tax details of UK citizens and stock control in supermarkets. Smaller databases may be used for storing details of your personal CD collection, for example. Using a computerised database is much faster than using a paper database, in which, for instance, filing cards are stored on a manual card index system. *The Phone Book* is an example of a paper database in which records are listed in alphabetical order of name. It is now possible to find telephone numbers on the Internet – this method uses a computerised database. Directory Enquiries accesses telephone numbers quickly because operators have access to computerised databases. Databases are used extensively by many organisations and businesses.

Access is a database application. It is very powerful with numerous helpful features. Some of these include searching, sorting, querying, reporting and outputting specified data in various ways (eg reports and forms). Some of these features are also available in spreadsheet programs, such as Excel. For New CLAIT it is acceptable to use Excel for this unit. However, knowledge of Access will be very useful generally and if you want to progress to CLAIT Plus. In this chapter, you will use only features necessary to edit, sort, search and print using simple databases. Different facets of Access will be explained as and when you meet them. Creating a database from scratch is not a requirement for New CLAIT. However, if you want to learn how to create one to gain a more thorough understanding of Access databases, you can work through Section 1 of the databases chapter in the CLAIT Plus part of this book.

Common database terms

Common database terms (general to all types of database applications) include:

File   A file is a collection of related records.

Record A collection of information for each item in a file is called a record.

Field   A record is divided into separate categories, known as fields. There are different types of field. The common ones are:

Alphabetic (in Access called *text*) fields. These contain text that is manipulated alphabetically.

Numeric (in Access called *number*) fields. These recognise numbers and sort in ascending or descending numerical order. *Note:* In Access DATE/TIME and CURRENCY fields can also be used as number fields where appropriate. The format of such fields is determined when the database is designed. For example, a date format could be 10/02/03, or 10 February 2003, or 10-Feb-02, depending on the database design. It does not matter which format you use to enter the date since Access will always follow the format set. When working with currency you should use only the numeric value, ie no £ symbol or commas. Access will automatically format it.

Alphanumeric (in Access called *text*) fields. These contain numbers and text that do not need to be sorted in number order, telephone numbers, for example.

An Access database file contains database *objects*. We will be using two database objects – *Tables* and *Queries*. We will meet all the above terms as we progress through this chapter.

1.2 Loading Access and an existing database

Exercise 1

Load Access and the database file **Fitness**.

Method

1   Load Access in the same way as loading other programs in the Microsoft Office suite:

From the **Programs** menu, select: Microsoft Access

The Access window appears, and you will notice that there are many similarities with the Word window, for example Title bar, Menu bar and Standard toolbar, which are all used in the same way as when using other Office applications.

2   On loading Access, a dialogue box also appears (Figure 5.1).

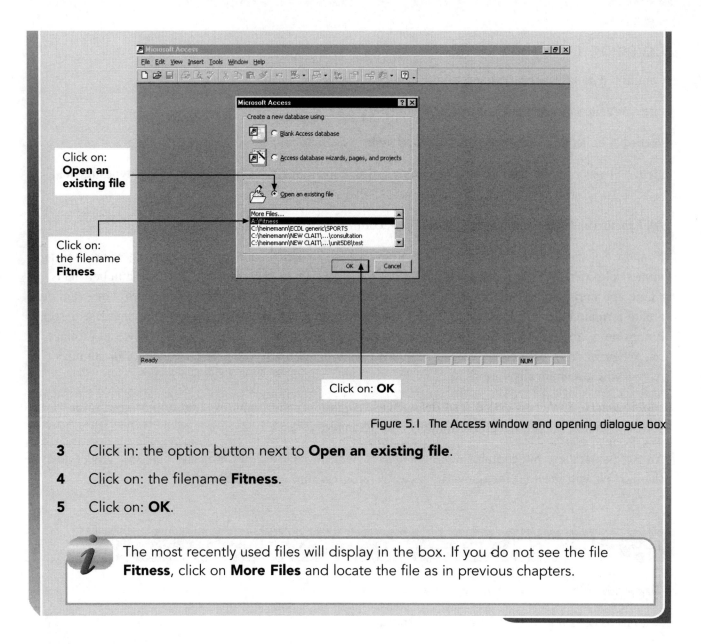

Click on:
**Open an
existing file**

Click on:
the filename
Fitness

Click on: **OK**

Figure 5.1 The Access window and opening dialogue box

3   Click in: the option button next to **Open an existing file**.

4   Click on: the filename **Fitness**.

5   Click on: **OK**.

> The most recently used files will display in the box. If you do not see the file **Fitness**, click on **More Files** and locate the file as in previous chapters.

1.3 Accessing the database table

Exercise 2

Load the database table **CLASSES**.

Method

> The window in Figure 5.2 enables you to access all *objects* of the database. For New CLAIT, you will only be working with the objects, *Tables* and *Queries*.
>
> The overall database filename is **Fitness**. Within this file there can be many objects, such as tables and queries that have their own individual names. In this case (Figure 5.2) the **Tables** button is selected (it looks as if it is pressed in) and the table attached to this database is named **CLASSES**. A table is used to store records, each record consisting of fields. We will access this table next. In Section 2 we will query the database in order to extract specified records only.

1 The **Fitness: Database** window is displayed (Figure 5.2).

2 With the **Tables** button selected in the **Objects** section, double-click on the table **CLASSES**.

Click on:
the **Tables**
button

Double-click
on: **CLASSES**

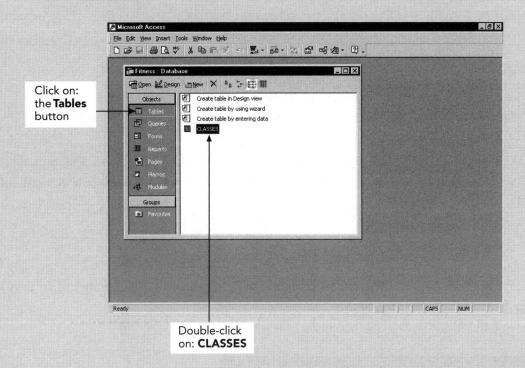

Figure 5.2 Fitness:Database window/Loading a table

3 The table is displayed (Figure 5.3).

Field names:
there are 7 fields in
this database

Records:
there are 16
records in this
database

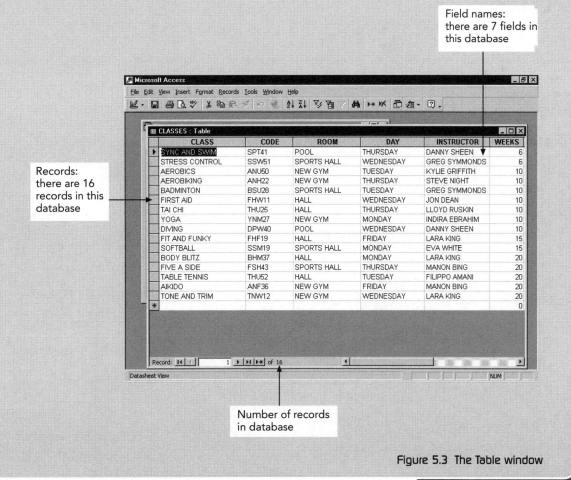

Number of records
in database

Figure 5.3 The Table window

Refer to Figure 5.3 and locate the following on your screen display:

1 Field names

There are seven fields in each record of this database. They are CLASS, CODE, ROOM, DAY, INSTRUCTOR, WEEKS, START DATE (you may need to use the scroll bar to view them all).

CLASS, ROOM, DAY and INSTRUCTOR are alphabetic (in Access *Text*) fields. CODE is an alphanumeric field (in Access *Text*) field. WEEKS is a numeric (in Access *Number*) field. START DATE is a numeric (in Access *Date*) field.

2 Records

One row of data represents one record. Therefore this database has 16 records. The number of records is displayed at the bottom of the table window.

1.5 Moving around the database table

Practise moving around the database.

Method

There are several ways to move around:

- Use the arrow keys.
- Use the **Tab** key.
- Click anywhere on the table.
- Use the navigation buttons at the bottom of the table (Figure 5.4).

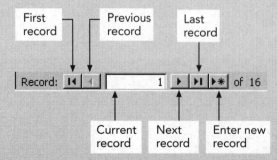

Figure 5.4 Navigation buttons

Exercise 5

Enter the following new records to the database:

CLASS	CODE	ROOM	DAY	INSTRUCTOR	WEEKS	START DATE
TENNIS	THM21	SPORTS HALL	MONDAY	EVA WHITE	10	16/09/02
JUDO	JNT40	NEW GYM	TUESDAY	MANON BING	15	10/9/02
FENCING	FSM31	SPORTS HALL	MONDAY	KYLIE GRIFFITH	20	9/09/02

Method

1 Move the cursor to the last empty row using one of the methods in Section 1.5 (Figure 5.5). Notice that the record number now shows 17.

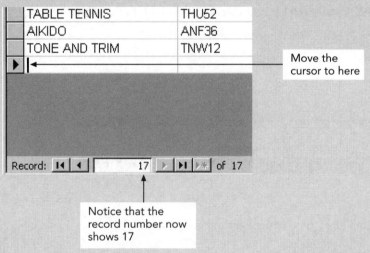

Move the cursor to here

Notice that the record number now shows 17

Figure 5.5 Adding a new record

2 Press: the **Caps Lock** key so that you are consistently using upper case letters to conform with the rest of the database entries.

3 Key in the data for each record in the appropriate fields, pressing **Enter** or **Tab** after each entry.

4 Proofread on screen. Notice that the START DATE of the FENCING class automatically changes to display 09 instead of 9 and 2002 instead of 02. (The database date field has been designed for this to happen.)

5 You should now have 19 records in the database.

Always check your work very carefully. It is very important that data is entered accurately. If it is not, results of searches (in the next section) will not work properly. Accuracy is essential for CLAIT assignments. When adding/amending always use the same case as the rest of the entries for the database fields. In New CLAIT it is essential that all data is displayed in full on printouts. Check the database on screen to see if any columns need widening. To widen a column:

1 With the table displayed, in the field headings row position the mouse on the line between the field headings. The pointer changes to a double arrow.

2 Hold down the left mouse button and drag to the right until the data is displayed in full.

3 Release the mouse button.

1.7 Deleting records

Exercise 6

FIRST AID on **WEDNESDAY** in the **HALL** has been cancelled. Delete this record.

Method

1 Click the row selection box to the far left of the record (Figure 5.6).

Click in this box to select the **FIRST AID** record → FIRST AID | FHW11 | HALL

Figure 5.6 Selecting a record

2 An arrow appears in the box; the entire record is highlighted.

3 Right-click anywhere on the selection.

4 A pop-up menu appears (Figure 5.7).

Figure 5.7 Deleting a record

5 Select: **Delete Record**.

6 You will be asked to confirm that you want to delete this record; click on: **Yes**.

Notice how the other records move up. It is important that you delete the record and not just the contents of the record since this would leave a blank row. Check to see the new number of records at the bottom of the table. It should now display 18.

1.8 Amending data

Exercise 7

Some of the data needs amending. Make amendments as follows:

1   The **CODE** for **SOFTBALL** should be **SSM26** and the **WEEKS** should be **12**.

2   **BADMINTON** should take place in the **NEW GYM**.

Method

1   Position the cursor in the place where you need to make the amendment.

2   Delete the incorrect data by pressing: **Delete** or the ← Del (Backspace) key.

3   Key in the correct data.

1.9 Replacing data

Exercise 8

In the **ROOM** field, use the codes as follows to replace the existing data:

POOL = P   **SPORTS HALL = SH**
NEW GYM = NG   **HALL = H**

Method

1   Select the **ROOM** field column by clicking on the name at the top of the column.

2   From the **Edit** menu, select: **Replace**.

3   The **Find and Replace** dialogue box is displayed (Figure 5.8).

4   Ensure the **Replace** tab is selected.

5   In the **Find What** box, key in **POOL**.

6   In the **Replace With** box, key in **P**.

7   Check that the **Look In** box displays the field that you want to amend, ie in this case **ROOM**.

8   Click on: **Replace All**.

9   You will be asked to confirm; click on: **Yes**.

10 Continue with the other codes.

11 When you have completed all the replacements, click on: the **Close** button of the **Find and Replace** box.

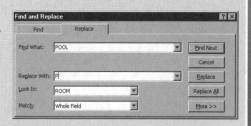

Figure 5.8 Find and Replace dialogue box

Using **Search and Replace** is extremely time-saving when you have a large number of records. You can also use **Search** to locate records in a large database to save having manually to scroll through all the records.

1.10 Printing the data in table format

Exercise 9

Print all the data in table format.

Method

(*Note:* It is best if the table fits on one page. This method shows how to do this.)

1 From the **File** menu, select: **Print Preview**.

2 From this you will see that the table is being split over two pages in portrait display. (Use the arrows at the bottom to view other pages.)

3 Click on: **Close** to return to the table.

4 To change to landscape display, from the **File** menu, select: **Page Setup**.

5 Click on: the **Page** tab and then in the **Landscape** option button. Click on: **OK** (Figure 5.9).

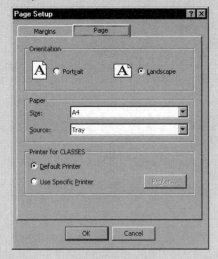

Figure 5.9 Changing to landscape display

6 Now check **Print Preview** again. It should now fit on one page. (The arrows at the bottom of the screen are greyed out.)

7 Return to the table, then from the **File** menu, select: **Print**.

8 The **Print** dialogue box is displayed.

9 Click on: **OK**.

10 Proofread your printout to ensure data is accurate and that all amendments have been made.

To make it easier to check through, you can sort the data. For a quick method to sort, see the quick reference at the end of this chapter.

1.11 Saving the database table

Exercise 10

Save the database table.

Method

1 Click on: the ⊠ **Close** button at the top right of the **Table** window.

2 The updated data is saved automatically. (*Note:* This is unlike most Office applications where you are reminded to save data.)

1.12 Saving and closing the database

Exercise 11

Save the database file **Fitness**.

Method

From the **File** menu, select **Close**.

 The components of the database file are automatically saved together. Each individual part, such as the table **CLASSES**, has been saved as we have progressed through the exercises. If any parts are not saved, you will be prompted to save before closing.

1.13 Exiting Access

Exercise 12

Exit Access.

Method

From the **File** menu, select: **Exit**.

Note: For the following two exercises you will need to access the Access files **Car sales** and **Holidays** on the CD-ROM.

Practice 1

1   Open the database **Car sales**.

2   Add the following new records to the database as follows:

    a CARTERS garage now has a **VAUXHALL CORSA**, colour is **RED**. It has **2** previous owners and is priced at **3495**. The MOT is due on **16/2/03**.

    b BROMLEYS garage now has a **FORD KA**, colour is **RED**. It has **1** previous owner and is priced at **2995**. The MOT is due on **2/1/03**.

    c DAVID PIKE garage now has a **FORD PUMA**, colour is **SILVER**. It has **1** previous owner and is priced at **6500**. The MOT is due on **12/5/03**.

3   The **LANDROVER DISCOVERY** at **SMYTHES** has been sold. Delete this record.

4   Make the following amendments and save the data:

    a The **NISSAN MICRA** at **BROMLEYS** is **GREEN** and has been reduced to **2995**.

    b At **DAVID PIKE** garage, the **SILVER FORD FIESTA's** MOT due date is **21/6/03**.

5   It has been decided to use codes in the **MAKE** field. Replace the existing entries as follows:

    FORD = FD
    RENAULT = RT
    VAUXHALL = VX
    NISSAN = NS
    LANDROVER = LR

6   Print all the data in table format.

7   Close the database and exit Access.

Practice 2

Remember: When working with currency, use the numeric value only, ie no £ symbols or commas. Access will automatically format the entry.

1   Open the database **Holidays**.

2   Add the following new records to the database as follows:

    a 3 nights, **HOTEL** accommodation in **BONN, GERMANY**. The code is **GB237** and the departure date is **13 March 2002**. The cost is **250**.

    b 2 nights, **APARTMENT** accommodation in **ST MALO, FRANCE**. The code is **FS388** and the departure date is **15 April 2002**. The cost is **162**.

    c 14 nights, **HOTEL** accommodation in **PERTH, AUSTRALIA**. The code is **AP589** and the departure date is **16 June 2002**. The cost is **1450**.

3 The **APARTMENT** accommodation in **PERTH, AUSTRALIA** costing **1199** should not have been entered. Delete this record.

4 Make the following amendments and save the data:

    a The departure date of the **APARTMENT** holiday code **GB455** in **BONN, GERMANY** should be **16 January 2002**.

    b The **HOTEL** accommodation in **ANTIBES**, code **FA541** should cost **350**.

5 It has been decided to use codes in the **COUNTRY** field. Replace the existing entries as follows:

FRANCE = FR
GERMANY = GE
SWITZERLAND = SW
AUSTRALIA = AU
BULGARIA = BU

6 Print all the data in table format.

7 Close the database and exit Access.

2 Manipulating data

In this section you will practise and learn how to:

- create and save queries
- select data on two criteria
- sort data numerically/alphabetically
- present only selected fields
- select data on one criterion
- print queries
- sort by date

 A database can be *sorted* into a certain order to match the task that you are carrying out, eg alphabetical order of surname or numeric order of account balance. There are two methods to sort the database. For quick table sorting, see the quick reference guide. For CLAIT assignments, you are usually asked to sort selected data and save it. In order to do this without overwriting any other data sort, you will need to create a query.

What is a query?

Once you have stored information in your database, you will want to query (question) the database to extract information, in other words *search* the database for specific information, eg all people who work on Fridays or all orders over £100. This section explains how to create and sort queries in Access.

2.1 Creating and saving a query, selecting data on one criterion

Exercise 1

Using the file **Fitness** saved in Section 1, set up the following database query:

1   Select all the classes that take place on **TUESDAY**.

2   Sort the data in ascending order of **WEEKS**.

3   Display all fields.

Method

1   Load Access and the database file **Fitness** saved at the end of Section 1.

2   In the **Objects** section of the **Fitness:Database** window, click on the: **Queries** button.

3   Double-click on: **Create query in Design view** (Figure 5.10).

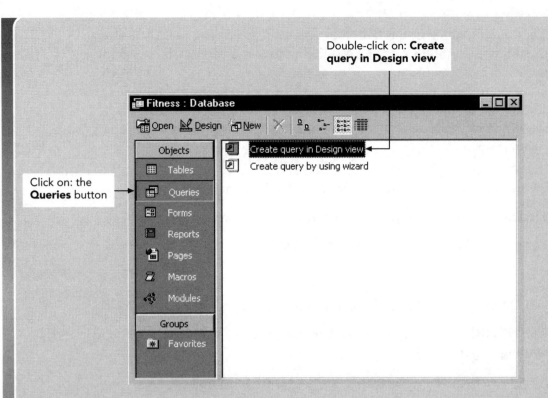

Double-click on: **Create query in Design view**

Click on: the **Queries** button

Figure 5.10 Creating a query

4 The **Show Table** box appears with the Table **CLASSES** selected (Figure 5.11)

5 Click on: **Add**, then on: **Close**.

Figure 5.11 Show Table box

6 The **Query – Design View** window is displayed (Figure 5.12).

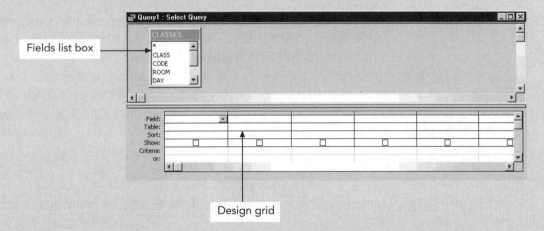

Fields list box

Design grid

Figure 5.12 Query Design

7 The fields of the **CLASSES** table are displayed in a Fields List box. Place the fields in the Design Grid as follows:

a In the **Design Grid**, in the **Field** row, click in: the first field column.

b Click on: the down arrow.

c Click on: the name of the field that you want to appear, ie **CLASS** (*Note:* **CLASS** not **CLASSES** since **CLASSES** is the name of the table, not a field name.)

d Click in: the next field column; click on: the down arrow.

e Click on: the name of the next field you want to appear, ie **CODE**.

f Repeat steps (d) to (e) until all the fields are on the grid (as in the **Field** row of Figure 5.13).

 There are other ways to place the fields in the Design Grid:

1 Double-click on: the field name that you want in the Design Grid.

2 Drag the field name on to the Design Grid.

8 In the field **DAY** column, click in: the **Criteria** row, then key in: **TUESDAY**.

9 In the field **WEEKS** column, click in: the **Sort** row, then click on: the down arrow, then on: **Ascending** (Figure 5.13).

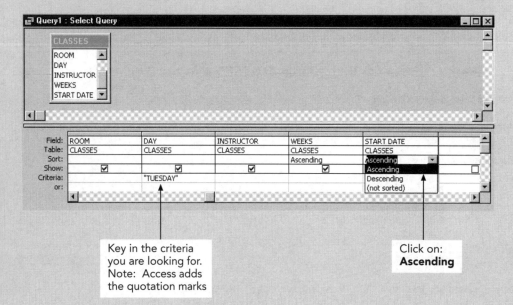

Key in the criteria you are looking for. Note: Access adds the quotation marks

Click on: **Ascending**

Figure 5.13 Entering criteria and sorting

 When sorting you can choose to sort in **Ascending** (alphabetic A–Z, or numeric lowest to highest, dates earliest to most recent) or **Descending** (alphabetic Z–A, or numeric highest to lowest, dates most recent to earliest). Although this chapter contains descending alphabetic sorts, alphabetic sorts for New CLAIT are always in ascending order, ie A–Z.

10 To save the query, from the **File** menu, select: **Save As**. Replace the default name **Query1** by deleting it and keying in the query name **Tues weeks ascending**. Click on: **OK** (Figure 5.14).

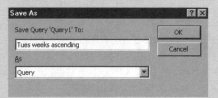

Figure 5.14 Saving the sorted query

11 Close the query window by clicking on: the **Close** button in the right-hand corner of the Design window.

12 You are returned to the **Fitness:Database** window.

13 To view the results of the query, double-click on: the query name (Figure 5.15).

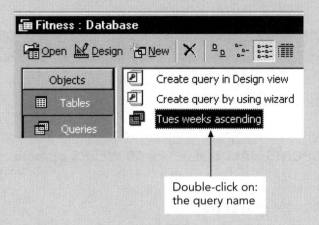

Double-click on: the query name

Figure 5.15 Viewing the Query results

14 The query result should look like Figure 5.16.

CLASS	CODE	ROOM	DAY	INSTRUCTOR	WEEKS	START DATE
BADMINTON	BSU28	NG	TUESDAY	GREG SYMMONDS	10	10/09/02
AEROBICS	ANU50	NG	TUESDAY	KYLIE GRIFFITH	10	10/09/02
JUDO	JNT40	NG	TUESDAY	MANON BING	15	10/09/02
TABLE TENNIS	THU52	H	TUESDAY	FILIPPO AMANI	20	10/09/02
*					0	

Figure 5.16 Result of query

 Scan the result of the query. If there is no data or if incorrect data is displayed, click on: the **View** button to return to Design view and check the query design.

 Click on: the **View** button again to return to the query result (this view is known as Datasheet view).

15 Click on: the **Close button** in the top right-hand corner of this window to return to the **Fitness:Database** window.

2.2 Printing a query

Exercise 2

Print the query saved as **Tues weeks ascending**.

Method

1 In the **Fitness:Database** window, click on: the **Queries** button.

2 Double-click on: **Tues weeks ascending**.

3 From the **File** menu, use **Print Preview** and **Page Setup** to print in landscape.

4 From the **File** menu, select: **Print**.

5 Click on: **OK**.

2.3 Creating and saving a query, selecting data on two criteria

Exercise 3

Set up the following database query:

1 Select all classes that take place in the **SPORTS HALL** that run for **10 WEEKS or more than 10 weeks**.

2 Sort the data into descending numerical order of **WEEKS**.

3 Display all fields.

> (greater than) symbol is obtained by holding down the **Shift** key and pressing the full stop key.

< (less than) symbol is obtained by holding down the **Shift** key and pressing the comma key.

The following symbols are used in queries:

=	is equal to
>	greater than (or more recent than in the case of a date)
<	less than (or before in the case of a date)
>=	greater than or equal to
<=	less than or equal to
<>	not equal to

Working with dates

Before 10 February 2001	<10 February 2001 (*Note:* You can use an abbreviated version of the date and it will change to the set format, eg 10/02/01.)
After 10 February 2001	>10 February 2001
10 February 2001 or after	>=10 February 2001
10 February 2001 or before	<=10 February 2001
10 February 2001 to 20 February 2001 inclusive	>9 February 2001 and <21 February 2001 *or* >=10 February 2001 and <=20 February 2001 *or* Between 10 February 2001 and 20 February 2001

In this instance, as we have already created a query, **Tues weeks ascending**, so we can use this as the basis for this query.

You could create a completely new query for this if you wanted to, but this would only duplicate effort.

Method

1   From the **Fitness:Database** window, click on: the **Queries** button, double-click on: the query **Tues weeks ascending**, then on: the **View** button to switch to Design view.

2   Delete the entry you keyed in for the original query, ie **TUESDAY** and the sort order, ie **Ascending** so that the original query data is cleared.

Field:	CLASS	CODE	ROOM	DAY	INSTRUCTOR	WEEKS	START DATE	
Table:	CLASSES	CLASSES	CLASSES	CLASSES	CLASSES	CLASSES	CLASSES	
Sort:						Descending		
Show:	☑	☑	☑	☑	☑	☑	☑	
Criteria:			"SH"			>=10		
or:								

3   In the field **ROOM** column and the **Criteria** row, key in **SH** and press: **Enter**.

4   In the field **WEEKS** column and the **Criteria** row, key in **>=10** and press: **Enter**.

5   In the field **WEEKS** column, click in: the **Sort** row, then click on: the down arrow, then on: **Descending**.

Figure 5.17 Selecting more than one criteria

6   Save the query as **SH 10 or more** and print.

2.4 Sorting by date

Exercise 4

Set up the following database query:

1   Select all classes that start **before 12/9/02** and run for **12 weeks or less**.

2   Sort the data into descending **START DATE** order.

3   Display all fields.

Method

1   Set up the query following one of the methods above. (For the **START DATE** criteria, key in **<12/9/02**.)

2   Save the query with a relevant descriptive name and print.

Exercise 5

Access the query saved in Exercise 4. Sort the query in ascending order of CLASS. Produce a print out displaying only the following fields:

CLASS, **INSTRUCTOR** and **START DATE**

Method

1   Access the query and display it in Design view.

2   Delete the **START DATE** sort by clicking on the down arrow in the START DATE **Sort** box and selecting: **(not sorted)**.

3   Select the requested **CLASS** sort.

4   In the **Show** row, remove the ticks, by clicking on them, in the fields that you do not want to display (Figure 5.18).

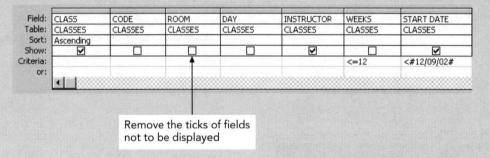

Field:	CLASS	CODE	ROOM	DAY	INSTRUCTOR	WEEKS	START DATE
Table:	CLASSES	CLASSES	CLASSES	CLASSES	CLASSES	CLASSES	CLASSES
Sort:	Ascending						
Show:	☑	☐	☐	☐	☑	☐	☑
Criteria:						<=12	<#12/09/02#
or:							

Remove the ticks of fields not to be displayed

Figure 5.18 Showing selected fields only

5   Save the query with a new name and print.

- You will notice that only the fields with ticks appear on the printout.
- *Remember:* it is always a good idea to check that your query is showing the correct result, so always view it before printing. If it is not showing what you think you have asked for, return to Design view by clicking the View toolbar button and checking the details you have entered.
- You can sort and search within the same query.
- When creating queries, Access adds quotation marks (in Design view) to the criteria you key in. You do not need to worry about this.
- If you are presenting selected fields, you do not need to enter all the database fields in the Design Grid. However, you will need to enter those that you are sorting or searching even if you do not need to display them.
- When working with tables and queries, in order to view all fields you can resize the field columns by dragging the field name row using the mouse (as shown below). Always check that the data is still displayed in full.

1 Hover the mouse over the line between the field names.

2 A double-arrow appears.

3 Hold down the left mouse button and drag to the left.

4 Release the mouse button.

Table   Query

Common errors

- Misspelling the criteria so that it does not find an exact match (this can also be due to a spelling error in the data in the database). Always proofread carefully.
- Making the criteria plural, ie **MONDAYS** instead of **MONDAY**. The query will not find **MONDAYS** as this is not what was entered in the database and therefore is not an exact match.
- Leaving spaces where they should not be.

2.6 Exit Access

Databases practice 2

Practice 3

1 Open the database **Car sales** saved in Practice 1, Section 1.

2 Set up the following database query:

    a Find all vehicles at **DAVID PIKE** garage.

    b Sort the selected records in alphabetical order of **MODEL**.

    c Display all fields.

    d Save the query.

    Print the query results in table format.

3 Set up the following database query:

    a Select all **RED** vehicles that have had **2** or fewer previous owners.

    b Sort the selected records into descending order of price.

    c Display only the fields **GARAGE**, **COLOUR**, **PREVIOUS OWNERS** and **PRICE**.

    d Save the query.

    Print the query results in table format.

4 Set up the following database query:

    a Select all vehicles with a price of less than **3500**.

    b Sort the records into ascending order of MOT due date.

    c Display only the fields **MAKE**, **MODEL** and **MOT DUE**.

    d Save the query.

    Print the query results in table format.

5 Close the file and exit Access with all the data saved.

Practice 4

1 Open the database **holidays** saved in Practice 2, Section 1.

2 Set up the following database query:

    a Find all holidays in **AUSTRALIA**.

    b Sort the selected records into descending order of **DEPARTURE DATE**.

    c Display all fields.

    d Save the query.

    Print the query results in table format.

3 Set up the following database query:

    a Select all **APARTMENT** accommodation with a departure date before **16 April 2002**.

    b Sort the selected records into alphabetical order of location.

c Display only the fields **LOCATION**, **CODE** and **DEPARTURE DATE**.

d Save the query.

Print the query results in table format.

4 Set up the following database query:

a Select all holidays of less than **7** nights costing more than **200**.

b Sort the records into ascending departure date order.

c Display only the fields **COUNTRY**, **ACCOMMODATION** and **NO OF NIGHTS**.

d Save the query.

Print the query results in table format.

5 Close the file and exit Access with all the data saved.

Databases quick reference for New CLAIT (Access)

Note: Since Access is a little different to other Office applications, this quick reference guide follows a different format to others in the book. There is a full reference guide, following the format of other quick reference guides, in Chapter 9.

Adding a record	**1** Position the cursor in the row under the last record and enter the information **2** Close the table **3** Data is saved automatically when you close the **Table** window
Closing the database	From the **File** menu, select: **Close** IMPORTANT: *Always close the database file properly*
Creating queries, sorting them, specifying simple criteria and printing queries	**1** If the database is not already open, open it so that the **Database** window is displayed **2** Click on: the **Queries** tab **3** Double-click: **Create query in Design view** **4** Select table. Click on: Add and then on: **Close** **5** The fields of the table are now displayed in a list box in the **Query** window **6** Place the fields that you need for your query in the field row of the query grid
Deleting an entire record	**1** Select the record by clicking in: the left window border next to the first field of that record **2** Press: **Delete** **3** Click on: **OK** to save the change
Editing records in a table	**1** Open the Table if it is not already open. (In the **Database** window, click on: the **Tables** tab, and double-click on: the table name) **2** Click on: the entry you wish to edit and key in the new data
Loading Access	**Start** menu, **Programs**, **Microsoft Access**
Opening a database file	**1** In the Access opening dialog box, click in: **Open an existing file** option button **2** Locate the file **3** Click on: the filename **4** Click on: **OK**
Opening a table	**1** In the **Database** window, click on: the **Tables** button **2** Double-click on: the table name
Printing a table	**1** Open the table you want to print **2** From the **File** menu, select: **Print** **3** Click on: **OK**
Printing on landscape	**1** Open the table you want to print **2** From the **File** menu, select: **Page Setup** **3** Click on: the **Page** tab, click on: **Landscape**, **OK**
Printing specific fields	Use the **Show** row in the grid to choose whether or not to display a particular field in the query A tick in the **Show** box means that the field will show, no tick means that it will not show. Click to toggle between them
Printing a query	With the query result on screen, from the **File** menu, select: **Print**
Quick sorting records	**1** Open the table if it is not already open **2** Select the field that you wish to sort by clicking on: the **Field Name** at the top of the field column **3** Click on: the ⬆ **Sort Ascending** button or on: the ⬇ **Sort Descending** button
Saving a query	**1** When you have finished designing your query, save it by selecting: **Save as** from the **File** menu **2** Key in an appropriate query name **3** Click on: **OK**

	4 Close the **Query** window **5** To see the results of your query, double-click on: the query name
Searching and replacing	**1** With the table open, select the field to search by clicking on: the **Field Name** **2** From the **Edit** menu, select: **Replace** **3** With the **Replace** tab selected, key in the data to find in the **Find What** box **4** In the **Replace With** box, key in the replacement data **5** Click on: **Replace All** **6** Click on: **Yes** **7** Click on: **Close**
Sorting a query	In the **Design** grid, click in: the **Sort** box in the appropriate field Select: **Ascending** or **Descending**
Specifying simple criteria	Use the **Criteria** row in the grid to specify the conditions in a specific field, eg **RED** in the **COLOUR** field

Hints and tips

Saving tables before and after amendments

When completing New CLAIT assignments, it can be very irritating if you spot that you have made an error(s) before making amendments and you now only have the amended table to work with. In such instances, the only answer is to retrace your steps, reversing the amendments so that you arrive back at the original table. This can be very tedious and produces a lot of errors.

To save your original table intact, follow the steps below:

1   With the table name selected in the **Database** window, click on: the **Copy** button.

2   Click on: the **Paste** button.

3   In the **Paste Table** box, key in the new table name; ensure **Structure and Data** is selected.

4   Click on: **OK**.

You will now have two exact copies of the same table. Make amendments to one of them, leaving the other intact.

Other tips

- Always proofread your work carefully. This is especially important with database work as one error could make sorting and searching incorrect.
- Be consistent with use of upper, lower, sentence or title case within fields.
- Ensure all data is displayed in full on printouts.
- Ensure records are fully deleted, ie do not leave a blank row by deleting the contents only.
- Have you made all the amendments requested?
- Have you replaced specified data?
- Always check that your query results are those expected.
- Are the queries sorted in the order requested?
- Do you have the correct number of printouts?

Databases: sample full practice assignment

Note: For this assignment you will need to use the Access database file, **Houses**, on the CD-ROM.

Scenario

You work as an Administrative Assistant for a large estate agent. Your job is to update the database of properties in the company's local offices as requested by the Office Manager.

Your Office Manager has asked you to amend and update the database of current properties for sale.

1   Open the database **Houses**.

Four new properties need to be added to the database.

2   Create records for the new properties as follows:

a   In the **MILTON KEYNES** Office there is a new property located in **WILLEN** that was registered on **19 September 2002**. The property ref is **M285** and the price is **199995**. The vendor's surname is **LUHRMANN** and there have been **0** viewings to date.

b   In the **MILTON KEYNES** Office there is a new property located in **FISHERMEAD** that was registered on **20 September 2002**. The property ref is **M790** and the price is **179999**. The vendor's surname is **JENSON** and there has been **1** viewing to date.

c   In the **OLNEY** Office there is a new property located in **PODINGTON** that was registered on **20 September 2002**. The property ref is **Y133** and the price is **69995**. The vendor's surname is **GALLWAY** and there have been **0** viewings to date.

d   In the **OLNEY** Office there is a new property located in **TURVEY** that was registered on **21 September 2002**. The property ref is **Y185** and the price is **78950**. The vendor's surname is **SMITH** and there have been **0** viewings to date.

3   Delete the record at the **MILTON KEYNES** office, vendor **GIULIANI**, property ref **M682**. This has been withdrawn.

4   It has been decided to use codes in the **OFFICE** field. Replace the existing entries as follows:

MILTON KEYNES	MK
BLETCHLEY	BY
WOLVERTON	WN
OLNEY	OL
STONY STRATFORD	SS
NEWPORT PAGNELL	NP

5   Two of the records need amending:

a   At the **WOLVERTON** office, property ref **W821**, the location should be **HODGE LEA**.

b   At the **MILTON KEYNES** office, the property with the vendor **JOHNSON** should be priced at **159995**.

Make these changes and save the amended data.

6 Print all the data in table format.

Your Office Manager would like to find out about viewings.

7 Set up the following database query:

 a Select all properties that have had less than **3** viewings.

 b Sort the data in alphabetical order of **VENDOR**.

 c Display only the fields **LOCATION**, **VENDOR** and **VIEWINGS**.

 d Save the query.

 Print the results of the query in table format.

 A prospective buyer is looking for a property for sale in the Milton Keynes office. She has already secured finance up to 160000.

8 Set up the following database query:

 a Select all properties in the **MILTON KEYNES** office under **160000**.

 b Sort the data in ascending order of **DATE REGISTERED**.

 c Display only the fields **PROPERTY REF**, **PRICE** and **DATE REGISTERED**.

 d Save the query.

 Print the results of the query in table format.

 The Office Manager would like you to find information about recently registered properties in the WOLVERTON office.

9 Set up the following database query:

 a Select all properties registered since the beginning of **AUGUST** in **WOLVERTON**.

 b Sort the data in descending order of **PRICE**.

 c Display only the fields **LOCATION**, **VENDOR** and **PROPERTY REF**.

 d Save the query.

 Print the results of the query in table format.

10 Close the file and exit the software with all the data saved.

PART 2
CLAIT Plus

In order to get the best from Part 2, it is an advantage if you have already worked through or achieved the units covered in Part 1 of this book. The skills to CLAIT level are not repeated in Part 2 but there are opportunities to practise them.

There are many new skills to learn for CLAIT Plus. You are guided through these step by step in small manageable chunks thus allowing you to concentrate on the skills themselves, rather than the detail required at this level. However, once you feel confident with your newfound abilities, you will be able to work through the sample full practice assignments for each unit. The quick reference guides will help to jog your memory as you progress. Before attempting an actual OCR assignment, it is a good idea to practise as many sample assignments as you can (your tutor will be able to guide you to good sources). This will ensure that you are fully prepared.

Create, manage and integrate files (Unit 1)

File management

Using Windows Explorer in this section you will practise and learn how to:

- understand more about computer storage structure
- move files/folders
- recognise file types

- create, name and rename files/folders
- create subfolders
- copy files/folders
- print file structure

Note: Before commencing on this chapter, it is recommended that you have worked through Chapters 2, 3 and 5 or that you have achieved Units 2, 4 and 5 at CLAIT Level 1.

For this section, you will need access to the folders **Plus Unit1 sec1** and **Chpt6 practice** on the CD-ROM.

1.1 Computer storage structure

Exercise 1

Open Windows Explorer to examine the computer's storage structure. This is termed the *hierarchical* structure. It is set out in a tree structure, branching off to different levels.

Method

1 From the Windows desktop, click on: the **Start** button.

2 Select: **Programs**, then click on: **Windows Explorer**.

3 The Explorer window is displayed.

4 The **Folders** pane will have a similar content to that in Figure 6.1.

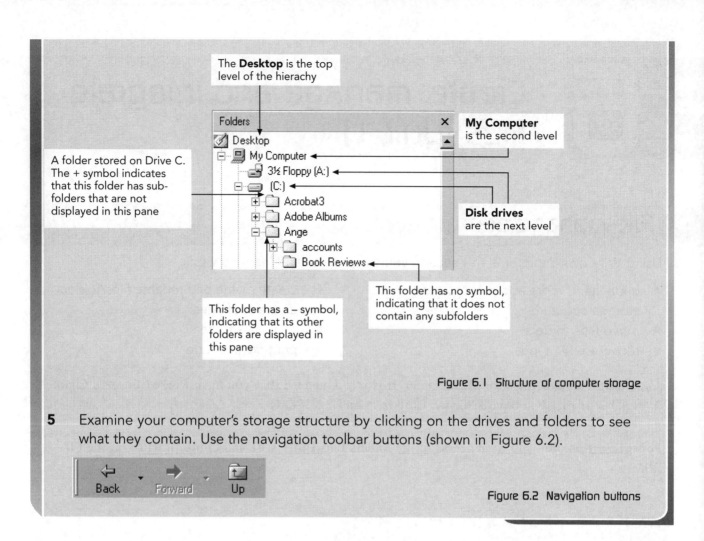

The **Desktop** is the top level of the hierachy

My Computer is the second level

A folder stored on Drive C. The + symbol indicates that this folder has sub-folders that are not displayed in this pane

Disk drives are the next level

This folder has a – symbol, indicating that its other folders are displayed in this pane

This folder has no symbol, indicating that it does not contain any subfolders

Figure 6.1 Structure of computer storage

5 Examine your computer's storage structure by clicking on the drives and folders to see what they contain. Use the navigation toolbar buttons (shown in Figure 6.2).

Figure 6.2 Navigation buttons

1.2 Creating and naming folders

Exercise 2

Create two folders at the same level, one with the name **Working (your initials)**, eg **working ajb**, and the other with the name **Testing (your initials)**.

Method

1 Select where you want the new folders to be stored by clicking on a location in the **Folders** pane so that the location becomes highlighted and the contents are displayed in the right-hand pane. (*Note:* If you are using Floppy Drive A (as in these examples) you will need to have a disk inserted in Drive A. You may need to ask your tutor for a suitable location.)

2 Right-click in a white space in the right-hand **Contents** pane. A menu appears (Figure 6.3).

3 Select: **New** and then **Folder**.

4 The new folder appears (Figure 6.4).

5 Key in the name for the new folder and press: **Enter**.

Figure 6.3 Creating a new folder

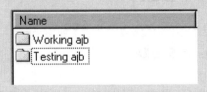

Figure 6.4 Naming a folder

6 Create the second folder in the same way.

7 You will now have two folders as shown in Figure 6.5. Notice that there is a + symbol next to the location, in the **Folders** pane, to denote these folders.

Name
☐ Working ajb
☐ Testing ajb

Figure 6.5 Two folders at the same level

Note: If your window has a different layout, you may be in **Web Page View**. If you want to change views, from the **View** menu, select **as Web Page** so that there is no tick next to it. There are also other View possibilities (eg List, Details).

1.3 Creating and naming subfolders

Exercise 3

Create a subfolder with the name **Draft** within the folder named **Working**.

Method

1 Double-click on: the folder named **Working**.

2 The two new folders you created in the last exercise are now displayed in the **Folders** pane (Figure 6.6). The **Working** folder has an open folder icon indicating that it is active.

Figure 6.6 Creating a subfolder

3 Follow steps 2–5 in the last exercise.

4 The new folder is displayed in the **Contents** pane and the **Working** folder has a + symbol next to it (Figure 6.7) denoting that it has contents, ie the **Draft** folder.

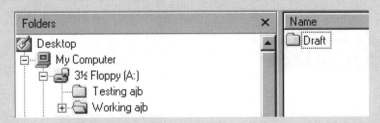

Figure 6.7 Subfolder is displayed in the Contents pane

By following the methods above you can create subfolders within subfolders, resulting in a similar structure to that shown below:

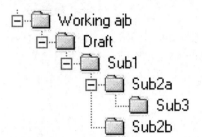

Draft is a subfolder in **Working**

Sub1 is a subfolder in **Draft**

Sub2a and **Sub2b** are subfolders in **Sub1**

Sub3 is a subfolder in **Sub2a**

1.4 Renaming folders/files

Exercise 4

Rename the folder **Draft** with the new name **Exercise**.

Method

1 Right-click on: the folder.

2 Select: **Rename** from the pop-up menu.

3 Key in the new name and press: **Enter**.

 Files can be renamed using the same method. Ensure that when renaming a file, if the file is displaying an extension, you remember to key in the file extension, ie after the actual name, the dot and letters, eg fame.doc (in this case the .doc. This denotes that it is a Word file. There is more about file extensions later in this section).

Note: For the following exercises you will need to access files on the CD-ROM that accompanies this book.

1.5 Copying files/folders

Exercise 5

Copy the file **Weather** from the CD-ROM (in the folder **Plus Unit1 sec1**) to the folder **Working**.

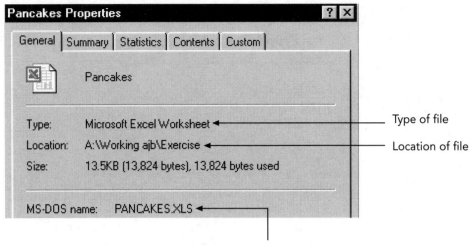

Type of file

Location of file

Filename with extension. *Note:* In this case the full name is shown. If the filename is more than 8 characters, it will be truncated

Figure 6.8 File properties

When you save a file, the computer automatically gives it an extension, ie **a Word file** named **XXXX** becomes **XXXX.doc**. Other common file extensions are:

Extension	File type	Icon
.doc	Word	
.txt	Plain text	
.xls	Excel	
.csv	Comma Separated Value datafile	
.mdb	Access	
.ppt	PowerPoint	
.htm	HTML, most commonly used on the World Wide Web	
.gif	graphics	

You can also use the toolbar buttons in Explorer to view file properties. Select the folder/file, then click on: the **Properties** button. Alternatively, click on: the **Views** button down arrow and select: **Details** to view listed file details.

File details are displayed as below:

Drag from here to the right to view full details of file type

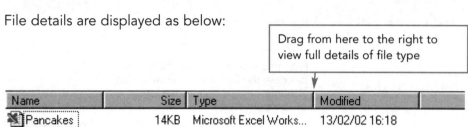

Name	Size	Type	Modified
Pancakes	14KB	Microsoft Excel Works...	13/02/02 16:18

Executable applications such as Word and Excel have a .EXE extension.

1.9 Printing file structure

Exercise 8

Produce a screen printout of the contents of the **Testing** and **Working** folders.
Ensure that your name is displayed on the printout.

Method

1 Select the folder **Testing** in the **Folders** pane so that its contents are displayed in the right-hand pane.

2 Press: the **Print Scrn** key. The screen is saved to the clipboard (a storage area). You will not see or be informed of this.

3 Load Word using the **Start** button.

4 With a new Word document open, click on: the **Paste** button. The Windows Explorer screen is pasted into Word. Reduce the size (using the corner handles to maintain its proportions) as necessary to fit on the page but still be legible.

5 Return to Windows Explorer by clicking its button on the taskbar.

6 Select the folder **Working** and click on the folder **Exercise** so that its contents are displayed.

7 Repeat steps 2–4.

8 You should now have the contents of the two folders on the page. Align as necessary.

9 Double-click and key in your name somewhere on the page (Figure 6.9).

[Your date]

Figure 6.9 Printing file structure

10   Save and print the Word document.

11   Close the file and exit Word.

1.10 Deleting files/folders

Revise from Chapter 1.

1.11 Exit Windows Explorer

 Some file maintenance can also be carried out within application programmes, such as Word and Excel. There is information in the Appendix about file maintenance in application programs.

Create, manage and integrate files practice

For these exercises you will need to access the folder **Chpt6 practice** on the accompanying CD-ROM.

Practice 1

1 Create a folder with the name **[your initials]Prac** in your own work area (you may need to ask your tutor about the best place for your work area).

2 Copy the folder **Chapt6 practice** to the folder **[your initials]Prac**.

3 The folder **Chapt6 practice** contains two subfolders. Move the file **fashion** from the folder **Green** to the folder **Red**.

4 In the folder **Green**, rename the file **house** as **building**.

5 Copy the file **quakes**, in the folder **Green**, to the folder **Red**.

6 Produce a screen printout of the contents of the folders **Green** and **Red**. Ensure that your name is on the printout.

Practice 2

1 Create a subfolder with the name **Yellow** in the folder **Red**.

2 Copy all the contents of the folder **Green** to the folder **Yellow**.

3 Delete the folder **Green**.

4 In the folder **Red**, delete the file **fashion**.

5 Copy the files **earth** and **spaceship** from the folder **Yellow** to the folder **Red**.

6 Produce a screen printout of the contents of the folders Yellow and Red. Ensure that your name is on the printout.

7 On the printout write the name of the type of files next to the filenames.

In this section you will practise and learn how to:

- open and save a text file in Word format
- apply headers and footers
- apply page numbering
- set widows/orphans
- join paragraphs
- insert special characters
- apply bullets and numbering

- set top/bottom margins, paper size and orientation
- set autofields (English format)
- copy text
- change case
- insert page breaks

Note: For the remaining sections in this chapter you will need to access the text file **bread**, **breadmaking** (a datafile), **wholegrain** (a spreadsheet file containing a chart) and **breadlogo** (a graphic file). These can be found on the accompanying CD-ROM. It is advisable to create a folder in your work area and copy the files to the new folder before you begin. In the examples I have created a folder **Factsheet** on a floppy disk and copied the files to it.

2.1 Opening and saving documents in other formats

Exercise 1

Open the text file **bread** and save it as a Word file using the filename **dough**.

Method

 The file **bread** is a text file in TXT format. This type of file contains simple no-frills text. It is a useful format because it can be accepted and read by a wide range of programs, including Word. It can be saved in Word in Word format.

1 Load Word.

2 From the **File** menu select: **Open**. The **Open** dialogue box is displayed.

3 In the **Look in** box, click on: the down arrow and then on the location of the file **bread**.

4 The file will not be displayed if **Word Documents** is selected in the **Files of type** box (Figure 6.10). (This is because it is a text file and not a Word file.)

5 Click on: the down arrow and select: either **All Files** or **Text Files**.

6 The file will now be displayed.

7 Click on: the filename.

8 Click on: **Open**.

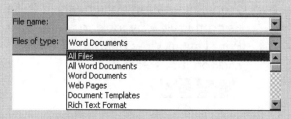

Figure 6.10 Selecting file type

9 The document appears (but without correction instructions).

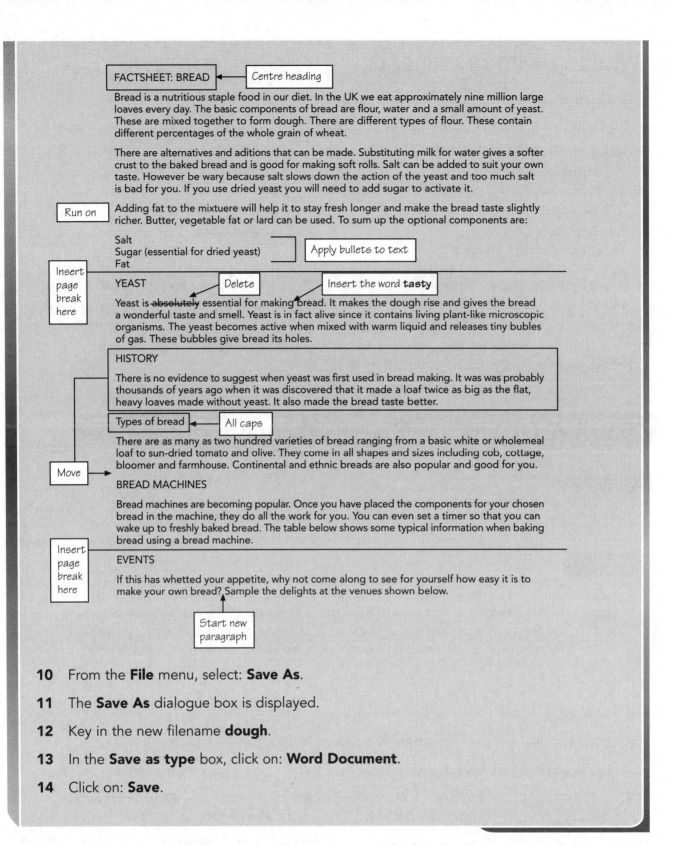

FACTSHEET: BREAD ← Centre heading

Bread is a nutritious staple food in our diet. In the UK we eat approximately nine million large loaves every day. The basic components of bread are flour, water and a small amount of yeast. These are mixed together to form dough. There are different types of flour. These contain different percentages of the whole grain of wheat.

There are alternatives and aditions that can be made. Substituting milk for water gives a softer crust to the baked bread and is good for making soft rolls. Salt can be added to suit your own taste. However be wary because salt slows down the action of the yeast and too much salt is bad for you. If you use dried yeast you will need to add sugar to activate it.

Run on → Adding fat to the mixtuere will help it to stay fresh longer and make the bread taste slightly richer. Butter, vegetable fat or lard can be used. To sum up the optional components are:

Salt
Sugar (essential for dried yeast)   Apply bullets to text
Fat

Insert page break here

YEAST   Delete   Insert the word **tasty**

Yeast is ~~absolutely~~ essential for making bread. It makes the dough rise and gives the bread a wonderful taste and smell. Yeast is in fact alive since it contains living plant-like microscopic organisms. The yeast becomes active when mixed with warm liquid and releases tiny bubles of gas. These bubbles give bread its holes.

HISTORY

There is no evidence to suggest when yeast was first used in bread making. It was was probably thousands of years ago when it was discovered that it made a loaf twice as big as the flat, heavy loaves made without yeast. It also made the bread taste better.

Types of bread ← All caps

There are as many as two hundred varieties of bread ranging from a basic white or wholemeal loaf to sun-dried tomato and olive. They come in all shapes and sizes including cob, cottage, bloomer and farmhouse. Continental and ethnic breads are also popular and good for you.

Move →

BREAD MACHINES

Bread machines are becoming popular. Once you have placed the components for your chosen bread in the machine, they do all the work for you. You can even set a timer so that you can wake up to freshly baked bread. The table below shows some typical information when baking bread using a bread machine.

Insert page break here

EVENTS

If this has whetted your appetite, why not come along to see for yourself how easy it is to make your own bread? Sample the delights at the venues shown below.

Start new paragraph

10 From the **File** menu, select: **Save As**.

11 The **Save As** dialogue box is displayed.

12 Key in the new filename **dough**.

13 In the **Save as type** box, click on: **Word Document**.

14 Click on: **Save**.

 When integrating documents, it is best to be in Print Layout View. Check that you are using this view by looking at the View buttons (bottom left of document area). The Print Layout View button is the third from the left and should be pressed in. If not, click on it to select it.

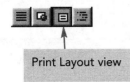

Print Layout view

There are amendments to be made to the document, as indicated on the hard copy. Before starting on these do the following exercises.

2.2 Using Page Setup

Exercise 2

Use **Page Setup** to make the following adjustments:

1 Set margins to: 2.5 cm top and bottom, 2 cm left and right.

2 Set paper size to A4 and portrait orientation.

Method

1 From the **File** menu, select **Page Setup**.

2 With the **Margins** tab selected, key in the new values in the **Top**, **Bottom**, **Left** and **Right** boxes (Figure 6.11).

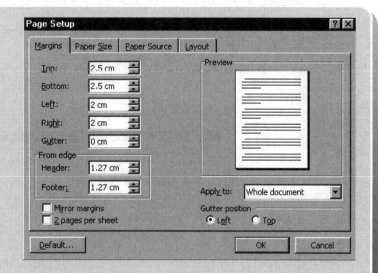

Figure 6.11 Changing margins

3 Click on: the **Paper Size** tab.

4 In the **Paper Size** box, select: **A4** (Figure 6.12).

5 In the **Orientation** section, click in: the option button to select: **Portrait**.

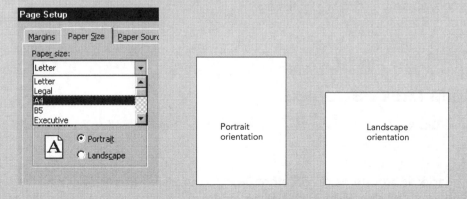

Figure 6.12 Selecting paper size and orientation

2.3 Applying headers and footers

Exercise 3

Create a header displaying your name.

Method

 Headers and footers are areas at the top and bottom (respectively) of printed pages so that details such as date and page numbers can be displayed. You will not see these in all views in Word, but they are displayed in **Print Layout View** and will be displayed in **Print Preview**.

1 From the **View** menu, select: **Header and Footer**. The **Header** or **Footer** box is displayed along with the **Header and Footer** toolbar (Figure 6.13).

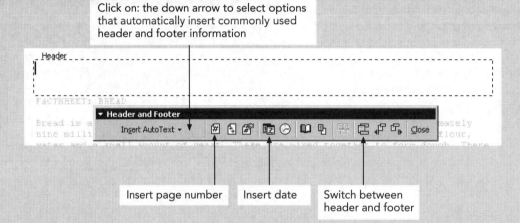

Click on: the down arrow to select options that automatically insert commonly used header and footer information

Insert page number   Insert date   Switch between header and footer

Figure 6.13 Applying a header/footer

 Using the buttons in Figure 6.13, automatic fields can be inserted. These buttons produce predetermined entries that can be formatted using the menu options. Text can be inserted manually where the cursor is flashing in the **Header** box.

2 Key in your name where the cursor is flashing.

3 Click on: **Close**.

Aligning in headers/footers

Pressing the **Tab** key will align centre and pressing it again will align to the right

or

Enter the header/footer items on different lines (by pressing **Enter** after each entry) and align using the toolbar buttons.

Exercise 4

Apply a footer to include an automatic date field (English date format: dd-mm-yy) and the filename. Add an automatic page number, right aligned. Do not show the page number on the first page.

It is important to check that the date is in the correct English format (incorrect date formatting is penalised in CLAIT Plus assignments). US dates have the format mm-dd-yy (ie the mm and dd in reverse order) so 06-08-02 would be 8th June 2002 in US format but 6th August 2002 in UK format.

Automatic page numbering is useful because it saves having to key in the page numbers on to individual pages and because the page numbers will change accordingly when new pages/page breaks are added.

Method

1. From the **View** menu, select: **Header and Footer** (see Figure 6.13).

2. Click on: the **Switch Between Header and Footer** button.

3. Click on: the **Insert Date** button.

4. Check that the date is displayed in English format. If not, you will need to set this option as follows:

   a. From the **Insert** menu, select: **Date and Time**. The **Date and Time** dialogue box is displayed (Figure 6.14).

   b. In the **Language** box, select: **English (U.K.)**.

   c. In the **Available formats** box, select the format required.

   d. Click on: **OK**.

   e. Delete the incorrect date by selecting it and pressing: **Delete**.

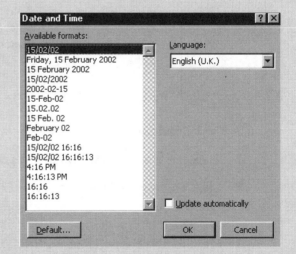

Figure 6.14 Setting date format

5. Leave a space by pressing: the **Tab** key.

6. Click on the **Insert Autotext** button and select: **Filename**.

7. Click on: **Close**.

Adding automatic page numbers

8. From the **Insert** menu, select: **Page Numbers**. The **Page Numbers** dialogue box is displayed (Figure 6.15).

Figure 6.15 Formatting page numbers

9 In the **Position** box, select: **Bottom of page (Footer)**.

10 In the **Alignment** box, select: **Right**.

11 Click in the box to remove the tick next to **Show number on first page**.

12 Click on: **OK**.

If you were not bothered about the positioning and showing of page numbers on the first page, you could have clicked on **Insert Page Number** from the **Header and Footer** toolbar. Notice that the **Page Numbers** dialogue box also allows further formatting by pressing the **Format** button, eg page numbering starting at a number other than one.

Note: You will not see the page numbers yet since you have only one page at the present time.

Check that the headers and footers are correct by zooming in with **Print Layout View** or in **Print Preview**.

In **Print Layout View**:

Using the page view magnification/zoom tool

1 Click on the down arrow in the **Zoom** toolbar box to reveal default zoom views.

2 Select: a zoom greater than 100% (the default) to enlarge text.

3 To revert back, select: zoom **100%**.

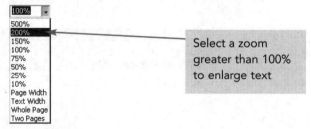

In **Print Preview**:

1 Click on: the Magnifier button, then on the text to magnify.

2 Click on: the text again to revert back to the original view.

3 Move between pages using the Navigation buttons at the bottom right of the window.

When not displaying the page number on the first page, Word has a habit of removing all other header and footer information from the first page. To rectify this:

From **Page Setup**, **Layout** tab, **Headers and Footers** section, ensure that **Different first page** is selected.

You will then be able to set the first page headers and footers separately. Ensure that you include and align all other information to be the same as on the following pages.

2.4 Editing a document

Exercise 5

Edit and amend the document as set out on page 176.

Method

The following tasks have been covered in Part 1:

- Centring, deleting and inserting text.
- Splitting paragraphs.
- Replacing text.
- Moving text.

Carry out these amendments where shown. At CLAIT Plus level, it is essential that line spacing between headings, subheadings and paragraphs is applied consistently. When you are editing, always check that the consistency of spacing is correct. Also check for consistency of spacing after full stops, commas and so on. Use the **Show/Hide** button.

The remaining editing and amending is covered in the following sections.

2.5 Applying bullets and numbering

Exercise 6

Apply bullets to the list as shown.

Method

Select the three lines of the list.

Click on: the ⊞ **Bullets** button.

Note: If the list has been indented, click on: the ⊞ **Decrease Indent** button.

Numbering is added in the same way using the ⊞ **Numbering** button. If you want to format the bullets/numbering further, from the **Format** menu, select: **Bullets and Numbering**. Select options that you require.

To turn Bullets/Numbering off

1 Select the line where you want to turn Bullets/Numbering off.

2 Click on: the **Bullets/Numbering** button as appropriate.

2.6 Joining paragraphs

 Joining paragraphs is sometimes known as running on.

Exercise 7

Join paragraphs two and three where shown.

Method

1 Position the cursor at the start of paragraph three, ie in front of the **A** in **Adding**.

2 Press: the ← **Del** (**Backspace**) key twice (top right of main keys).

3 Check for consistency of spacing.

2.7 Changing case

Exercise 8

Change the text **Types of bread** to capitals (upper case) as shown.

Method

1 Select the text to change.

2 From the **Format** menu, select: **Change Case**. The **Change Case** box is displayed (Figure 6.16).

3 Click in: the **UPPERCASE** option button.

4 Click on: **OK**.

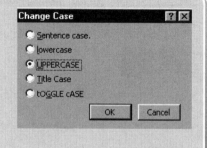

Figure 6.16 Changing case

2.8 Inserting page breaks

Exercise 9

Insert page breaks where shown.

1 Position the cursor in front of the first letter of the line where the page break is to be inserted.

2 From the **Insert** menu, select: **Break**.

3 The **Break** dialogue box appears. Ensure that the **Page break** option button is chosen and click on: **OK** (Figure 6.17).

4 Repeat for the other page break.

Figure 6.17 The Break dialogue box

 It is important to set out the pages so that they are easy to read. Check that the default setting for **Widow/Orphan** control (**Format** menu, **Paragraph**, **Line and Page Breaks**) is ticked. This ensures that paragraphs are not split so that one stray line of text appears at the bottom or top of a page. Always check that headings are not split from the text to which they refer.

There are soft and hard page breaks. As your text reaches the bottom margin of a page, a soft page break is automatically inserted by Word. This will reposition itself should you add or delete text from the document. A hard page break is inserted by you. Its position will always remain constant until you decide to alter it.

To delete a hard page break

1 Ensure that you are in **Normal View** by selecting it from the bottom left corner of the document window.

Normal View

2 Position the cursor on the page break (dotted line).

3 Press: **Delete**.

 Instead of using the arrow keys to see the next/previous page, click on **Previous Page** or **Next Page** on the vertical scroll bar.

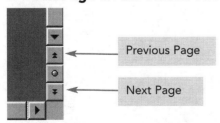

Previous Page

Next Page

Use the **Multiple Pages** button to see all pages at once.

Exercise 10

At the end of the document, leave one line space and insert the following text:

This factsheet was compiled by Hélène Melot, © Château Claude.

Method

1 Position the cursor at the end of the document (Press: **Ctrl + End**).

2 Ensure that you leave a line space after the final paragraph.

3 Key in the text up to the **H** of **Hélène**.

4 From the **Insert** menu, select: **Symbol**. The **Symbol** box is displayed (Figure 6.18).

5 With the **Symbols** tab selected and **(Normal text)** displayed in the **Font** box, click on: the symbol to insert, in this case the **é** (as shown selected).

6 Click on: **Insert**.

7 When keying in the rest of the text, insert the other symbols in the same way.

 Note the symbols that are available. There are other interesting and useful symbols available by selecting **Wingdings** in the **Font** box. If the font of the symbol does not match the font you are using, select the symbol and change the font in the normal way by using the **Font** box.

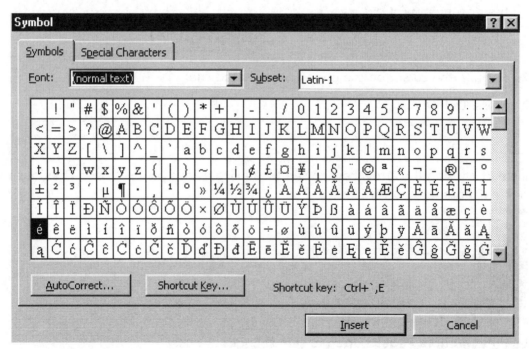

Figure 6.18 Inserting symbols

2.10 Copying text

Exercise 11

Copy the sentence that you have just keyed in so that it appears as the final sentence of the first paragraph.

Method

1. Select the text to copy.
2. Click on: the **Copy** button.
3. Position the cursor where you want the text to be copied to.
4. Click on: the **Paste** button.
5. Check for consistency of spacing.

2.11 Spellchecking

Exercise 12

Run the spellchecker through the document.

Method

This was covered in Part 1.

Note: Leave specialist words as they are, eg Factsheet.

At CLAIT level, spellchecking was not a requirement but was covered in Part 1 because it is such a useful tool. At CLAIT Plus level, spellchecking is a requirement. Correct any misspelt words and delete any repeated words that the spellchecker finds. However, remember that the spellchecker (and grammar checker) makes mistakes. Specialist words and brand names will be highlighted by the spellchecker. These should not usually be altered unless specifically requested. Always check that you are using the English (UK) spellchecker. This is displayed with the title of the **Spelling and Grammar** box. If not, change to the UK setting in the **Dictionary language** box.

2.12 Proofreading

Exercise 13

Proofread the document against the hard copy to check that the tasks set have been completed, consistency of spacing has been maintained and keyed in text is accurate. Correct any errors.

2.13 Saving and printing

Exercise 14

Save the document in Word format with the filename **doughdraft** and print one copy. Proofread the printed copy because sometimes it can be difficult to spot errors on screen.

Create, manage and integrate files (Unit 1)

3 Working with tabular data

In this section you will practise and learn how to:

- insert a table into a document
- change column/cell attributes: width, alignment
- apply gridlines, borders and shading
- encode data as specified

3.1 Inserting a table

Exercise 1

Open the Word document **doughdraft** saved at the end of the last section. Insert the following table at the end of the document. Ensure dates are in English (UK) format. Use codes for the hosts as follows:

H = Hélène, J = Jenny, M = Mark, Mi = Michael, C = Columbus, Jy = Jyoti

Venue	Directions	Date	Time	Hosts
Park Road	From the train station, turn right under the underpass. Turn left and follow the road straight on. Park Road is on the left.	16/10/02	15:00	Hélène, Jenny, Mark
Lake View	From the Town Hall, walk up the hill to the Cathedral. Turn left at The Swan Inn into Lake View.	18/10/02	09:00	Jyoti, Michael, Mark
Green Park	From the Bus Station's West exit, turn right. Continue straight on to Green Park.	21/11/02	10:00	Columbus, Hélène, Jyoti
Finchdale Road	This is opposite St Andrew's church in the centre of town.	22/11/02	15:30	Jyoti, Michael, Mark
Briar's Heath	From the Bus Station, take the first right up the hill to St Annes Road. Take the first on the left.	25/11/02	12:00	Columbus, Hélène, Jyoti

Tables provide an excellent way of displaying data so that it is easy to read. There are other methods to indent and line up data and these are mentioned briefly at the end of this section and in the Appendix. Coding data saves keying in. It also saves space in the table so that other columns can be widened, making them easier to read. The table has more clarity if the headings are not split between lines. In this instance, the **Directions** column could be widened.

1 With the document open, position the cursor where you want the table to be.

2 Hold down the left mouse button over the 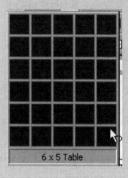 **Insert Table** button: a grid appears.

3 Drag the mouse across and down the grid to result in the number of columns and rows required for the table (5 columns and 6 rows, including the headings, Figure 6.19). Release the mouse.

Figure 6.19 Setting cells for a new table

4 The empty table appears in your document.

5 Key in the table's text, pressing: **Tab** to move to the next entry position (or use the arrow keys).

6 Proofread carefully against copy.

 If you press **Enter** by mistake, a line space will appear. Press: the ← **Del** (**Backspace**) key to remove the line space.

3.2 Changing column widths

Exercise 2

Change the width of the columns so that the entries fit more exactly, making the contents easier to read.

Method

 Tables are created with standard cell widths and heights. You can choose to adjust individual columns or change column widths for the entire table. In this table, it would be a good idea to widen the column **Directions** to make the contents easier to read. The columns **Date**, **Time** and **Hosts** could be narrowed.

Changing individual column widths

1 Select the column to change by hovering at the top of the first row of the column until the pointer turns into a thick black arrow (Figure 6.20).

> When the thick black arrow is showing, click the mouse to select the column

Directions	D
From the train station, turn right under the underpass. Turn	1(

Figure 6.20 Selecting a column

2 Click the mouse. The column is highlighted.

3 Hover over the right column border until the pointer turns into a double arrow.

4 Drag the right column border to the required position.

5 Release the mouse.

6 Similarly, make the **Date**, **Time** and **Hosts** columns narrower.

Exercise 3

Change column widths using **AutoFit**.

Method

1 Using the **Undo** button, undo the column widths set in the last exercise. (Several clicks required.)

2 Click anywhere in the table.

3 From the **Table** menu, select: **AutoFit**, **AutoFit to Contents**.

Note the other options in this menu item. **AutoFit to Window** is useful if you have narrowed the table too much or if you change page orientation. **Distribute columns evenly** is useful too. In CLAIT Plus you are penalised if data is not displayed in full and words are split.

3.3 Aligning cell contents

Exercise 4

Align the table contents as follows:

Column headings	**Centred**
Row headings	Left
Text	Left (wrapped)
Numeric	Right
Date/Time	Centre

1   Select the cells to align by dragging the mouse over them.

2   Right-click on the selection.

3   From the pop-up menu, select: **Cell Alignment**.

4   Select: the alignment you want.

5   Repeat until all cells have been aligned.

 Using the middle row of the **Cell Alignment** selection is usually sufficient for CLAIT Plus purposes. For efficiency, work on a selection (ie all the Row Headings at once) and not just single cells.

3.4 Gridlines, borders and shading

 Borders and shading are used to make the table easier to read. By default, the table will automatically have borders around the cells. When you remove the borders you will see the table's gridlines. These are greyed out, denoting that they will not appear on a printout but are there as a guide while you work. To hide gridlines, with the cursor positioned in the table, from the **Table** menu, select: **Hide Gridlines**. To redisplay select: **Hide Gridlines** again. This toggles the gridlines on and off.

Exercise 5

Remove the borders from the table.

Method

1   Position the cursor anywhere in the table and from the **Table** menu, select: **Select**, then: **Table**.

2   From the toolbar, click on the down arrow next to the **Border** button. Click on: **No Border** (Figure 6.21).

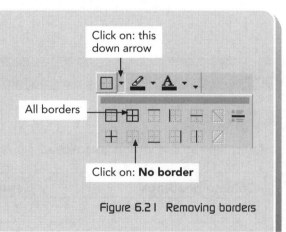

Figure 6.21 Removing borders

Notice that the gridlines are now displayed. Practise removing/adding them as above.

Note the other border options available and experiment with adding/taking away borders.

Exercise 6

Add borders round the whole table and between cells.

Method

Follow the method above, this time selecting: **All Borders**.

Exercise 7

Add shading to the **Column headings** row only.

Method

1 Select the **Headings** row.

2 Right-click over the selection.

3 Select: **Borders and Shading** to access the **Borders and Shading** dialogue box (Figure 6.22).

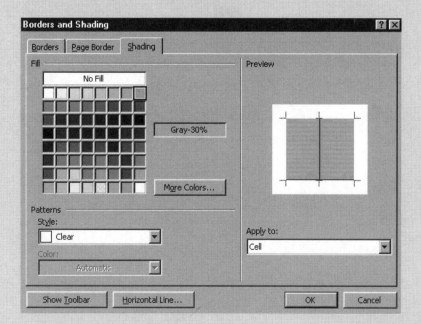

Figure 6.22 Borders and Shading dialogue box

4 With the **Shading** tab selected, in the **Fill** section, click on: a colour. (*Note:* A light shade of grey is a suitable choice for a black and white printout.)

5 Click on: **OK**.

3.5 Save document

Save the document as **doughdraft1** and print one copy of page 3 only.

Method

1. In the **Print** dialogue box, **Page Range** section, click in: the **Pages Option** button.
2. Key in: **3**.
3. Click on: **OK**.

3.6 Close the file and exit Word

Other methods of indenting
Using tabs is another method of indenting and lining up text, but it is not as easy as using the Table facility. Never use the space bar to line up text! Text may look as if it is lined up on the screen, but will not look lined up on the printout.

Using default tabs
By default, tabs are set every 1.27 cm from the left margin. Press the **Tab** key to move to the next tab stop. Tabs can be set up to replace the default settings.

Indenting text
Text can be indented from the margin using the **Increase Indent** button.

Importing

In this section you will practise and learn how to:

- import an image
- import a chart
- import a datafile
- format these objects as requested

 When working with integrated documents it is important that you follow the guidelines below. In CLAIT Plus you will be penalised if you do not adhere to them. Ensure that text, images, graphs and lines are not superimposed. Imported data must not be split across pages. Graphs/charts must be positioned within the margins of the page.

4.1 Importing an image

Exercise 1

Open the Word document **doughdraft1** saved at the end of the last section. Import the image **breadlogo** at the top of the first page. Align it to the right of the page. Maintain its original proportions.

Method

1. With the document open, position the cursor at the top of the first page.

2. Press: **Enter** to create a line space.

3. From the **Insert** menu, select: **Picture**, then **From File** (Figure 6.23).

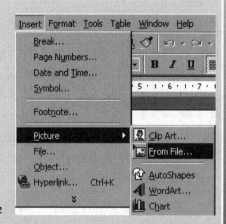

Figure 6.23 Inserting an image

4. The **Insert Picture** dialogue box is displayed (Figure 6.24).

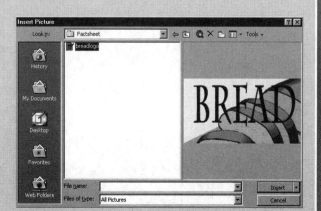

Figure 6.24 Insert Picture dialogue box

5 In the **Look in** box, select the location of the file.

Note: The **Files of Type** box is displaying **All Pictures** because you chose to insert a picture. The file is in gif format (a graphic format).

6 Click on: the filename to see a preview.

7 Click on: **Insert**.

8 The image is inserted in the document.

9 Click on the image to select it.

10 Align using the Word toolbar buttons.

11 Resize by dragging the handles from a corner of the image (this will ensure that its proportions are maintained).

12 Save the document with the same filename.

4.2 Importing a datafile

Exercise 2

Insert the datafile **breadmaking** underneath the last sentence of the paragraph with the subheading **BREAD MACHINES**. Show all borders on the imported datafile. Format as follows:

Column headings	Sans serif font	Point size 12	Centre, bold, shaded
Text			Left align
Numeric (ie FLOUR, BAKE, TOTAL TIME)			Right align

Method

1 Position the cursor in the Word document where the datafile is to be inserted.

2 From the **Insert** menu, select: **File**. The **Insert File** dialogue box is displayed (Figure 6.25).

Figure 6.25 Insert File dialogue box

3 In the **Look in** box, select the location of the file.

4 In the **Files of type** box, select: **All Files**.

5 Click on: the file and then on: **Insert**.

6   The file is inserted into the document (Figure 6.26).

```
TYPE,SIZE,FLOUR,BAKE,TOTAL TIME
BASIC WHITE,SMALL,2 cups,45 min,2 hr 45 min
BASIC WHITE,LARGE,3 cups,50 min,2 hr 50 min
WHOLEMEAL,SMALL,2 cups,45 min,4 hr 20 min
WHOLEMEAL,LARGE,3 cups,55 min,4 hr 30 min
FRENCH,N/A,2 cups,65 min,3 hr 10 min
SWEET,N/A,3 cups,50 min,3 hr 25 min
```

Figure 6.26 The datafile will look like this

Note: The datafile is in CSV format, so we need to convert it to table format.

7   Select the datafile so it is highlighted.

8   From the **Table** menu, select: **Convert**, then: **Text to Table**.

9   The **Convert Text to Table** dialogue box is displayed (Figure 6.27).

Figure 6.27 Convert Text to Table dialogue box

10 In the **AutoFit behavior** section, click in: the **AutoFit to contents** option button.

11 Click on: **OK**.

12 The datafile now looks like Figure 6.28.

TYPE	SIZE	FLOUR	BAKE	TOTAL TIME
BASIC WHITE	SMALL	2 cups	45 min	2 hr 45 min
BASIC WHITE	LARGE	3 cups	50 min	2 hr 50 min
WHOLEMEAL	SMALL	2 cups	45 min	4 hr 20 min
WHOLEMEAL	LARGE	3 cups	55 min	4 hr 30 min
FRENCH	N/A	2 cups	65 min	3 hr 10 min
SWEET	N/A	3 cups	50 min	3 hr 25 min

Figure 6.28 datafile converted to table

13 Align and shade as requested using the methods described in Section 3. Set font, set point size and emphasis as requested. The datafile will now look similar to Figure 6.29.

TYPE	SIZE	FLOUR	BAKE	TOTAL TIME
BASIC WHITE	SMALL	2 cups	45 min	2 hr 45 min
BASIC WHITE	LARGE	3 cups	50 min	2 hr 50 min
WHOLEMEAL	SMALL	2 cups	45 min	4 hr 20 min
WHOLEMEAL	LARGE	3 cups	55 min	4 hr 30 min
FRENCH	N/A	2 cups	65 min	3 hr 10 min
SWEET	N/A	3 cups	50 min	3 hr 25 min

Figure 6.29 datafile contents aligned and shaded as requested

14 Ensure that the imported datafile is still positioned within the margins. (Look at the ruler to ensure that it has not slipped across the margins.) If it has, drag the table border of the side that is over the margin back to within the margin. From the **Table** menu, select: **Table**. From the **Table** menu (again), select: **AutoFit to Contents**.

15 Save the document with the same filename.

When importing from other programs, data can sometimes become adrift from its original placing. Always check that imported data is as it should be by opening the original file and scanning through. This datafile is an Excel file saved in CSV format so it can be opened in Excel.

Exercise 3

Insert the bar chart named **wholegrain** after the first paragraph of the document **doughdraft1**. Ensure it is legible. Use serif font. Add a border to frame the chart.

Method

1   Position the cursor where you want the chart to be inserted.

2   You may need to press: **Enter** twice to ensure that the chart does not run right up to the text.

3   Load Excel and open the file **wholegrain**.

4   If the chart data and not the chart is displayed, display the chart by clicking on the appropriate Sheet tab at the bottom of the grid area (Figure 6.30).

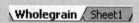

Figure 6.30 Changing sheets

5   Select the entire chart by clicking in a white space outside the plotted chart area.

6   Click on: the **Copy** button.

7   Switch back to the Word document by clicking on the document's button on the taskbar (Figure 6.31).

Figure 6.31 Switching programs on the taskbar

8   Click on: the **Paste** button.

9   The chart is inserted into the document.

10   Close the Excel file and close Excel by right-clicking on the file's button on the taskbar and selecting: **Close** from the pop-up menu. If prompted, do not save changes to the Excel file.

11   Resize the chart by dragging the corner handles inwards (Use the corner handles to preserve the proportions.)

12   Check that the chart still fits between the margins.

13   Format the font as requested, ie serif, and ensure that the chart is legible as follows:

Note: When reducing the size of the chart to fit between the margins, the font may have become very small and difficult to read.

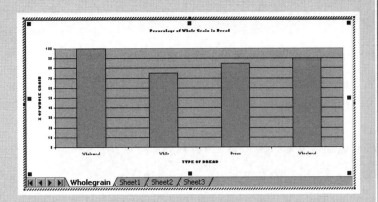

a Double-click on the chart so that it has a border, as shown in Figure 6.32.

Figure 6.32 Chart is selected for editing

b Double-click on each text item in turn to set font and font size so that the chart is legible.

c Click in a white space to deselect the chart.

Adding a border

14 Select the chart by clicking on it once.

Either:

Use the Outside Borders toolbar button

or

15 From the **Format** menu, select: **Borders and Shading**. The **Borders** dialogue box is displayed (Figure 6.33).

Figure 6.33 Adding a border

16 With the **Borders** tab selected, in the **Settings** section, click on: **Box**.

17 In the **Apply to** box, ensure that **Picture** is selected.

18 Click on: **OK**.

Note: You may be asked to import another type of chart, eg a pie chart. Use the same method as that detailed above.

4.4 Save document

Save the document as **dough integrated** and print one copy.

4.5 Close the file and exit Word

5 Adding styles

In this section you will practise and learn how to:

- understand the reasons for house styles
- apply styles

5.1 About house styles

Companies and organisations have their own *house styles*. A style is the way the text is formatted so that it takes on a specific appearance. Using house styles gives documents a similar look and feel. For example, all letters sent out are set out in the same way, all reports produced are set out in the same way and so on. This helps people to recognise company documentation and distinguish it from other documents. It is also easier to locate information, such as customer references and account numbers, since these will always be in the same position on the document.

Instead of using the default **Normal** document template in Word, you can set up templates that contain the house style of the company or organisation. This is more efficient than having to format text each time you create a document, especially in longer documents, as you will discover in Section 5.2.

5.2 Applying text styles

Exercise 1

Apply the following text styles to the document **dough integrated** saved at the end of the last section. Use single line spacing except for the bulleted list, which should have double line spacing.

Feature	Font	Point size	Style	Alignment
Heading	Serif	16	Bold	Centred (already done)
Subheadings	Serif	12	Italic	Left
Body text	Serif	11		Justified
Bullet text	Serif	11	Bold	Left
Tables	Serif	12		

Note: There are many serif (and sans serif) fonts. When working on a document it looks neater if you use the same font throughout (unless requested otherwise). The document is already in a serif font (ie Courier) but there are other serif fonts that are easier to read, eg Times New Roman.

1 Load Word and open the file **dough integrated**.

Applying a style for the heading

2 Click on: the down arrow of the [Normal] **Style box** on the **Formatting** toolbar and see if there is a style that suits your needs for the heading, ie serif font, 16 point size, bold (also aligned centre).

3 If a style that matches your needs is not listed, you will need to create one as follows:

a Select the heading.

b Format the heading as requested.

c From the **Format** menu, select: **Style**. The **Style** dialogue box is displayed (Figure 6.34).

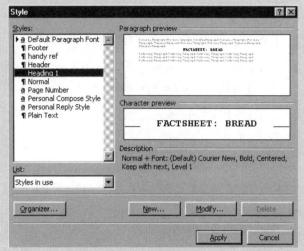

Figure 6.34 Style dialogue box

d Click on: **New**. The **New Style** dialogue box is displayed (Figure 6.35).

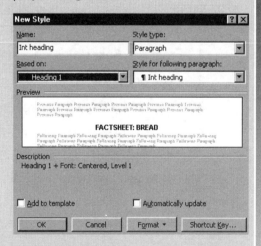

Figure 6.35 New Style dialogue box

e In the **Name** box, key in a name for the style, eg **Int header**.

f Click on: **OK**.

g You are returned to the **Style** dialogue box.

h Click on: **Apply**.

i Look in the **Style** box and you will see that the new style is now listed.

j If you need to add any more headings, you can select the next heading, and click on the style and all the formatting can be done in one go.

Applying a style for subheadings

1 Follow steps 2 and 3 above.

2 Ensure that you apply the style to all the subheadings.

Note: Left alignment is the default so does not need to be set.

Applying body text style

1 Follow steps 2 and 3 as for the heading, but after step 2(e) click on the **Format** button.

2 From the menu, select: **Paragraph**.

3 Note that you can select options from the **Paragraph** box, such as **Alignment** – set this to **Justified** and **Line spacing** (not required in this case).

4 Ensure that you apply the style to the other body text.

Applying bullet text style

Follow the methods above. Remember to set alignment to **Left**.

Applying table style

Follow the methods above.

When setting up more than one style, you can create all of the styles in the New Style dialogue box without closing it between selecting new styles as follows:

1 From the **Format** menu, select: **Style**.

2 Click on: **New**.

3 In the **New Style** box, key in a style name in the **Name** box.

4 lick on: **Format** and make selections using the options, eg **Font** and **Paragraph**, clicking on: **OK** in between options.

5 When you are happy with the new style, click on: **OK** to return to the **Style** dialogue box.

6 Click on: **New** to create the next new style.

7 When all of the new styles have been set, click on: **Apply**.

8 The styles will now be listed in the toolbar drop down **Style** box. The new styles can be assigned to the relevant text in the document by selecting the text and then the new style from the drop-down list.

There are other ways to format a short document quickly. To copy formatting from one paragraph of body text to another:

1 Select: the text with the formatting to copy.

2 Double-click on: the **Format Painter** button.

3 Select the text to copy the formatting to. The formatting is copied across.

4 Repeat as necessary.

5 Press: **Esc** to turn the **Format Painter** off.

5.3 Final check

Do a final check for consistency of spacing and positioning of imports. Check that the styling is correct.

5.4 Save document

Save the document with the filename **Int complete** and print one copy.

5.5 Close the file and exit Word

Create, manage and integrate files quick reference for CLAIT Plus

Windows Explorer

Action	Keyboard	Mouse	Right-mouse menu	Menu
Copy file/folder	Select the file/folder			
	Ctrl + C	Click: the 📋 **Copy** button	**Copy**	**Edit**, **Copy**
	Click where you want to copy the file/folder			
	Ctrl + V	Click: the 📋 **Paste** button	**Paste**	**Edit**, **Paste**
Create a new folder	Select where you want the new folder to be			
			New, **Folder**	**File**, **New**, **Folder**
Create a subfolder	Select the folder in which you want the subfolder to be and follow the steps for creating a new folder.			
Delete a file/folder	Select the file/folder			
	Delete		**Delete**	**File**, **Delete**
Display contents of folder		Double-click: the folder		
Find files/folders	**Start**, **Find**, **Files or Folders** or in Windows Explorer **File** menu, **Find**			
Move file/folder	Select the file			
	Ctrl + X	Click: the ✂ **Cut** button	**Cut**	**Edit**, **Cut**
	Click where you want to move the file/folder to			
	Ctrl + V	Click: the 📋 **Paste** button	**Paste**	**Edit**, **Paste**
Printing file structure	Press: **Print Scrn** Load Word, click on: the 📋 **Paste** button			
Recycle Bin, restore files	Double-click on the **Recycle Bin** icon Select the file you want to restore			
			Restore	**File**, **Restore**
Recycle Bin, empty			**Empty Recycle Bin**	
Rename file/folder			**Rename**	**File**, **Rename**
Select files *Adjacent*	Click: the first file Holding down: **Shift**, click: the last file			
Non-adjacent	Click: the first file Holding down: **Ctrl**, click: each file in turn			
View all file/folder attributes		Click: the 🔲 ▾ **Views** button arrow, **Details**		
View individual file/folder attributes	Select file/folder			
		Click: the 📋 **Properties** button	**Properties**	**File**, **Properties**

Word

Action	Keyboard	Mouse	Right-mouse menu	Menu
Change case				**F**ormat, **Change Case**
Copy text	Select: the text to be copied			
	Ctrl + C **Ctrl + V**	Click on: the 📋 **Copy** button Click on: the 📋 **Paste** button	**Copy** **Paste**	**E**dit, **C**opy **E**dit, **P**aste
English date format				**I**nsert, **Date and Time**
Font	Select the text you want to change			
		Click: the ▼ down arrow next to the **Font** box Select: the font you require	**Font**	F**o**rmat, **Font** Select: the required font from the **Font:** menu
Formatting, copy	Select text to copy			
		Click: the 🖌 **Format Painter** button Double-click to copy to several pieces of text		
Headers and Footers				**V**iew, **H**eader and Footer Select: **Autofields** using the **Header and Footer** toolbar buttons
Insert image, file, chart, spreadsheet		Use Cut and Paste method		**I**nsert, *either* **Picture**, **O**bject, **File** Resize using handles
Lists, bulleted and numbered	Click: the ▤ ▤ **Numbering** *or* **Bullets** button		**Bullets and Numbering**	F**o**rmat, **Bullets and Numbering**
Margins				**F**ile, **Page Set**u**p**, **Margins** (also select **Paper Size** and **Orientation** using the tabs in this box)
Open an existing text file	**Ctrl + O**	Click: the 📂 **Open** button		**F**ile, **Open**
	In the **Look in** box, select the appropriate location Select: **All Files** or **Text Files** in the **Files of Type** box Click on: the filename Click on: **Open**			
Page break, add	**Ctrl + Enter**			**I**nsert, **B**reak, OK
Page break, delete	In **Normal** View, place the cursor on the page break Press: **Delete**			
Page numbering				**I**nsert, **Page N**u**mbers** Select the required options
Page Setup				**F**ile, **Page Setup** (Choose from **Margins**, Paper **Size**, **Paper Source**, **Layout**)
Paper size	(See Page Setup)			

Action	Keyboard	Mouse	Right-mouse menu	Menu
Paragraphs – splitting/joining	*Splitting*: Move the cursor to the first letter of the new paragraph Press: **Enter** twice *Joining*: Move the cursor to the first character of the second paragraph Press ← (Backspace) twice (Press the spacebar to insert a space after a full stop)			
Save file in Word format				**File**, **Save As** Select **Word Document** in the **Save as type box**
Special characters/ symbols, inserting				**Insert**, **Symbol**
Spellcheck	**F7**	Click: the ✅ **Spelling** button		**Tools**, **Spelling and Grammar**
Styles	Select from the [Normal ▾] **Style** box drop-down list			**Format**, **Style**
Tables (see Section 3)		Click: the ▦ **Insert Table** button		**Table**, **Insert**, **Table**
Widows and Orphans				**Format**, **Paragraph**, **Line and Page Breaks** Select: **Widow/Orphan control**
Zoom	Click: the [100% ▾] **Zoom** button			**View**, **Zoom**

Hints and tips

- Proofread and spellcheck carefully.
- Always display data in full.
- Use English (UK) date formats and the spellchecker.
- Code information when requested.
- Adhere to House Style Sheet formats.
- Check headers and footers.

Create, manage and integrate files: sample full practice assignment

You work at the local Community College and you have been asked to produce a document to advertise a forthcoming Weekend Workshop.

To produce the document you will need the following files:

- A text file (**recycling** stored in a folder **plusint**) with a draft of the document that you will add to, amend and import the files below.
- A spreadsheet (**household** stored in folder **imports**) containing a chart showing typical household rubbish.
- A datafile (**waste** stored in folder **imports**) containing details of waste from a selection of countries.
- A graphic file **dustbin** stored in folder **imports**.

You will also need to consult the:

- House Style Sheet
- Draft Document
- Lectures and Workshops List

You will need to use system software and application software that will allow you to:

- manage files and folders on a system;
- combine text, graphics and datafiles; and
- control page layout, columns and use of tables.

All your work must be carried out and saved within the folder **plusint**.

HOUSE STYLE SHEET

Page setup

- Use A4 paper
- Use portrait orientation
- Margins:
  top   2 cm
  bottom   2.5 cm
  left   1.5 cm
  right   1.5 cm
- Header: candidate name, filename
- Footer: automatic date field (English format dd-mm-yy)
- Automatic page number, right aligned
- Use single line spacing (except where indicated)

Text style

Feature	Font	Point size	Style	Alignment	
Heading	Sans serif	14	Bold	Centred	
Subheadings	Sans serif	12	Bold, Italic	Left	
Body	Sans serif	10		Justified	
Bullet text	Sans serif	10	Bold	Left	
Tables	Sans serif	10	With gridlines	Column heading	Centred, italic, shaded
				Text	Left (wrapped)
				Numeric	Right
				Date	Right
Imported datafile	Sans serif	11	With gridlines	Column/row headings	Centred, bold, no shading
				Text	Left
				Numeric	Right
				Date	Right
Graph/chart text	Sans serif	Legible			

- Line spacing between headings, subheadings and paragraphs should be applied consistently
- Widows and orphans must be avoided
- Text, images, graphs and lines must not be superimposed
- Imported data must not be split across pages
- Graphs/charts must be positioned within the margins of the page
- Do not display a page number on the first page of the document
- Spellcheck all documentation. Specialist words and brand names have already been checked and no changes should be made to them

Exercise

As you will be working with a number of files to create the final document, you will need to set up a folder.

1   In your working folder **plusint**, create a new folder and name it **final**.

2   Copy the files **recycling**, **household**, **waste** and **dustbin** into the folder **final**.

3   Using suitable application software, open the text file **recycling** and save it in your software's normal file type using the filename **conserve** in the folder **final**.

4   Using the file **conserve** and referring to the draft document, make the changes shown.

5   Insert the following paragraph at the end of the document:

Please telephone Jeanna Quail on Bedford 600700 if you would like to book a place or if you require further details. The office is open from 9 am and closes at 4 pm Monday to Friday. Note that there are no charges for this event.

6   Search the document and replace the word **lectures** with **talks** wherever it appears.

7   Apply the house style to the document as detailed in the House Style Sheet. Ensure that all amendments have been made and that any spelling errors have been corrected.

8   Save the document in the folder **final**.

9   Print one copy of the document and close the file.

10   Rename the folder **final** as **(your initials)unit1**.

11   Within the folder **plusint**, create a new folder and name it **graphics**.

12   Move the file **dustbin** from the folder **(yourinitials)unit1** to the **graphics** folder.

13   Delete the files **recycling**, **household** and **waste** from the folder **(your initials)unit1**.

14   Produce evidence in the form of a screen printout of the contents of the **graphics** and **(yourinitials)unit1** folders. Ensure that your name is clearly visible on the screen print.

Insert the graphic **dustbin** here, and align it to the right

WEEKEND WORKSHOP ON RECYCLING ← Centre heading

The weekend workshop on recycling is scheduled to take place on 14/15 September 2002. It is envisaged that there will be places for fifty delegates. Speakers have been chosen from the local community. They will deliver lectures and workshops and be on hand to answer any queries that may arise.

Run on

The issues addressed will be wide-ranging - starting with recycling from a historical perspective to present day issues. If you want to know about recycling, then this is definitely the place to be.

WHAT IS RECYCLING?

Recycling is the process of recovering and reusing waste products. More than 50% of household waste could be recycled. Currently we recycle only about 10%. Some of the contents of of a typical household dustbin are shown in the chart below. The lectures will elabborate on this issue.

Delete

Insert the bar chart here, from the **household** spreadsheet. Ensure that it is within the margins and is legible. Add a border to frame the chart.

HISTORY

Recycling is not new. In the home, not very long ago, it was commonplace to darn socks if holes appeared. Clothes would be handed down to siblings. Today we just throw things away and buy new. During wartime, larger scale recycling took place. There were shortages of essential materials so collections were organised of things like:

Silk
Rubber
Aluminium   Apply bullets to text

In present times recycling and its benefits have become widely recognised. Recycling is now a major component of the management of waste.

Insert page break here

What to recycle ← ALL CAPS

Most recyclable products have a recycling symbol on them. This usually takes the form of the Mobius Strip now a universal symbol of recycling. The German mathematician and astronomer, Ferdinand Mobius, discovered the Mobius Strip in 1858. It is a continuous loop with one surfface and one edge formed by twisting one end of a long rectangular strip 180° and attaching this end to the other. The shape of the Mobius Strip expresses transformation and so the process of transforming waste material into useful resources.

start new paragraph

bold

Insert page break here

Recycling has become a universal priority. The table below shows household waste generated (in thousands of tonnes) in 1995 by six countries including the UK. Note: the GDP is in millions of dollars and the Rank is amount per capita.

Double line spacing for this section only

Insert the datafile **waste** here

Insert page break here

IN THE OFFICE

There are many things that you can do in the office to save energy and materials. These include switching things off when you are not using them and not throwing away your old computer. Instead give it away (many charitable organisations will be pleased to have it), trade it in or recycle the parts. You can reduce papper consumption by not printing out everything. Always use recycled paper and keep a scrap box for junk mail and other waste paper. Then either use it for scrap paper notes or recycle it.

SELECTION FROM THE WEEKEND

The table gives details of some lectures and workshops that take place before noon. So if you only have a morning to spare, please come along.

Move

Create a table here. The information to use is shown on the **lectures and workshops list**. Check the data before you begin so that you identify the number of columns and rows that will be required. Use the headings LECTURER, DATE, VENUE, DESCRIPTION. You should only include lectures that start before noon. VEW4E should be coded.

Lecture Hall	LH
Green Room	GR
Library	LY
Seminar Room	SR

You must display all gridlines. Ensure that only the specified data is included and that all the data is visible.

We look forward to welcoming you.

LECTURE	Introduction to Recycling
DATE	14/09/02
TIME	09:30
LECTURER	James Walsh
VENUE	Lecture Hall
DURATION	1 hour
DESCRIPTION	A general introduction about the process of recovering and reusing waste products. Types of waste. A brief history of recycling.
CODE	JW193LH

LECTURE	Actions for Recycling
DATE	14/09/02
TIME	11:00
LECTURER	Jenny Long
VENUE	Lecture Hall
DURATION	1 hour 15 minutes
DESCRIPTION	Simple things that everyone can do to ensure efficient recycling. Types of products that are recyclable. Where to recycle them.
CODE	JL11LH

LECTURE	Computers and Recycling
DATE	15/09/02
TIME	11:00
LECTURER	Timothy Mann
VENUE	Green Room
DURATION	1 hour
DESCRIPTION	Why you should not throw your old computer in the bin. What you can do with it. Who might want it and why?
CODE	TM11GR

LECTURE	The Paperless Office
DATE	15/09/02
TIME	13:30
LECTURER	Rhian Davies
VENUE	Library
DURATION	1 hour
DESCRIPTION	Why are we using more paper then ever? How can we cut down on wastage?
CODE	RD133L

LECTURE	Recycling Labelling
DATE	14/09/02
TIME	13:30
LECTURER	Gabrielle Fiorentini
VENUE	Green Room
DURATION	30 minutes
DESCRIPTION	Practical workshop. Examination of common household rubbish. What is the Mobius Loop? What do the recycling labels tell us?
CODE	GF133GR

LECTURE	The Wheelie Bin
DATE	14/09/02
TIME	10:00
LECTURER	José Fernandez
VENUE	Seminar Room
DURATION	30 minutes
DESCRIPTION	The bin of the 21st century? What goes in it? Its history and use.
CODE	JF10SR

LECTURE	Landfill and Incineration
DATE	15/09/02
TIME	15:00
LECTURER	Amelda Jacobs
VENUE	Library
DURATION	1 hour
DESCRIPTION	Ways of getting rid of waste. Advantages and disadvantages
CODE	AJ15L

LECTURE	Using Recycled Products
DATE	15/09/02
TIME	09:30
LECTURER	Aidan O'Neill
VENUE	Green Room
DURATION	30 minutes
DESCRIPTION	Choosing recycled products. Can all products be made from recycled materials?
CODE	AN093GR

LECTURE	Packaging
DATE	14/09/02
TIME	16:00
LECTURER	Hugh Samuels
VENUE	Seminar Room
DURATION	1 hour
DESCRIPTION	Workshop looking at packaging on various products. How much packaging is enough? Does packaging have an impact on saleability?
CODE	HS16SR

Chapter 7

Spreadsheets using Excel (Unit 2)

I ‖ Importing, amending and printing

In this section you will practise and learn how to:

- open and import a generic file
- amend column widths
- wrap cell contents
- set English (UK) date format
- sort data maintaining integrity
- print
  - alter margins
  - select paper size and orientation
  - add headers and footers with automatic fields
  - fit to specified number of pages
  - selection
  - display row/column headings on printout
  - apply/remove gridlines

Note: Before commencing on this chapter, it is recommended that you have worked through Chapter 3, or that you have achieved Unit 4, Spreadsheets, at CLAIT Level 1. For the exercises in this section you will need to access the file **concerts** on the CD-ROM.

This chapter uses the file **concerts** as its starting point. This file contains information on a series of charity concerts. The sections that follow contain various tasks that take you through building this spreadsheet to produce data for income, costs and analysis.

I.I ‖ Accessing files in other formats

Exercise I

Import the datafile **concerts** into Excel.

There are spreadsheet applications other than Excel. datafiles created in other applications can be saved in different formats. Some formats can be opened and read by applications other than those that the datafile was created and saved in. This is useful when sharing and transferring files. *CSV (comma separated values)* is one of those formats. As its name implies the data is separated by commas. In CLAIT Plus datafiles to be imported are supplied in CSV format.

1   Open Excel.

2   From the **File** menu, select: **Open**.

3   The **Open** dialogue box is displayed (Figure 7.1).

4   In the **Look in** box, select the location of the file.

5   To display the file in the box, in the **Files of type** box change to: **All Files**.

6   Click on: the filename, then on: **Open**.

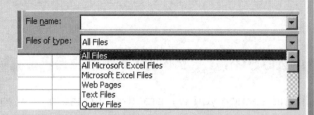

Figure 7.1 Selecting file type

1.2 Saving the file in Excel format

Exercise 2

Save the datafile with the name **charity** in Excel format.

Method

1   From the **File** menu, select: **Save As**.

2   The **Save As** box is displayed (Figure 7.2).

3   In the **Save in** box, select the location.

4   In the **File name** box, key in the new filename.

5   In the **Save as type** box note that CSV is displayed; change this to: **Microsoft Excel Workbook**.

   Note: In Excel a spreadsheet file is referred to as a *workbook*.

Figure 7.2 Saving file in Excel format

Exercise 3

Amend all column widths to 12 digits.

Method

1   Using the **Zoom** control on the toolbar, change the zoom so that you can see all the spreadsheet, eg 50% (Figure 7.3).

Figure 7.3 Changing the Zoom

2   Select all the spreadsheet columns.

3   From the **Format** menu, select: **Column**, then **Width** (Figure 7.4).

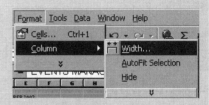

Figure 7.4 Changing column width to an exact measurement

4   The **Column Width** box is displayed (Figure 7.5).

5   In the **Column Width** box, key in the new width.

6   Click on: **OK**.

Figure 7.5 Column Width box

In Excel the default column width is approximately nine numeric characters. For CLAIT Plus assignments you will lose marks if data is not displayed in full. When data is not displayed in full it can render a printout useless since, for instance, there may be more than one name beginning WILL, eg WILLIAMS or WILLIAMSON or WILLKINSONS. When only the first letters are displayed it would be impossible to differentiate between them. In order to display data in full, you will need to demonstrate changing column width to an exact measurement (contents remain on one line) and wrapping contents of text cells (text flows on to next line(s) but remains on the same row, ie retains its cell reference), as in Section 1.4.

Exercise 4

There are cell headings remaining that still do not display in full. Wrap the contents of the following cells:

In the INCOME section, NO OF TICKETS, TICKETS SOLD, TICKETS REMAINING.

In the OUTGOING COSTS section, STAGE HANDS.

Method

1 Select the cell(s) to wrap by either selecting them one by one or select them all together by holding down the **Ctrl** key when selecting.

2 From the **Format** menu, select: **Cells**.

3 The **Format Cells** dialogue box is displayed (Figure 7.6).

4 With the **Alignment** tab selected, in the **Text control** section, click in: the **Wrap text** box so that a tick is displayed.

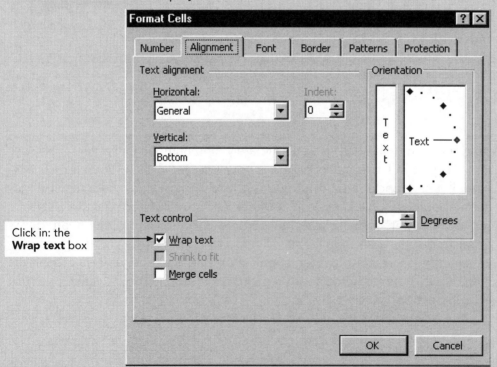

Click in: the **Wrap text** box

Figure 7.6 Wrapping text

5 Click on: **OK**.

6 Using the **Zoom** control return zoom of 100%.

1.5 Changing column width

Exercise 5

As an exception to setting columns to 12 digits above, widen column B so that all the venue names in this column are displayed in full.

Method

As in the New CLAIT section, ie *either* drag the column border *or* double-click on the column border.

1.6 Changing date format on spreadsheet data

Exercise 6

Change the cells that contain dates to the format **dd/mm/yy**, ie English UK date format.

Method

 If the date format is set to English US, it will display as, for example, 09/23/02 and not 23/09/02, ie mm/dd/yy instead of dd/mm/yy format. This results in months exceeding 12 in the month section as in the example. Therefore the dates are incorrect and any date that you enter will be incorrectly formatted.

You need to ensure that dates are in English (UK) format. You will be penalised in CLAIT Plus assignments for using dates in non-English format.

You may also be asked to enter an automatic date in a header or footer. See Section 1.10.

1   Check to determine the format of the dates.

2   If you need to change them, select the cells containing the dates.

3   From the **Format** menu, select: **Cells**.

4   The **Format Cells** dialogue box is displayed.

5   With the **Number** tab selected, select: **Custom**.

    Note: It is necessary to select **Custom** rather than **Date** because date does not have an English UK type of the format dd/mm/yy.

6   In the **Type** box, key in: **dd/mm/yy** (Figure 7.7).

7   Click on: **OK**.

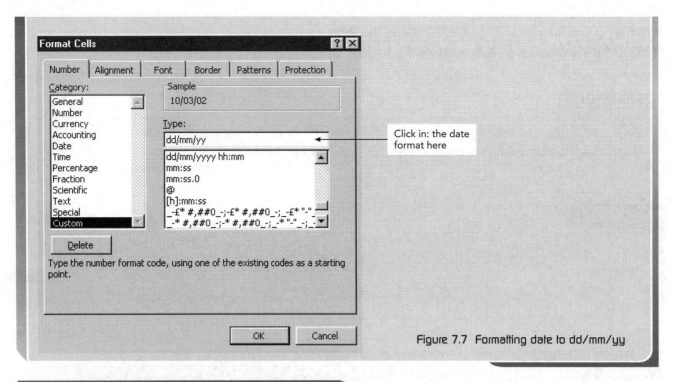

Figure 7.7 Formatting date to dd/mm/yy

1.7 Sorting data

Exercise 7

In the INCOME section, sort the data in the VENUE CODE column by code.

Method

 When sorting data in spreadsheets, it is important that any corresponding data is kept with the sorted data. For instance, if only the VENUE CODE column is selected and sorted, the corresponding columns (ie VENUE, DATE and TICKETS SOLD) would not change their position on the spreadsheet and so would not relate to the correct VENUE CODE, ie the integrity of the corresponding data would be lost. To ensure that this does not happen, it is necessary to select the corresponding cells as well as the cells to sort.

1   Select the VENUE CODE cells together with the corresponding cells VENUE, DATE, and TICKETS SOLD.

2   From the **Data** menu, select: **Sort**.

3   The **Sort** box is displayed (Figure 7.8).

4   In the **Sort by** box, select: **Column A** (or **VENUE CODE**) and **Ascending**.

5   In the **My list has** section, click on: the relevant box – ie have you selected the headings for the data as well as the data itself? If so click in: **Header row**, if not click in: **No header row**. *Note:* You do not want to include the header row in the sort and this ensures that it is not included with the rest of the data.

6   Click on: **OK**.

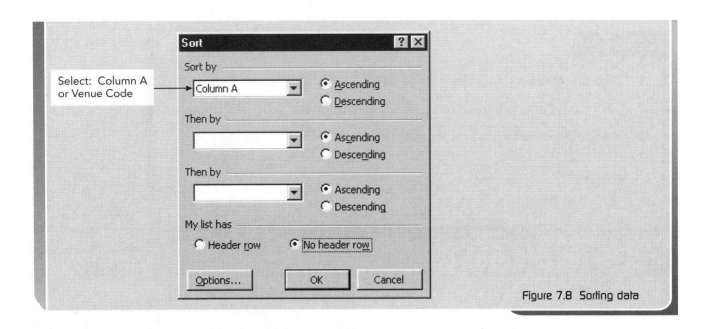

Figure 7.8 Sorting data

1.8 Changing margins

Exercise 8

Change the spreadsheet margins so that they are:

Top	2 cm
Bottom	2 cm
Left	1 cm
Right	1 cm

Method

1. From the **File** menu, select: **Page Setup**.

2. The **Page Setup** dialogue box is displayed.

3. Select: the **Margins** tab.

4. Key in the margin widths requested (Figure 7.9).

5. Click on: **OK**.

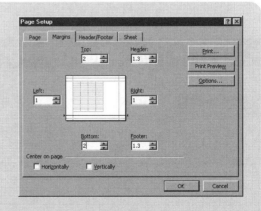

Figure 7.9 Setting margins

1.9 Selecting paper size, orientation and fitting to a specified number of pages

Exercise 9

Select A4 paper and landscape orientation. Ensure that a printout will be on one page only.

1   From the **File** menu, select: **Page Setup**.

2   With the **Page** tab selected, in the **Orientation** section, select: **Landscape** (Figure 7.10).

3   In the **Paper size** box, select: **A4**.

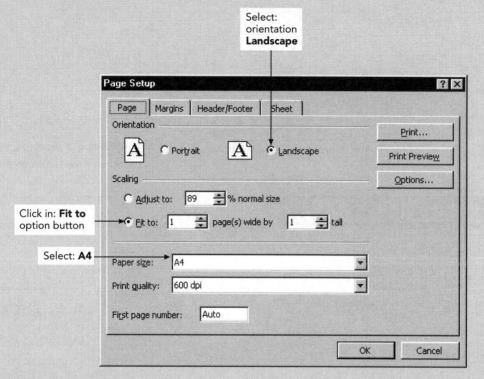

Select: orientation **Landscape**

Click in: **Fit to** option button

Select: **A4**

Figure 7.10 Setting orientation, paper size and number of pages

4   In the **Scaling** section, click in: the option button **Fit to** and select: **1** in the page(s) boxes.

5   Click on: **OK**.

1.10 Adding headers and footers

Exercise 10

Add a header to include your name and centre number.

Add a footer to include an automatic date (in English UK format), page number and filename.

Method

1   From the **File** menu, select: **Page Setup**.

2   The **Page Setup** dialogue box is displayed.

3   Select: the **Header/Footer** tab (Figure 7.11).

4   Click on: the **Custom Header** button.

5   The Header box is displayed (Figure 7.12).

6 Key in the header text in the boxes. (To move from section to section, use the **Tab** key or click in the section boxes.)

7 Click on: **OK**.

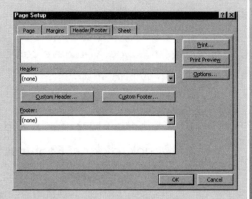

Figure 7.11 Adding headers/footers

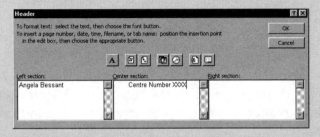

Figure 7.12 Adding a header

8 Click on: the **Custom Footer** box.

9 The **Footer** box is displayed.

10 Use the buttons to insert an automatic date, page number and filename as follows:

a Position the cursor in the section where you want the automatic field to be inserted.

b Click on: the relevant button from those shown in Figure 7.13.

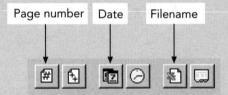

Figure 7.13 Automatic entry buttons

11 The automatic entries are displayed as shown in Figure 7.14.

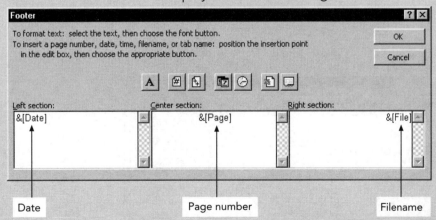

Figure 7.14 Inserting automatic fields in headers/footers

12 Click on: **OK**. You will see a preview of the header/footer. Check that the date is in English UK format. (If not, see the INFO box below.)

13 Click on: **OK**.

If the automatic date is not in English (UK) format you need to change it as follows:

Save the work you have completed to date

In the Windows desktop:

1   Click on: **Start**.
2   From the **Start** menu, select: **Settings**, **Control Panel**.
3   Double-click on: **Regional Settings**.
4   With the **Regional Settings** tab selected, check that: **English (United Kingdom)** is chosen. If not select it from the drop-down list.
5   Select: the **Date** tab.
6   Select: the date style you want.
7   Click on: **Apply**.

It is a good idea to check that you are displaying English UK date format before starting on the spreadsheet since, if you need to alter it, you will probably have to restart the computer before it is activated.

1.11 Printing with gridlines and row/column headings

Exercise 11

Print the spreadsheet showing gridlines and row and column headings, ie the new numbers and column letters.

Method

1   From the **File** menu, select: **Page Setup**. **The Page Setup** dialogue box is displayed.
2   With the **Sheet** tab selected, in the **Print** section, click in: the **Gridlines** box so that a tick appears and click in: the **Row and column headings** so that a tick appears (Figure 7.15).
3   Click on: **Print**.
4   The **Print** dialogue box is displayed.
5   Click on: **OK**.

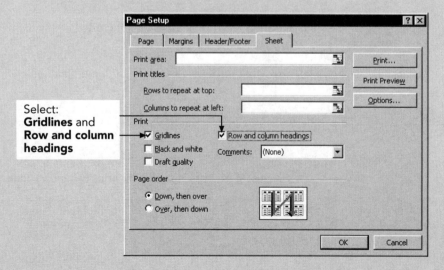

Figure 7.15 Printing gridlines and column/row headings

1.12 Printing a selection

Exercise 12

Print the VENUE and DATE cells (including their headings, ie VENUE and DATE, and row and column headings) only, with all settings as for the last printout.

Method

1   Select the cells to print.

2   From the **File** menu, select: **Print**.

3   In the **Print** box, **Print what** section, select: **Selection** (Figure 7.16).

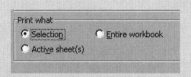

4   Click on: **OK**.

Figure 7.16 Printing a selection

 Setting a page ready for printing is an important and useful habit. Changing page orientation ensures that the spreadsheet fits the page in the most logical way. For instance, if you have long columns and short rows, portrait is more appropriate. The opposite is true for landscape orientation. Changing margins can make the spreadsheet look neater on the page and can free up more space to make it fit. Adding headers and footers (such as filename and date) enables location of the file easier at a later date. The more information you have the easier it will be to find.

1.13 Save file

Save the file retaining the name **charity** and Excel format.

1.14 Close the file and exit Excel

In this section you will practise and learn how to:

- work with formulae
- name cells
- use mathematical operators + -* /
- use functions: SUM, AVERAGE, COUNT/COUNTA/COUNTIF, MIN, MAX
- print formulae

 ## Working with formulae

At CLAIT Plus level you will be expected to be able to work out a range of formulae and have references to cells not only within the same worksheet but also to cells in worksheets in other spreadsheet files. To assist you in this, you are provided with a *Formula Sheet*. This does not contain the actual formulae themselves but it serves as a guide to the makeup of the formulae. For the exercises that follow a formula sheet is provided so that you can get used to the format. At this stage, since you are still learning, you will also be guided through the creation of formulae. You may find it beneficial to use the Zoom toolbar facility from time to time to zoom out so that more of the spreadsheet is displayed whilst working on it. The sample full practice assignment provides practice without guidance.

When learning how to construct formulae, it is a good idea to check the results on a calculator to ensure that your formulae are doing the calculations you want. Remember, there may be a small difference between the results in some instances. This is because Excel works on the values it has stored and not on the displayed values. For instance, if you have formatted values to one decimal place, Excel will still work with the stored value that may be to many decimal places.

Excel follows arithmetic protocol when carrying out calculations. It will perform multiplication and division first and then addition and subtraction. Sometimes you will need to force Excel to carry out the calculation in a different order. As in arithmetic, this can be achieved by adding brackets around the appropriate part, eg when cells A1, A2 and A3 contain the numbers 4, 3 and 2 respectively. A1+A2* A3 in numbers is 4 + 3 % 2 which Excel would calculate to be (carrying out the multiplication first) 10. Placing brackets around the addition section forces Excel to perform the calculation differently. (A1+A2)*A3 in numbers is (4 + 3) % 2 and gives the result 14.

Throughout this section, model formulae are provided. Try to work out the formulae for yourself before looking at those given.

FORMULA SHEET (formulae for this section)

Tickets remaining	Subtract the tickets sold from the number of tickets
Revenue	Multiply the number of tickets sold by the named cell **ticketprice**
Total revenue	Add together the revenue for each venue

Total number of tickets available (venue codes beginning with A)	Add together the number of tickets for all venues with codes beginning with A
Total number of tickets sold (venue codes beginning with A)	Add together the tickets sold for all venues with codes beginning with A
Total number of tickets available (venue codes beginning with B)	Add together the number of tickets for all venues with codes beginning with B
Total number of tickets sold (venue codes beginning with B)	Add together the tickets sold for all venues with codes beginning with B
% of tickets sold	Divide the tickets sold by the number of tickets and multiply by 100

2.1 Practising simple calculations

Exercise 1

Open the file **charity** saved in Section 1. In the NO OF TICKETS column, enter the numbers as follows:

CODES ending with:

WE 4000
AF 5000
EV 6000

It is very important that you are accurate in entering all numerical data into spreadsheets. A single mistake can have an unplanned effect on other cells, making the data incorrect.

Exercise 2

In the TICKET SALES section, generate the figures for the number of tickets remaining for all the venues.

Method

Refer to the Formula Sheet, generate the figure for the first venue and replicate down the TICKETS REMAINING column for the other venues.

When working at this level you will be creating formulae that have references to cells that are in other parts of the spreadsheet, ie not in the same row or column. Instead of keying in the cell reference, a quicker way of adding a cell reference to a formula is by clicking on the cell to be included. The cell reference is then automatically inserted into the formula.

Exercise 3

In the INCOME section, calculate the total for the NO OF TICKETS and replicate this formula to generate totals for TICKETS SOLD and TICKETS REMAINING.

2.2 Naming cells

Exercise 4

In the ANALYSIS section, name the cell that contains the ticket cost, ie 60, **ticketprice**.

Method

 Excel allows you to give a meaningful descriptive name to a cell or to a range of cells. You can then use this name as part of a formula. This can make formulae shorter and easier to understand. It is particularly useful for large spreadsheets, when working with multiple spreadsheets or for spreadsheets that are not often used, as it reminds you of what the formulae are about.

1 Click on the cell to name, ie in this case **B14**.

2 From the **Insert** menu, select: **Name**, then: **Define**.

3 The **Define Name** dialogue box is displayed.

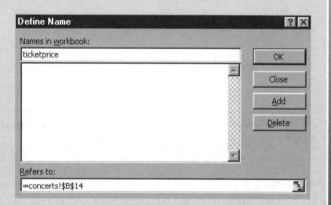

Figure 7.17 Naming a cell

4 In the **Names in workbook** box, enter the name **ticketprice** (Figure 7.17).

 In the **Refers to** box, the worksheet name and cell reference are given in the form of:

=concerts!\$B\$14

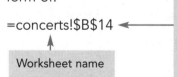
Worksheet name

Cell reference
This has a \$ symbol inserted in front of the column letter and in front of the row number. This denotes that the cell has been given an absolute reference, ie it will not change even when copied or replicated

In this case the worksheet has the name **concerts**.

5 Click on: **OK**.

6 You will notice that the name **ticketprice** appears in the **Name box** (Figure 7.18) instead of the usual cell reference.

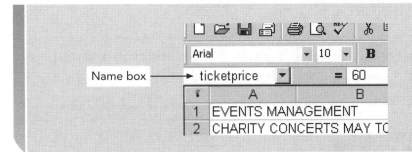

Figure 7.18 Name box

2.3 Using a named cell in a formula

Exercise 5

In the cell adjacent to the TICKETS REMAINING heading, enter the heading REVENUE. Refer to the Formula Sheet and generate a figure for the revenue for each of the venues and a Total revenue. Use a named cell in the formula.

Note: Adjacent means next to or adjoining.

Method

When creating the formula do not use the reference B14 but use the cell name. Do this by clicking on it to select it or by keying in the cell name (not reference) in the formula. The formula for the first venue is:

=E18*ticketprice

2.4 Practising more formulae

Exercise 6

In the ANALYSIS section, in the CODE column enter A and B in the two rows underneath this heading.

Exercise 7

In the INCOME section, in the cell below TOTALS, enter the heading TOTALS A. In the cell below this enter the heading TOTALS B.

Using the Formula Sheet, generate a formula to calculate the total number of tickets available and the total number sold at venues with codes beginning with A in the cells adjacent to TOTALS A.

Using the Formula Sheet, generate a formula to calculate the total number of tickets available and the total number sold at venues with codes beginning with B in the cells adjacent to TOTALS B.

In the ANALYSIS section, refer to the Formula Sheet and generate the percentage of tickets sold at venues with codes beginning A and at venues with codes beginning B.

2.5 Using the COUNT function

 COUNT is a useful function. Use it to count the number of cells in a range. There are three different versions that you need to be aware of:

=COUNT(cell ref:cell ref)	Numbers and dates are counted within a specified range. Any cells containing no entries or text entries are not counted.
=COUNTA(Cell ref:cell ref)	This counts cells with text entries but it will also include any non-blank entries such as numbers or dates.
=COUNTIF(Cell ref:cell ref,"criteria")	This counts the cells, determines if they meet a specific criteria (in this example greater than 100) and returns the result. The criteria can be number or text based. For example, if you are looking to count all names of Ann, the formula could be =COUNTIF(A1:A10,"Ann").
	Use the operators:
	> greater than < less than <> not equal to = equal to >= more than or equal to <= less than or equal to

Exercise 9

In the ANALYSIS section, in the NO OF VENUES WITH THIS CODE column, generate a formula to count the numbers of codes beginning with A and B. Use one of the COUNT functions.

Method

In this case, since we are counting codes (ie text entries), use COUNTA. Formulae are:

=COUNTA(A18:A26)
=COUNTA(A27:A35)

In the ANALYSIS section, add a new column heading LESS THAN 500 adjacent to the %TICKETS SOLD heading. Wrap this new heading.

Generate a formula to count the number of venues with codes beginning with A that have less than 500 tickets left. Do the same for venues with codes beginning with B.

Method

In this case, since we are looking for a specific criteria, ie less than 500, use COUNTIF. Formulae are:

=COUNTIF(F18:F26,"<500")
=COUNTIF(F27:F35,"<500")

Because of the way the COUNT function calculates (ie it includes values of 0 in some of its calculations) it is very important that when replicating formulae you do not replicate zero values over what should be left as blank cells. Ensure that you delete such zero entries when they occur.

2.6 Using the functions AVERAGE, MAX and MIN

The AVERAGE, MAX and MIN functions are used to generate the average, maximum and minimum values in a cell range.

Using the AVERAGE function
If you want to find the average of five numbers you need to add up the numbers and divide by 5 so, for example, in a cell range (A1 to A5) you could use a formula:

=SUM(A1:A5)/5

However if you add another cell to this range, thus making six numbers, then the formula would be incorrect. You would need to divide by 6 not 5. To overcome this, you can use the AVERAGE function. So using the example above the formula would be:

=AVERAGE(A1:A5)

You can also find averages of numbers that are not in an adjacent cell range using commas to separate the cell references:

=AVERAGE(A1,A6,B7,C4)

Using the MAX and MIN functions
The MAX and MIN functions are used in a similar way. For example, if you wanted to find the maximum value in a cell range, the formula could be:

=MAX(A1:A5)

or

=MAX(A1,A6,B7,C4)

Use the MIN function in the same way to find the minimum value:

=MIN(A1:A5)

or

=MIN(A1,A6,B7,C4)

Note: You cannot shorten the word AVERAGE.

Exercise 11

In the ANALYSIS section, in the cells A9, A10 and A11, enter the headings AVERAGE TICKET REVENUE, MAX REVENUE, MIN REVENUE. Wrap the cells as necessary.

In the corresponding adjacent cells, use formulae to generate the results using the REVENUE column of the TICKET SALES section (use the functions AVERAGE, MAX and MIN).

Method

Use the formulae:

=AVERAGE(G18:G35)
=MAX(G18:G35)
=MIN(G18:G35)

2.7 Save spreadsheet

Save your spreadsheet with the name **Charity2** and print in landscape on one page. Ensure all cell contents are displayed in full.

Note: Do not alter column widths – use **Fit to page**.

2.8 Print copy

Print a copy of the spreadsheet with the formulae displayed in full. Print in landscape on one page.

Note: Do not alter column widths – use **Fit to page**.

2.9 Check your printouts with the sample answers

2.10 Close the file and exit Excel

More calculating

In this section you will practise and learn how to:

- work with formulae to project results
- work with absolute and relative cell references
- use functions: SQRT, IF

FORMULA SHEET (*formulae for this section*)

If statement (Yes, No)	IF tickets remaining is more the 600, return the value "Yes", otherwise return the value "No"
Stage Hands cost per venue	Multiply the Cost per Hr by the Hrs per Venue
Marshalls cost per venue	Divide the NO OF TICKETS by 500 and multiply by the Marshalls cost per Hr
Fencing required	Square root of 250 multiplied by 2
Fencing cost	Fencing required multiplied by the cost per metre
Toilet cost per venue	Multiply the MISC figure by the NO OF TICKETS and then by the cost per toilet
Totals	Add the Stage Hands, Marshalls and Toilets costs and add on the fencing cost

3.1 Making projections

Open the file **Charity2** saved in Section 2.

 Spreadsheets are very useful if you need to project different results by asking 'what if...?' For example what if just one value, such as ticket price in this spreadsheet, is changed? The results of calculations would change accordingly and would be quite different. It is extremely useful to be able to project different results when deciding on things such as pricing of goods, pay rates and so on.

Exercise 1

Change the ticket price to 70.

Add to the header: Ticket price £70.

Print out the REVENUE column only to see what affect this has had.

Notice the effect changing one cell has had on other sections of the spreadsheet.

Exercise 2

Change the ticket price to 50.

Add to the header: Ticket price £50.

Print out the REVENUE column only to see what affect this has had.

Exercise 3

Change the ticket price back to its original value of 60.

3.2 Using the IF function

The IF function is used to test a specified condition and return a verdict. As an example, in this spreadsheet you could determine the scale of profit made using the condition IF REVENUE is greater than 20000 return a verdict of Excellent, if not return a verdict of Good.

The formula for this would be:

=IF(G18>20000,"Excellent","Good"), ie
=IF (test,"value if true", "value if false")

Exercise 4

In the TICKET SALES section, insert a new column with the heading ADVERTISE after the heading REVENUE.

Refer to the Formula Sheet, use the IF function to test whether the events need further advertising because ticket sales are low. If the Tickets Remaining are more than 600 it is worth advertising so indicate Yes, otherwise indicate No.

Method

The formula in this case is:

=IF(F18>600,"Yes","No")

Replicate this to the other cells in the column.

When replicating formulae, the cell references change to reflect their new position. A relative cell reference will change relatively to its position on the spreadsheet. By contrast, an absolute cell reference will not change even if it is replicated or moved to another part of the spreadsheet. If you need to make a cell reference absolute, add a $ sign in front of the column letter and another $ sign in front of the row number or press: **F4** when the cell is active. For example, cell reference C8 becomes $C$8 when it is absolute.

Exercise 5

In the ADDITIONAL FIELD REQUIREMENTS section, enter the Stage Hands cost per hour of 6.50 in cell I6. Wrap the STAGE HANDS text in the cell so that it displays in full.

Enter the Marshalls cost per hour of 7.00 in cell I7.

Change the heading in cell J5 to **Hrs per Venue**.

Enter 10 for the Stage Hands Hrs per Venue.

In the OUTGOING COSTS section, using the Formula Sheet, enter a formula to generate the Stage Hands cost per venue. You must use absolute cell references in the formula.

Method

1   Click on cell I18 (where you want the result to appear).
2   Enter the = sign.
3   Click on cell I6 (Stage hand cost per hr) so that the cell is active and its reference appears on the formula bar.
4   Press: the **F4** key ($ signs appear in the cell reference to assign it absolute status).
5   Enter the * symbol.
6   Click on cell J6 (Stage hand hrs per venue) so that the cell reference appears on the formula bar as before.
7   Press: the **F4** key (to make the reference absolute).
8   Press: **Enter**.
9   Replicate the formula for the other venues.

Note: You can insert the $ symbols by hand if you prefer. If you do not use absolute cell references in this formula you will not be able to replicate it. Try the formula again without making the cells absolute to see what results you get.

Exercise 6

In the OUTGOING COSTS section, using the Formula Sheet, enter a formula to generate the Marshalls cost per venue. You must use absolute cell references in the formula.

1. Click on cell J18 (where you want the result to appear).

2. Enter =**D18/500***

3. Click on cell I7 (Marshall cost per hr) so that the cell is active and its reference is displayed on the formula bar.

4. Press: the **F4** key (to make the cell reference absolute).

5. Press: **Enter**.

6. Replicate the formula for the other venues.

3.4 Using the SQRT function

The square of a number is the number multiplied by itself:

2 multiplied by 2 = 4, ie 4 is the square of 2, sometimes written as 22 or 2 squared.

Floor covering is often priced in square metres so if you needed a carpet for a room of 2 metres by 2 metres you would need 4 square metres:

3 multiplied by 3 = 9, ie 9 is the square of 3, sometimes written as 32 or 3 squared

4 multiplied by 4 = 16, ie 16 is the square of 4, sometimes written as 42 or 4 squared and so on.

The square root of a number is the original number in the examples above:

The square root of 4 is 2
The square root of 9 is 3
The square root of 16 is 4 and so on.

Square root symbol is ÷ so the square root of 16 could be written as ÷16 = 4. Excel has a function **SQRT** that works out the square root of a given number.

Exercise 7

Practise the SQRT function.

Method

1. In an empty cell at the bottom of the spreadsheet, say G41, enter the number **16**.

2. In another cell enter the formula **=SQRT(G41)**.

3. The result 4 is displayed in the cell.

4. Change the number in cell G41 to 9 to result in 3 being displayed.

5. Now change the number in cell G41 to 25 and then to 81 (results 5 and 9 respectively).

6 Now try the number 147 and notice that the square root of a number does not have to be an integer but can have many decimal places.

7 When you have finished practising delete the cell entries in this exercise.

Exercise 8

In this exercise you need to work out the amount of fencing required to fence part of a field to be used as a parking area for the event organisers. You have been allocated a square space of approximately 250 square metres and will need to provide fencing for two sides of the parking space (the other sides are the existing field fencing). In the ADDITIONAL FIELD REQUIREMENTS section, in the cell below the heading FENCING, using the Formula Sheet generate a formula to calculate the length of fencing required.

Method

Click on the cell H10 and enter the formula:

=SQRT(250)*2

This formula is derived from the square root of the space required, ie 250 square metres (this gives the length of one side of the square) multiplied by 2 to give the total for 2 sides.

Exercise 9

In the cell below H10, enter 5.00 (the cost of the fencing per metre). Using the Formula Sheet, generate a formula in the FENCING column of the OUTGOING COSTS section that calculates the total cost of the fencing. Use absolute cell references. DO NOT REPLICATE THIS FORMULA.

Method

The formula is:

=$H$10*$H$11

3.5 More formulae practice

Exercise 10

Additional toilet facilities are required at the venues. In the ADDITIONAL FIELD REQUIREMENTS section, in the cell below the heading PORTABLE TOILETS, enter 100.00, the cost in pounds per toilet.

In the OUTGOING COSTS section, using the Formula Sheet, generate a formula to calculate the toilet cost per venue. Use absolute cell references in the formula. Replicate the formulae for each venue.

Formula is:

=$I$14*D18*$I$10

Exercise 11

In the OUTGOING COSTS section, add a column headed TOTALS, adjacent to the FENCING column. Using the Formula Sheet, create a formula to generate the total outgoing costs for each venue. Use an absolute cell reference in the formula.

Method

Formula is:

=SUM(I18:K18)+$L$18

3.6 Save spreadsheet

Save the spreadsheet with the filename **charity3**.

3.7 Print copies

Remove the ticket price from the header. Print two copies with landscape orientation, one showing the data and one showing the formulae.

3.8 Check your printouts with the samples provided

3.9 Close the file and exit Excel

Working with more than one spreadsheet file

In this section you will practise and learn how to:

- open more than one spreadsheet file
- understand spreadsheet linking and using linked data in formulae

4.1 Open file

Open the file **charity3** saved at the end of Section 3.

4.2 Opening more than one spreadsheet file

 Working with more than one spreadsheet file
At CLAIT Plus level you will work with more than one spreadsheet file to link cell data. Linking data can prove very useful because when one of the linked spreadsheets is updated, other linked spreadsheets are automatically updated at the same time.

When opening a new Excel file, the file actually contains (by default) three worksheets. These can be accessed by clicking on the relevant sheet tabs or using the arrow navigation buttons at the bottom of the Excel window (Figure 7.19). These sheets are known collectively as an Excel workbook and are saved together in the same file. More sheets (including chart sheets) can be added to the workbook at any time.

Figure 7.19 Accessing sheets

The sheets can be named so that they are easy to recognise. It is useful to have worksheets that contain related data in the same Excel file.

A CSV format file contains only one worksheet and this is automatically named with the same name as the CSV filename. In this section the Excel file saved in Section 1 that was originally in CSV format will be used. Notice that the worksheet in this file is named **concerts** (the original CSV format filename). Also notice that even when saved in Excel format there is still only one worksheet.

Exercise 1

Open a new spreadsheet file.

Method

Click on: the ☐ **New** button.

Exercise 2

On the new spreadsheet, in cell A1, enter the title:

CHARITY CONCERTS COSTINGS PREVIEW

 When working on related spreadsheet data it is often a good idea, instead of opening a new spreadsheet file, to use a worksheet within the original file. This way the sheets will be saved together in one file. (You can switch to a new worksheet using the sheet tabs at the bottom of the spreadsheet window.) However, the examples in this section demonstrate how to work with two separate spreadsheet files.

4.3 Switching between spreadsheet files

When spreadsheet files are open they have a button displayed on the taskbar. The file that is active on screen has a button that looks as if it is pressed in. In Figure 7.20 the new spreadsheet file **Book2** is active and displayed on screen. To display the other file you need to click on its button on the taskbar.

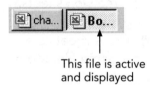

This file is active
and displayed

Figure 7.20 Switching between spreadsheet files

4.4 Linking spreadsheet data

Exercise 3

In column A, in a row below the title, create a link to the column heading VENUE in the **charity3** spreadsheet file. Ensure the link is relative and not absolute so that you can replicate this column to show all venue names.

Method

1   Click on the cell in column A where you want the heading to appear.

2   Key in the = sign.

3   Switch to the **charity3** file by clicking on its button on the taskbar.

4   Click on the cell (VENUE) that you want to copy.

5   The formula for the cell is displayed on the formula bar, as in Figure 7.21. Notice that this is made up of the spreadsheet filename **charity3.xls**, followed by the worksheet name **concerts**, followed by the cell reference **B17**. The cell reference is absolute (it has $ signs). This needs to be changed to a relative reference. To do this, whilst the cell is active, press: the **F4** key until the $ signs are removed.

6 Press: **Enter**.

7 The cell content is placed in the new spreadsheet cell.

8 Replicate this cell so that all the venues are displayed on the new spreadsheet.

9 Widen the column so that its contents are displayed in full.

```
=[charity3.xls]concerts!$B$17
```

Figure 7.21 Linking a cell to another spreadsheet file

Exercise 4

In column B create a link to the TICKETS REMAINING heading. Ensure the link is relative and not absolute so that you can replicate this column. Wrap the heading in the cell and widen it so that the words are not split over lines.

Method

Use the method as in Exercise 3.

4.5 Using linked data in formulae

Exercise 5

Add a new column headed PROFIT TO DATE next to the TICKETS REMAINING column. Wrap the cell contents. Calculate the profit to date.

Profit to date   Subtract the outgoing costs totals from the revenue from the **charity3** spreadsheet

Use relative not absolute cell references so that the formula can be replicated.

Method

1 Click in the cell below the new heading.

2 Key in =

3 Switch to the **charity3** spreadsheet by clicking on its button on the taskbar.

4 Click in the cell of the first venue of the REVENUE column.

5 With this cell still active, press: the **F4** key to remove all the $ signs (make the cell relative).

6 Key in the – sign.

7 In the OUTGOING COSTS section, click in the cell of the first venue of the TOTALS column.

8 With this cell active, press: the **F4** key to remove the $ signs (make the cell relative).

9 Press: **Enter**.

10 The first result is displayed on the new spreadsheet.

11 Replicate this so that the profit for all the venues is calculated.

4.6 Save spreadsheet

Save the new spreadsheet with the name **costings** and save the **charity3** spreadsheet with the name **charitylinked**.

4.7 Print in portrait

Print one copy in portrait display of the spreadsheet **costings** displaying the data. Ensure the data is displayed in full. Add your name, centre number and automatic filename to the header.

4.8 Print in landscape

Print one copy in landscape display of the spreadsheet **costings** displaying the formulae. Note that the formulae are very long so you will need to widen columns so that the formulae are displayed in full.

 When you need to widen columns to display formulae in full, it is best to save the spreadsheet first, widen the columns and then close the spreadsheet (not saving the changes, ie the cell widths). You can then reopen the saved spreadsheet with the cell widths intact and change back to displaying data instead of formulae.

4.9 Check the printouts with the samples provided

4.10 Close both spreadsheet files and exit Excel

5 Formatting

In this section you will practise and learn how to:

- display a variety of formats
- set text orientation
- apply borders
- align cell data (vertical/horizontal)
- hide rows/columns

5.1 Open spreadsheet

Open the spreadsheet file **Charitylinked**, saved in Section 4.

5.2 Displaying data using a variety of formats

 When working on CLAIT Plus assignments you will be given a *House Style Sheet* that details the formatting required on the spreadsheet. For the purposes of learning new skills there is no House Style Sheet in this section. You will be able to practise using one in the sample full practice assignment at the end of this chapter. You may remember some of the formatting from the CLAIT section but you can revise it here.

When entries are not manually formatted, they are set at the default **General** format. If you make an error when formatting and want to return cells to their original format, select: **General** from the **Category** list in the **Format Cells** dialogue box, **Number** tab selected.

Note: Exercises 1 to 11 refer to the **charitylinked** spreadsheet.

Percentages

Exercise 1

Format cell I14 containing 0.001 as a percentage to one decimal place.

Method

Click on: the **% Percent Style** button.

Note: You may need to use the **Increase Decimal** button if it displays a result of 0%.

Be careful when applying **Percent Style**. Always check that the percentage is what you expect. If you want a cell to display 10.4%, you must ensure that the entry is in decimal format (ie 0.104) and may need to click on: the **Increase Decimal** button to display the 4. If you key in 10.4 and then format using the **Percent Style** button you will get the percentage of 1050%.

When keying in percentages, instead of using the **Percent Style** button, you can key in the % symbol after the number. The cell will automatically format as a percentage.

Currency/monetary amounts

Exercise 2

Format all monetary amounts to 2 decimal places and no £ sign.

Method

1   Select the cells to format. Hold down the **Ctrl** key when selecting to select them together.

2   From the **Format** menu, select: **Cells**.

3   The **Format Cells** dialogue box is displayed (Figure 7.22).

4   Click on: the **Number** tab.

5   In the **Category** list, click on: **Currency**.

6   In the **Decimal Places** box, select: **2**.

7   In the **Symbol** box, select: **None**.

8   Click on: **OK**.

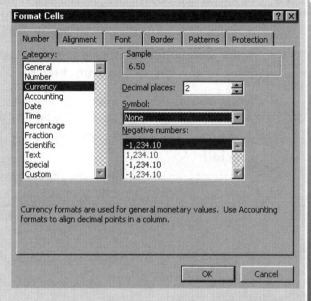

Figure 7.22 Formatting monetary amounts

Use the **Format Cells** box, **Number** tab, **Currency** to make other selections – eg using a £ sign, displaying a different number of decimal places or an integer (whole number) and selecting how negative numbers appear, eg with a minus symbol or/and in red.

Numbers

Exercise 3

Format all other numbers on the spreadsheet to have no decimal places.

Method

1 Select the other numbers.

2 From the **Format** menu, select: **Cells**.

3 The **Format Cells** dialogue box is displayed (Figure 7.22).

4 Click on: the **Number** tab.

5 In the **Category** list, click on: **Number** (Figure 7.23).

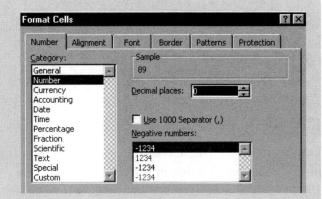

Figure 7.23 Formatting numbers

6 In the **Decimal Places** box, select: **0**.

7 Click on: **OK**.

 Notice that you can select negative number formats.

Date

Exercise 4

Format all dates to display in the format 12-Feb-02.

Remember: All dates must be in English (UK) format.

Method

1 Select the cells with dates as above.

2 Access the **Format Cells** dialogue box (as above).

3 Select: the **Number** tab.

4 In the **Category** box, select: **Date** (Figure 7.24).

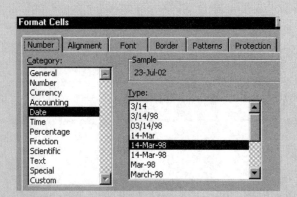

Figure 7.24 Formatting dates

5 In the **Type** box, click on: the format required.

6 Click on: **OK**.

Time of day

The spreadsheets in these sections do not have any time entries. You may be asked to use a time format in a CLAIT Plus assignment. If so, follow the steps above then:

1 In the **Category** section, select: **Time** (Figure 7.25).

2 In the **Type** box, click on: a specific format.

3 Click on: OK.

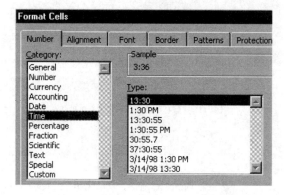

Figure 7.25 Formatting time

 In CLAIT Plus assignments you may be asked to format time meaning a measurement of time and not meaning time of day, for example, the time taken to do something, eg 3.44 minutes. In such cases use the **Number** format.

5.3 Merging cells to centre headings across cells

Exercise 5

Merge the cells on the top row so that the spreadsheet title EVENTS MANAGEMENT is centred across all columns of the spreadsheet that contain data.

Method

1 Select the cells in row 1 that are in columns that contain data (Figure 7.26). You may want to change the **Zoom** toolbar button to see all the spreadsheet.

2 Click on: the ▦ **Merge and Center button**.

Merging and centring makes the spreadsheet neater and easier to read. When an entry is merged and centred it still retains its original (and only its original) cell reference, in this case A1 (displayed in the **Name Box**). This is useful to know when you are amending such cell entries.

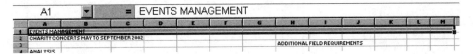

Figure 7.26 Merging cells to centre across cells

Exercise 6

Merge and centre the following headings across the cells that make up their sections:

ANALYSIS, ADDITIONAL FIELD REQUIREMENTS, INCOME (include the ADVERTISE column) and OUTGOING COSTS

Note: In the ANALYSIS section, wrap the heading NO OF VENUES WITH THIS CODE.

Method

Follow the method as in Exercise 5.

5.4 Aligning cell data horizontally and vertically

Exercise 7

Set all column headings to have alignment as follows:

Horizontal alignment: Left for columns of text and right for columns of numbers (including date).

Vertical alignment: Centre.

Wrap any remaining cells that do not display in full.

Method

1 Select the cells to align.

Horizontal alignment
2 Align horizontally using the toolbar buttons.

Vertical alignment
3 With the cells selected, from the **Format** menu, select: **Cells**.

4 The **Format Cells** dialogue box is displayed.

5   Click on: the **Alignment** tab (Figure 7.27).

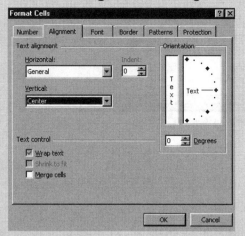

Figure 7.27 Setting vertical alignment

6   In the **Text alignment** section, in the **Vertical** box, select: **Centre**.

7   Click on: **OK**.

Notice how the headings have centred vertically in the cells. Aligning cells in this way gives the spreadsheet more clarity and makes it look neater.

5.5 Setting text orientation

Exercise 8

Set the orientation of the text in the cell containing the column heading ADVERTISE to 90 degrees. Change the row height so that ADVERTISE is displayed as one word. Right align the entries in this column.

Method

1   Click on the relevant cell to select it.

2   Access **Format**, **Cells**, **Alignment** as in Exercise 7 (Figure 7.27).

3   In the **Orientation** section, change the degrees to **90**.

4   Click on: **OK**.

5   Widen the row by hovering the cursor in the row numbers on a line between the rows (a double-headed arrow appears, Figure 7.28).

6   Drag the cell border to the required position.

Figure 7.28 Changing row height

Setting text orientation in this way means that columns can be narrower. This can be quite useful on larger spreadsheets since it saves space thus allowing you to see more of the data on the screen.

5.6 Setting font and font size and font style

Exercise 9

Set the font and font sizes as follows:

Feature	Font	Font size	Style
Main title and subtitle	Sans serif	14	Bold and italic
Section headings	Sans serif	12	Bold
Column headings and all other headings	Sans serif	11	No emphasis
Body	Sans serif	10	No emphasis

Method

Select the cells in turn and use the toolbar buttons to select the font type and format as requested.

Note: You may now need to widen cells to display data in full.

 Remember to set the correct font type. **Arial** is a sans serif font and **Times New Roman** is a serif font.

5.7 Applying borders

Exercise 10

Add a box border round the main heading and round the section headings.

Method

1   Select the cells where you want to add borders.
2   Click on: the down arrow of the **Borders** button.
3   The borders selection is displayed (Figure 7.29).
4   Click on: the most appropriate border.

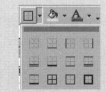

Figure 7.29 Applying borders

Borders differ from gridlines since they need to be applied manually and can be applied anywhere on the spreadsheet. Gridlines are applied/or are applied not to the whole sheet when printed.

5.8 Hiding columns/rows

Exercise 11

Hide the columns B, C, D and E.

Method

1. Select: the columns to hide.

2. From the **Format** menu, select: **Columns**, then: **Hide**.

Notice: A thick line appears where the columns are hidden. Looking at the column letters you can see which columns are hidden.

When you want to redisplay hidden columns

1. Select the column on each side of those hidden.

2. From the **Format** menu, select: **Column, Unhide**.

 Hiding columns is useful if you want to view more of the spreadsheet on screen. When printing it is sometimes useful to have a copy with columns hidden (eg not needing to absorb more data than is needed makes for more clarity and confidential data is not displayed).

5.9 Practising formatting

Exercise 12

Open the spreadsheet **costings** and practise some of the formatting skills that you have learnt.

5.10 Save spreadsheets

Save both spreadsheets with the names **charity(your initials)** and **costings(your initials)**. Remember to check that all data is displayed in full.

5.11 Print both the spreadsheets with page setup as requested

Page Setup

Use A4 paper

Use landscape orientation for the **charity** spreadsheet and portrait orientation for the **costings** spreadsheet

Do not show gridlines or row and column headings

Margins	top	2.5 cm
	bottom	2.5 cm
	left	1.5 cm
	right	1.5 cm
Header	automatic date field (English format dd/mm/yyyy) and page number	
Footer	filename, candidate name and centre number	

5.12 Unhide columns

Unhide the columns in the **charity(your initials)** spreadsheet and reprint.

5.13 Close both spreadsheets and exit Excel

Action	Keyboard	Mouse	Right-mouse menu	Menu
Absolute cell reference	Add **$** sign in front of the cell reference column letter and in front of the cell reference row number or press: **F4** when cell is active			
Align cell entries (horizontally and vertically)	Select cells to align			
		Click: the relevant button: ≡ ≡ ≡ 🔢	**Format Cells**	**Format, Cells**
				Format, Cells
			Select the **Alignment** tab Select from the **Horizontal/Vertical** drop-down menu as appropriate	
Autofill	Select the first cell, drag the **Fill Handle** across the cells			
Bold text	Select cells to embolden			
	Ctrl + B	Click: the **B** **Bold** button	**Format Cells**	**Format, Cells**
			Select the **Font** tab Select: **Bold** from the **Font style**: menu	
Borders	Select the cells that you want to add a border to			
		Click on the down arrow of the ⊞ , **Borders** button. Select the border you require	**Format Cells, Border** tab	**Format, Cells, Border** tab
Columns, changing width of		Drag the column border C ↔ D to fit the widest entry	Select the column(s) by clicking (and dragging) on the column ref box (at top of column)	
			Column Width Key in the width you want	(For an exact measurement) **Format, Column, Width** Key in the width you want *or* **Format, Column, AutoFit Selection**
Currency/ monetary amounts/ symbols		Click: the 💱 **Currency** button for UK currency		**Format, Cells, Number, Category, Currency**, select: symbol to use
Date, add automatic	From the **View** menu, select: **Header and Footer** Click: **Custom Header** Click: where you want the date to appear Click: the 🗓 **Date** button			
Date, format			**Format cells, Category, Custom/Date, Type**	**Format, Cells, Category, Custom/Date, Type**
Date, set UK format				**Start, Settings, Control Panel, Regional Settings, English (United Kingdom), Date** tab

Action	Keyboard	Mouse	Right-mouse menu	Menu
Decimal places		Click: the ↑.0/.00 **Increase Decimal** button to increase the number of decimal places Click: the .00/↓.0 **Decrease Decimal** to decrease the number of decimal places	**F**ormat cells Select: the **Number** tab Click: **Number** in the **Category**: menu Select the number of decimal places you need	**F**ormat, C**e**lls
Fit to page				**F**ile, **Page Set**u**p**, **F**it to (1) **Page**
Formulae, functions	Click on the cell where the result is required			
	Use: **=SUM(cell ref:cell ref)** for adding a range of cells *or* Click: Σ **AutoSum** button Click and drag over the cell range Press: **Enter**			
	Use: **=AVERAGE(cell ref:cell ref)** to find the average value in a range of cells			
	Use: **=COUNT(cell ref:cell ref)** to count the number and dates in specified range			
	Use: **=COUNTA(cell ref:cell ref)** to count text entries in a specified range			
	Use: **=COUNTIF(cell ref:cell ref, "criteria")** to count cells with a specified criteria			
	Use: **=IF(test, "value if true", "value if false")** to return a value for the given test			
	Use: **=MAX(cell ref:cell ref)** to find the maximum value in a specified range			
	Use: **=MIN(cell ref:cell ref)** to find the minimum value in a specified range			
	Use: **=SQRT(value)** to work out the square root of a number			
Formulae, operators	+ add - subtract * multiply /divide Arithmetic protocol: multiplication and division have priority over addition and subtraction. Use brackets to force otherwise			
Headers and footers including automatic fields (see Date UK format)				**V**iew, **Header and F**ooter, **Custom Header/Footer** Select: automatic fields in **Header/Footer** box
Help	**F1**			**Help** **Microsoft Excel Help**
	Shift + F1			**H**elp, What's **T**his?
Hide columns	**Ctrl + 0**		**Hide**	**F**ormat, **C**olumn, **Hide**
Hide rows			**Hide**	**F**ormat, **R**ow, **Hide**
Integers (whole numbers)		Click: the .00/↓.0 **Decrease Decimal** button until you have reduced the number of decimal places to zero	**F**ormat Cells Select: the **Number** tab Click: **Number** in the Category menu Change the number of decimal places to zero	**F**ormat, C**e**lls

Action	Keyboard	Mouse	Right-mouse menu	Menu˙
Link data between spreadsheets	Click on the cell where you want lined data to appear Key in = Switch to sheet where the data is to come from and click on relevant cell Press: **Enter**			
Margins				**File**, **Page Setup**, **Margins** tab
Merge cells	Click on the relevant cells Click on the ▦ **Merge and Center** button			
Move to top of document	**Ctrl + Home**			
Move to end of document	**Ctrl + End**			
Name cells	From the **Insert** menu, select: **Name**, **Define** Key in: the name Click: **OK**			
New file	**Ctrl + N**	Click: the 🗋 **New** button		**File**, **New**
Numbers, format			**Format cells**, **Number**	**Format**, **Cells**, **Number**, **Category**, **Number**
Open an existing file (including generic file)	**Ctrl + O**	Click: the 🗁 **Open** button		**File**, **Open**
	Select: the drive required Select: the filename (If a generic file) select: **All Files** in **Files of type** box Click: **Open**			
Page number, adding	From the **View** menu, select: **Header and Footer** Click: **Custom Header** Click: where you want the date to appear Click: the # **Page** button			
Page Setup	From the **File** menu, select: **Page Setup** Choose from **Margins**, **Paper Size**, **Paper Source**, **Layout**			
Paper size and orientation	See Page Setup			
Percentages, numbers as		Click: the **%** **Percent Style** button	**Format cells**, **Number**, **Category**, **Percentage**	**Format**, **Cells**, **Number**, **Category**, **Percentage**
Print column and row headings and/or gridlines				**File**, **Page Setup**, **Sheet**
Print in landscape/ portrait	From the **File** menu, select: **Page Setup** Click: the **Page** tab Select: **Landscape/Portrait** Click: **OK**			
Print selection	Select the cells to print			
	Ctrl + P			**File**, **Print**
	Select: **Selection** Click: **OK**			

Action	Keyboard	Mouse	Right-mouse menu	Menu
Remove text emphasis	Select text to be changed			
	Ctrl + B (remove bold)	Click: the appropriate button: **B** *I* U	**Format Cells**	**Format**, **Cells**
	Ctrl + I (remove italics)		Select the **Font** tab	
	Ctrl + U (remove underline)		Click: **Regular** in the **Font Style**: menu	
Replicate (copy) formulae	Select: the cell with the formula to be copied Drag the mouse from the bottom right corner of the cell over the cells to copy to Release mouse			
Restore deleted input	**Ctrl + Z**	Click: the ↶ **Undo** button		**Edit**, **Undo**
Save file in a different file format	Save as above, select from **Save as type**			
Selecting non-adjacent cells	Select the first cell(s), hold down **Ctrl** and click the others			
Remove selection	Click in any white space			
Sheets, adding				**Insert**, **Worksheet**
Changing	Click on appropriate sheet tab			
Copying		Use **Copy** and **Paste** buttons	Right-click on sheet tab. Select: **Move** or **Copy**. In the **Before** sheet section, select appropriate sheet. Ensure **Create a copy** is ticked. Click: **OK**	
Deleting			Right-click on Sheet tab. Select: **Delete**	
Renaming			Right-click on sheet tab. Select: **Rename**	
Sorting data	Select cells (and all related data cells) in the range to sort			
		Click: the ↑ **Ascending** or the ↓ **Descending** button		**Data**, **Sort**
Spellcheck	Move cursor to top of document			
	F7	Click: the ✓ **Spelling** button		**Tools**, **Spelling**
Switch between open spreadsheet files		Click on the spreadsheet's minimised button on the taskbar		

Action	Keyboard	Mouse	Right-mouse menu	Menu
Text formatting:	Select cell(s) to format		**F**ormat, **C**ells, **Font** tab	**F**ormat C**e**lls, **Font** tab
font, size, style, orientation	**Ctrl + B** Embolden **Ctrl + I** Italicise **Ctrl + U** Underline	*Select font and font size:* **Font** and **Font Size** boxes *Style:* Click: the relevant toolbar button on the formatting toolbar	*For orientation:* **Alignment** tab	*For orientation:* **Alignment** tab
Undo	**Ctrl + Z**	Click: the ↶ **Undo** button		**E**dit, **U**ndo
Unhide columns	Select the columns on either side of the hidden ones			
	Ctrl + Shift + 0		**U**nhide	**F**ormat, **C**olumn, **U**nhide
Unhide rows	Select the rows on either side of the hidden ones			
			Unhide	**F**ormat, **R**ow, **U**nhide
Wrap cell contents			**F**ormat Cells, **Alignment**	**F**ormat, **C**ells, **Alignment**, **Wrap** text

Hints and tips

- Check and double check. All spreadsheet data must be accurate.
- Check that all data and formulae are displayed in full. Truncating data is a common reason to lose marks.
- There are many small but significant tasks. Ensure that you work through methodically.
- Always use relative, absolute and named cells in formulae when requested.
- Always use functions in formulae when requested.
- Display row and column headings on printouts when requested.
- Ensure you have the correct number of printouts.
- When requested, have you printed a selection and not the entire sheet?

Spreadsheets: sample full practice assignment

Scenario

You are working as an Administrative Officer for a Hotel Company. You produce reports for the Manager.

The first report is to be set up using the specified data. It details bookings at the Hillside Hotel following special promotional offers for the Easter weekend. You will provide details of the revenue from the bookings together with the extra staffing costs required for the increase in trade. You will provide some comparisons if the special offer prices are altered.

The second report uses data from the first task and summarises the revenue generated with special offers and compares this data with the previous year's Easter bookings.

For Task 1 you will need the file **hillside**: a datafile containing details of special promotional Easter bookings.

For Task 2 you will need the file **summary**: a datafile containing details of last year's figures for the Easter weekend.

You will need to refer to the:

- House Style Sheet
- Formula Sheet.

To perform your tasks you will need to use application software that will allow you to:

- manipulate and format numeric data
- use live data from one spreadsheet to another.

HOUSE STYLE SHEET

Page setup

- Use A4 paper
- Use landscape orientation
- Margins:

top	2 cm
bottom	2.5 cm
left	2 cm
right	1.5 cm

- Header: automatic date field (English format, eg dd/mm/yy) and filename
- Footer: candidate name, centre number and page number

Text style

Feature	Font	Font size	Style	Alignment
Main title Subtitle	Serif	16	Bold, capitals Framed together by border	Centred across all columns that contain data
Section headings	Serif	12	Bold, italic Framed by border	Centred across the columns that make up the section
Column headings	Serif	10	No emphasis	Horizontal: centre Vertical: top
Body	Serif	10	No emphasis	Left unless otherwise stated

The section headings in this assignment are:

Special promotions, Extra Staffing, Bookings, Staffing costs, Promotion types

Number style

Feature	Font	Font size	Style	Alignment
Monetary amounts	Serif	10	2 decimal places Do not show monetary symbol unless specified	Right
Date	Serif	10	English format (eg dd/mm/yy)	Left
Other numbers	Serif	10	0 decimal places unless specified	Right unless specified

FORMULA SHEET

To complete the tasks you will need to use a variety of different cell references (relative, absolute, mixed and named cell) in the formulae. The following information has been provided to help you with your tasks.

Cost	Multiply the normal cost per person by the number of paying guests per room and then multiply by the number of nights, ie 4, and add the parking cost (the formula must contain an absolute cell reference and a named cell)
Promotional discount	Multiply the cost (generated above) by the discount (use an absolute cell reference)
Total of cost	Add together costs for all rooms
Total of promotional discount	Add together promotional discount for all rooms
Actual cost	Cost minus promotional discount
Kitchen/Restaurant/ Reception/Concierge	No of guests divided by 5 multiplied by rate per hour (use an absolute cell reference)
Totals	Add together costs for all rooms for each column, ie Kitchen, Restaurant, Reception and Concierge
Count hotel code types	Use a COUNT function to generate totals for each type and the overall total of all types (you must use a COUNT function)
Total of all types	Use a COUNT function to generate the total of all types (do not add the types)
If statement	If the Actual cost is greater then last year's cost, display **Profit**, otherwise display **Loss**

Task 1

Your first task is to produce a report showing the bookings and extra staffing for the special promotions Easter weekend.

1   Open the datafile **hillside** and save it in your software's normal file type. Use the filename **promotions**.

2   All the information needs to be visible. Amend all column widths to 12 digits to ensure all the data is displayed in full. Wrap to the column headings: **Type of break with code**, **Normal cost per person**, **No of paying guests per room**, **Promotional discount**.

3   In the **Special promotions** section, in the cell below the column headed **Discount**, enter **0.1** and format this cell to be a percentage with 2 decimal places.

4   In the **Special promotions** section, in the cell adjacent to the text **Parking (£)** enter **2.5** and name the cell **parkcost** (this is the total parking cost for 4 days and also qualifies for discount).

5   In the **Bookings** section, refer to the Formula Sheet and generate the figure for the **Cost** and the **Promotional discount** for the first room. Replicate the formulae for each of the rooms.

6   In the **Totals** row, using the Formula Sheet, generate totals for the **Cost** and **Promotional discount** columns.

7   Insert a new column headed **Actual cost** after the column headed **Promotional discount**. Refer to the Formula Sheet and generate a figure for the first room to display the difference between the promotional cost and the normal cost. Replicate this formula for the other rooms. Generate a formula for the total figure in the **Totals** row.

8   In the **Staffing costs** section, refer to the Formula Sheet and generate the figures for the **Kitchen**, **Restaurant**, **Reception** and **Concierge** per room.

9   In the **Totals** row, refer to the Formula Sheet and generate a formulae to total these columns.

10 One of the rooms has been included in error (it is now used for storage). Delete the whole row for Room code **49A**.

11 Some extra rooms need to be included. Insert the following data in the **Booking** section

Room code	Hotel code	No of paying guests per room
15B	S	2
44C	SP	3
22A	SB	2
27C	S	5

12 Copy any necessary formulae. Maintain any absolute and named cells in the formulae.

13 Sort the **Room Code** column in ascending order. Ensure associated data is also sorted.

14 In the **Promotion types** section at the bottom of the spreadsheet, enter the heading **Number** adjacent to the heading **Hotel code**. Wrap the heading **Hotel code**.

15 Refer to the Formula Sheet and count the number of **Hotel code** types. In column A below **Type SD**, enter **Total**. Generate the total number of rooms in the adjacent column. (Do not add the types of the cell entries you have just calculated.)

16 Your manager wants to know what the effect on the **Actual cost** would be if the % discount is increased to **15%** and decreased to **7%**.

In the **Special Promotions** section:

Change the percentage to **15%**. In the **Bookings** section, the **Total Actual cost** will change. This figure should be displayed next to the cell **Decrease discount** in the **Promotion types** section.

Change the percentage to **7%**. In the **Bookings** section, the **Total Actual** cost will change. This figure should be displayed next to the cell **Increase discount** in the **Promotion types** section.

Return the percentage to its original value of 10%.

Wrap the text in the cells containing the text **Increase discount** and **Decrease discount**.

17 In the **Totals** section, in the **Max**, **Min** and **Avg** columns, enter a formula to calculate the maximum, minimum and average income for the rooms from the **Actual costs** column.

18 The rooms coded ending with A now have personal safes in them. Add an S to all of the room codes ending with A – eg 49A to 49AS

19 In a cell below the title and subtitle enter the date: **19 June 2002**.

20 You should apply the house style to your work.

21 As an exception to the house style in the **Max**, **Min** and **Avg** columns, set the text orientation for all these column headings to a **90** degree angle. Both horizontal and vertical alignment should be set to centre. Ensure all data is displayed in full.

22 As an exception to the house style in the **Promotions type** section, display a £ sign and no decimal places for the **Decrease discount** and the **Increase discount** figures.

23 Save your work retaining the filename **promotions**.

24 Select the **Special Promotions** section of the spreadsheet. Using only 1 page, print this extract showing the figures. Make sure all data is displayed in full. The orientation, margins, header and footer should be as specified on the House Style Sheet.

25 Select the **Bookings** section only. Using only 1 page, print this extract showing the formulae. Make sure that all the formulae are displayed in full. Include row and column headings and gridlines on this print. The orientation, margins, header and footer should be as specified on the House Style Sheet.

26 Select the **Promotion types** section only. Using only 1 page, make two prints of this extract, one showing the formulae, the other the data. Make sure that all the formulae and data are displayed in full. Include row and column headings and gridlines on these prints. The orientation, margins, header and footer should be as specified on the House Style Sheet.

27 Select the **Staffing costs** section only. Using only 1 page, make two prints of this extract, one showing the formulae and the other showing the data. Make sure that all the formulae are displayed in full on the formulae print and that all data is shown in full on the data print. Do not include row and column headings and gridlines on these prints. The orientation, margins, header and footer should be as specified on the House Style Sheet.

Task 2

Your second task is to use data from the first task and make a summary of the revenue generated by the special discount.

1   Open the datafile **summary** and save it in your software's normal file type. Use the filename **profitability**.

2   All the information must be visible. Amend all column widths to 12 characters.

3   In column A and on a row below the title, adjacent to the heading **Last year**, create a link to the spreadsheet **promotions** to the column heading **Room code** in the **Bookings** section. Ensure that the link is relative and not absolute.

4   Replicate the codes in the **Room code** column on the **profitability** spreadsheet.

5   In the column adjacent to the column heading **Last year**, create a link to the heading **Actual cost** on the **promotions** spreadsheet, **Bookings** section. Ensure that the link is relative and not absolute.

6   Replicate the data in the **Actual cost** column on the **profitability** spreadsheet.

7   In the column adjacent to the column heading **Actual cost**, insert the heading **Profit**.

8   Refer to the Formula Sheet and generate an IF statement to show whether there is a Profit or a Loss.

9   Ensure that all columns are 12 digits wide. Apply house style to the spreadsheet as detailed on the House Style Sheet. As an exception to the House Style, centre the data in the **Profit** column.

10 Save the spreadsheet file retaining the name **profitability**.

11 Hide the columns **Last year** and **Actual cost**.

12 Print the spreadsheet showing the data with these columns still hidden. Include row and column headings on this print. Ensure all data is displayed in full.

13 Unhide the columns **Last year** and **Actual cost**.

14 Print a copy of the spreadsheet displaying the formulae. Ensure all formulae are displayed in full.

Graphs and charts using Excel (Unit 9)

 Accessing data source/exploded pie charts

In this section you will practise and learn how to:

- access data in other formats
- create an exploded pie chart
- add a header and footer
- select data set
- format a chart
- set orientation

Note: Before commencing on this chapter, it is recommended that you have worked through Chapters 3 and 4, or that you have achieved Units 4 and 7 (Spreadsheets and Graphs and Charts) at CLAIT Level 1. For the exercises in this section you will need to access the file **aviation** on the CD-ROM.

1.1 Accessing data in other formats

 For CLAIT Level 1, data was supplied in Excel format. For CLAIT Plus, data is supplied in CSV format – a generic format. Data for graphs is derived from many different sources and saved in various applications. It is not always possible to read this data in all types of software. Therefore supplying the data in generic format so that it can be read by other applications is often essential. Graphs and charts can then be created from the data in the application you normally use.

Exercise 1

Open the file **aviation**.

Method

1. Load Excel.
2. From the **File** menu, select: **Open**.
3. The **Open** dialogue box is displayed.
4. In the **Look in** box, select the location of the file.
5. Since the file is in CSV format it will not automatically be displayed.
6. In the **Files of type** box, select: **All files**.
7. The file should now be displayed.
8. Double-click on the file to open it.

Exercise 2

Create an exploded pie chart to display the **NUMBER OF PASSENGERS** travelling at the different **AIRPORTS**.

Give the chart the title **AIRPORT PASSENGERS** and a subtitle **YEAR 1997**.

Do not use a legend but ensure that each pie segment is distinctive.

Format the data labels on the pie chart so that a label and percentage are displayed for each portion of the pie.

Method

1   Select the data to chart, ie cells A5 to B10.

Always examine the data carefully to ensure that you are charting the correct data and only the data requested. For instance, in this case we should not include the totals row.

At CLAIT Plus level, data sets will be in rows or columns, ie:

MAX TEMP	6	7	10	13	17	20	22	21
MIN TEMP	2	2	3	6	8	12	14	13

Data series (Max Temp and Min Temp values) in rows

C	D
J	F
6	7
2	2
13	14
6	7

Data series (J and F values) in columns

Excel is usually able to determine whether to plot data from rows or columns. This decision is displayed at Step 2 of the Chart Wizard, ie Series in Rows or Columns.

Data can come from a single data set (as in pie charts) or a number of data sets (eg for comparisons). Sometimes you will need to select a subset of a large data set, eg you may have all the data for several years and you are asked to chart only some of those years. You are also expected to be able to select non-adjacent data, ie data that is not next to each other on the spreadsheet. You will practise all these selections as you progress through the chapter.

2   Create the chart using the Chart Wizard in the normal way:

   a   At Step 1 ensure that you select **Exploded Pie** (the bottom left pie type).

   b   At Step 3 key in the title and subtitle into the **Chart title** box (the subtitle will be set later). *Note:* On this chart you do not need to display a legend since all the data is to be displayed next to the pie. Display a legend when this is not the case.

   c   At Step 4, save the chart on a new sheet by selecting **As new sheet**.

Exercise 3

Emphasise the segment for **Manchester** by pulling it away from the rest of the chart.

Method

1 With the chart displayed, click on the chart to select it.

2 Click on: the pie segment for **Manchester** so only that segment is selected (Figure 8.1).

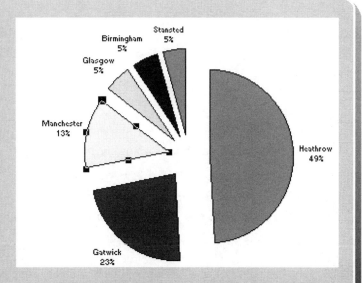

Figure 8.1 Selecting an individual segment

3 Drag the segment outwards so that it looks similar to Figure 8.2.

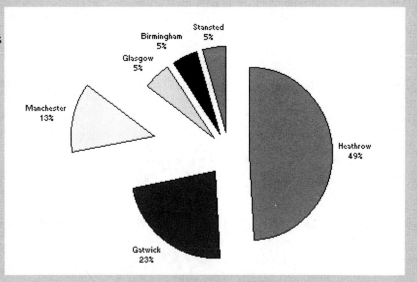

Figure 8.2 Manchester segment is emphasised

Exercise 4

Shade the segments so that they are distinguishable when output to a black and white printer. *Note:* You will notice that the chart segments are distinctive in colour but may not be distinctive in black and white.

1 Select an individual segment (as above).

2 Right-click on the segment.

3 From the pop-up menu, select: **Format Data Point** (Figure 8.3).

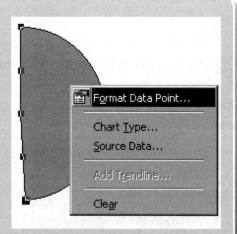

Figure 8.3 Formatting data points

4 The **Format Data Point** box is displayed (Figure 8.4).

5 With the **Patterns** tab selected, in the **Area** section, click on: the **Fill Effects** button.

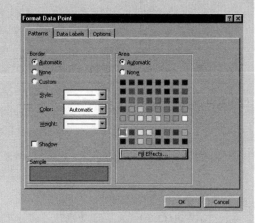

Figure 8.4 Accessing Fill Effects

6 The **Fill Effects** box is displayed (Figure 8.5).

7 Select: the **Pattern** tab.

8 Click on: a pattern; a sample is displayed. *Note:* You can change the colour in the **Foreground** box if necessary. (Changing to black is a good idea for a black and white output.)

9 Click on: **OK**.

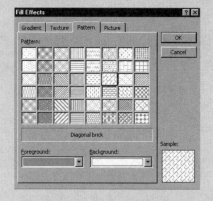

Figure 8.5 Selecting a pattern

10 Repeat for other indistinct segments, ensuring that the patterns are distinguishable. *Note:* Some of the segments can remain as they are. Check them in **Print Preview**.

There are other **Fill Effects** to select, eg **Gradient** and **Texture**. Experiment with these so that you know how to apply them.

For CLAIT Plus assignments you will be given *House Style Guidelines* so that all the charts you are asked to create look similar in appearance. House style is very important to companies and organisations. It gives them their own distinctive and recognisable look. You will work with House Style Guidelines in the sample full practice assignment at the end of the chapter.

Exercise 5

For the purposes of this exercise, display a legend for the chart. Format the chart as follows:

Typeface: serif
Text size:
title   20 pt bold
subtitle   18 pt italic
data labels 14 pt
legend   14 pt

 The default font in charts is Arial. This is a *sans serif* font. Serifs are small lines that stem from the upper and lower ends of characters. *Serif* fonts have such lines. Sans serif fonts do not have these lines. Examples:

Times New Roman is a serif font.
Arial is a sans serif font.

Method

1   Select the chart title by clicking on it.

2   Position the cursor in front of the letter **Y** of **Year** and press: **Enter** so that the subheading is in a new line.

3   Select the title by dragging the mouse over it and format it as specified using the toolbar buttons.

4   Select the subtitle and format it as specified.

5   Select the data labels by clicking on them.

6   Format using the toolbar buttons.

7   In this instance the labels are now overlapping. To remedy this, select an individual data label by clicking on it when all data labels are selected. Drag it to a position where it does not overlap. (*Note:* A line from the label to the segment will automatically appear if the label is positioned away from the pie.) Repeat with other data labels as necessary.

Display a legend by selecting the chart and then right-clicking in the chart area, ie not on the pie segments. From the pop-up menu, select: **Chart Options**. Select: the **Legend** tab and click in: the **Show legend** box. Click on: **OK**. *Note:* Here the legend is being inserted for practice only. A legend is not required for this pie chart because all information is displayed on data labels.

8   Format the legend by clicking on it to select it.

9 Format using the toolbar buttons.

10 Resize the legend box as necessary by dragging the handles so that all the text is fully visible.

11 Check that the legend boxes are distinguishable. If not change the segment fill to which the box refers.

1.6 Adding headers and footers

Exercise 6

Add a header displaying your name and a footer displaying your centre number.

Method

1 With the chart displayed, from the **View** menu, select: **Header and Footer**.

2 The **Page Setup** dialogue box is displayed with the **Header/Footer** tab selected (Figure 8.6).

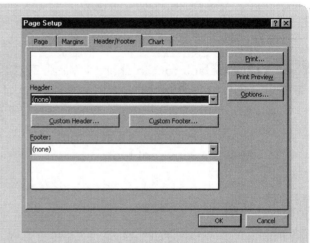

Figure 8.6 Adding a header/footer

3 Click on: the **Custom Header** button.

4 Key in: your name in any of the sections.

5 Click on: **OK**.

6 Click on: the **Custom Footer** button and repeat with the footer text.

7 Click on: **OK**.

1.7 Saving the file

Exercise 7

Save the file.

1.8 Setting orientation for printing

Exercise 8

Set the orientation for printing to landscape and print one copy. *Note:* Landscape has the widest side at the top. Portrait has the narrowest side at the top.

Method

1   From the **File** menu, select: **Page Setup**.

2   The **Page Setup** dialogue box is displayed (Figure 8.6).

3   With the **Page** tab selected, in the **Orientation** section, click in the **Landscape** option button (Figure 8.7).

4   Click on: **Print**.

5   Click on: **OK**.

Figure 8.7 Setting orientation

 When setting orientation, you may find that in some cases the objects (eg Legend, text boxes) need repositioning on your chart.

1.9 Close the file and exit Excel

2 Bar charts

In this section you will practise and learn how to:

- select non-adjacent data
- align labels
- create bar charts with several data sets
- use fill effects for bars

Note: For the exercises in this section you will need to access the file **transport** on the CD-ROM. You may also want to look at the file **transport1 data in rows**, also on the CD-ROM.

2.1 Selecting non-adjacent data

Exercise 1

From the file **transport**, select relevant data to produce a comparative vertical bar graph plotting **DISTANCE TRAVELLED** during the years shown (four in all) against **MODE** of travel.

Method

1 Load Excel.

2 Open the file **transport** (this is a generic file so will need to be opened as in Section 1).

3 Select the cells containing the MODE of travel, ie A5 to A15.

4 Hold down the **Ctrl** key and select the data for the years, ie C5 to F15.

In this example the data to chart is in columns. The **transport1 data in rows** file has exactly the same content as the **transport** file, but the data is transposed and is in rows. For comparison, you might like to try charting from this file's data after you have completed this section. As you learnt in the CLAIT section, Excel sometimes wrongly assumes which data to chart. You will need to remedy this. See the CLAIT section if you have forgotten how.

Always check that you are charting the data requested as you proceed through the Chart Wizard and after your chart is completed. If you have charted incorrect data, you can either delete the chart by right-clicking on its sheet tab at the bottom of the window and pressing: **Delete** (this is a bit drastic) *or* right-click in the chart area, select: **Source Data** and select accordingly.

Exercise 2

Create a comparative vertical bar chart with a legend as follows:

Title: **DISTANCE TRAVELLED 1970–2001 (per person, per year)**
x axis title: **MODE OF TRAVEL**
y axis title: **MILES TRAVELLED**

Format the labels on the x axis to have an alignment of 90 degrees.

Format the y axis scale Min 0, Max 390, Interval 30, set numbers to two decimal places.

Apply a different fill effect to each of the four bar sets so that they are easily distinguishable when printed.

Method

1 Create the chart in the normal way using the **Chart Wizard**.

2 Save the chart on a new sheet.

2.3 Aligning labels on the x axis

Method

1 Double-click on the x axis labels.

2 The **Format Axis** box is displayed.

3 Click on: the **Alignment** tab (Figure 8.8).

4 Use the arrows to set the degrees to 90.

5 Click on: **OK**.

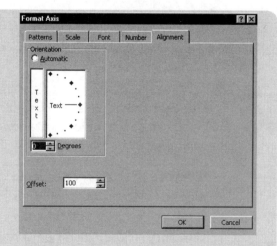

Figure 8.8 Setting alignment of axis labels

 You can also set the degrees to a negative number. Try this to see what the effect on alignment is. As well as using the **Degrees** box, you can set the alignment by moving the hand in the graphic box (above the **Degrees** box).

2.4 Formatting the *y* axis

Method

1 Double-click on: the *y* axis values.

2 The **Format Axis** box is displayed (Figure 8.8).

3 Click on: the **Scale** tab.

4 In the **Value (y) axis scale** section, set the **Minimum** and **Maximum** values as requested. In the **Major Unit** box, set the interval at 30 (as requested).

Note: Do not click on: **OK**. Move to next section.

2.5 Setting number format on the *y* axis

Method

1 Click on: the **Number** tab.

2 In the **Category** section, select: **Number** (Figure 8.9).

3 In the **Decimal Places** box, select: **2**.

4 Click on: **OK**.

Figure 8.9 Formatting numbers

 The **Format Axis** box is very useful. With the **Number** tab selected (as shown in Figure 8.9), you can select various categories and then format the category further. Amongst these are:

- **Number** – Set as integer, ie no decimal places or with a set number of decimal places. Select a 1000 comma separator and the negative numbers format (eg coloured red and with a minus sign).
- **Currency** – Select number of decimal places and £ sign displayed/not displayed. You can display other monetary signs. Format negative amounts.
- **Date** – Select the format for the date, eg 12/12/02 or Dec-02 or D.

You will have the opportunity to practise different formats as you progress through the chapter.

2.6 Applying a different fill effect to data series

Method

1 Click on: a data bar to select all data bars for that representation.

2 Right-click on the data bar.

3 From the pop-up menu, select: **Format Data Series**.

4 Proceed as for pie charts.

5 Repeat with the other three data bar sets.

6 Check with **Print Preview** that the bars are distinguishable.

7 Keep an eye on the legend and check that it too displays distinguishable fill effects. (Sometimes the legend is too small to display the fill. This may rectify itself when you format the chart, ie the legend may be in a larger font.)

2.7 Formatting the chart to house style

Exercise 3

Format the chart as follows:

Typeface: sans serif
Text size:

title	18 pt bold and italic
x axis title	14 pt bold
y axis title	14 pt bold
text on x axis	12 pt
numbering on y axis	12 pt
legend	12 pt

Add a footer including your name and centre number.

Method

1 Format the titles by selecting them and using the toolbar buttons.

2 Format the text on x axis by double-clicking on the x axis labels.

3 The **Format Axis** box is displayed.

4 Select: the **Font** tab.

5 Select: the options required and click on: **OK**.

6 Repeat steps 2–5 for the y axis numbering.

7 Format the legend as in Section 1.

8 Add a footer as in Section 1.

2.8 Save the file and print the chart in landscape orientation

2.9 Close the file and exit Excel

3 Line-column graphs

In this section you will practise and learn how to:

- understand the purpose of line-column graphs
- create a line-column graph:
  - format axis labels including date, setting currency format and negative numbers
  - fill plot area
  - add a text box
  - set line style and weight
  - display in portrait/landscape orientation

Note: For the exercises in this section you will need to access the file **bank** on the CD-ROM.

3.1 What is a line-column graph?

A typical line-column graph looks like Figure 8.10. It has columnar bars to represent one data series. This is plotted with another data series, represented by a line, on the same axis. The columns can be compared against the line. In this example, the columns represent actual grades achieved by students (students are labelled A, B, C and so on) and the line represents the average grade achieved by all the students in this sample. From this, we can easily see that seven students achieved the average grade or above and only four were below the average grade.

In this example the line is straight because it is plotting an average. However, in some graphs the line will not be straight (Figure 8.11). The graph in Figure 8.10 has just one columnar data set but it is also possible to plot more than one data set in columns, as in Figure 8.11. The line on this graph is not a straight line because the average is of the two tests for each individual student, not the average for the whole group.

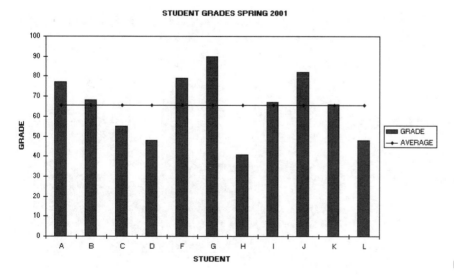

Figure 8.10 Line-column graph 1

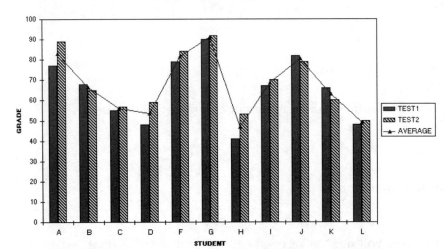

STUDENT GRADES FOR TWO TESTS

Figure 8.11 Line-column graph 2

3.2 Creating a line-column graph

Exercise 1

Access the file **bank** and create a line-column graph to plot the monthly **BANK BALANCE** (as columns) along with the **AVERAGE BALANCE** (as a line) against **MONTH**.

Title: **BANK BALANCE 2001**
x axis title: **MONTH**
y axis title: **£**

Display a legend showing actual **BALANCE** and **AVERAGE**.

Method

1   Load Excel and access the file **bank** (it is in generic format).

2   Select only the relevant data to plot.

3   Use **Chart Wizard** to plot the graph:

   a   At Step 1, select: the **Custom Types** tab.

   b   Select: **Line-Column**.

   c   Proceed with the graph in the normal way (Figure 8.12).

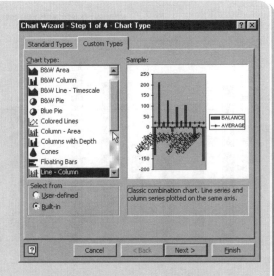

Figure 8.12 Selecting a line-column graph

4   The graph now looks like Figure 8.13.

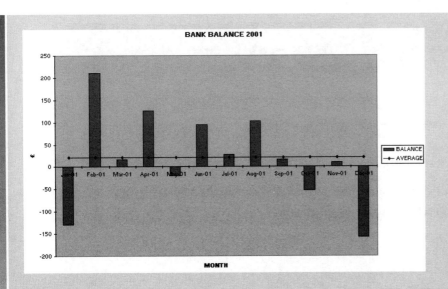

Figure 8.13 Line-column graph

Note: You will notice that because some of the bars have negative values these are displayed as columns below the x axis line.

3.3 Formatting x axis date labels

Exercise 2

Format the x axis so that the months appear with only a capital letter, ie **J** (January), **F** (February) and so on.

Method

1   Double-click on: the x axis labels.

2   The **Format Axis** box is displayed (Figure 8.14).

3   With the **Number** tab selected, ensure **Date** is selected in the **Category** box.

4   In the **Type** box, select the month's initial only format (as shown).

5   Click on: **OK**.

Note: Other formats are available for the date. Select these from this box when required. Select: **Custom** if you do not see the format you want.

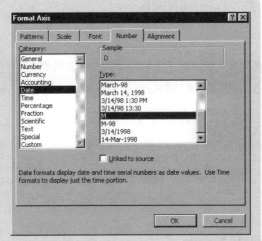

Figure 8.14 Formatting dates on the x axis

Exercise 3

Format the *y* axis as follows:

Scale: Min -240, Max 240, Interval 40.

Set the numbers to currency, ie displaying a £ sign with two decimal places. Ensure that negative numbers appear in red and with a minus sign.

Method

1   Set the scale in the normal way from the **Format Axis** box.

Setting numbers to currency

2   Double-click on: the axis values.

3   In the **Format Axis** box, select: the **Number** tab.

4   In the **Category** box, select: **Currency**.

5   Ensure there is a **£** sign in the **Symbol** box.

6   In the **Negative** numbers box, select: the example with the **minus** sign and £ sign (as shown).

7   In the **Decimal places** box, **2** is the default for the **Currency** category, so it can remain unchanged in this instance.

8   Click on: **OK**.

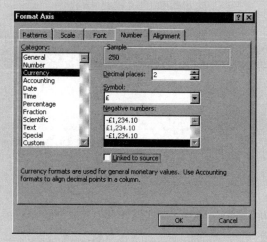

Figure 8.15 Setting numbers to currency

3.5 Setting line weights and markers

Exercise 4

Give the **AVERAGE** line a thicker weighting and remove the markers. (*Note:* The markers appear on the line at the plotted data points.)

Method

1   Double-click on: the line.

Setting line weighting

2   The line is selected and the **Format Data Series** box is displayed (Figure 8.16).

3   With the **Patterns** tab selected, in the **Line** section, select: **Custom**.

4   In the **Weight** box, click on: the down arrow and select: a thicker weighting.

Removing the markers

5 In the **Marker** section, click on: **None**.

6 Click on: **OK**.

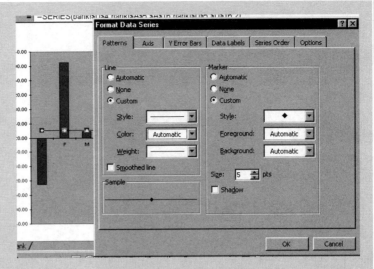

Figure 8.16 Setting line weights and markers

 Look at the different options in the **Format Data Series** box, **Patterns** tab selected. As well as the weighting, you can choose the style and colour of the line. You can choose a different style and colour for the markers too.

3.6 Setting plot area background fill

Exercise 5

Apply a two-colour fill to the plot area of the graph.

Method

1 Double-click on: the plot area (anywhere in the box that displays the bars and line, but not on the bars or line).

2 The **Format Plot Area** box is displayed (Figure 8.17).

3 Click on: the **Fill Effects** button.

4 The **Fill Effects** box is displayed (Figure 8.18).

5 Select: the **Gradient** tab.

6 In the **Colors** section, select: **Two colors**.

7 Select: **Color 1** and **Color 2**.

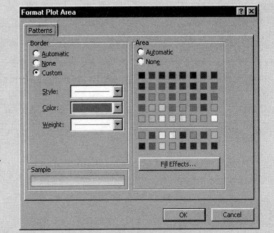

Figure 8.17 Formatting the Plot Area

Note: Do not select colours that are too similar because these will not be distinguishable on the printout. If you select colours that are too dark you will not be able to see the graph's bars and lines! You will need to experiment to see what works best.

8 Click on: **OK**.

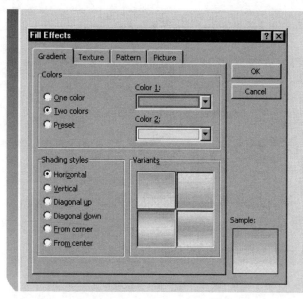

Figure 8.18 Fill Effects box

 Note: Many other options can be accessed in the **Format Plot Area** and **Fill Effects** boxes. For instance, you can select a **Texture** or **Pattern** fill or no fill at all. You can also set borders for the graph.

3.7 Display the graph in portrait orientation

Method

As in previous sections, using Page Setup.

3.8 Adding a text box

Exercise 6

Add three text boxes to the graph and place them in the plot area, as follows:

Below the x axis	**Overdrawn**
Above the x axis and below the Average line	**Credit**
Above the Average line	**Above Average Credit**

Method

1   Ensure that the **Drawing** toolbar is displayed (usually at the bottom of the screen). If it is not displayed, from the **View** menu, select: **Toolbars**. Click on: **Drawing** so that a tick is displayed next to it.

2   Click on: the ⬛ **Text Box** button.

3   In the appropriate place in the plot area, drag out a box large enough to fit the text.

(*Note:* You can alter the size of the box later so you do not need to be accurate.)

4   Key in the text.

5   Resize the box using the handles and reposition it by dragging to the preferred location.

Adding a visible border to a text box

6   On the **Drawing** toolbar, with the text box selected, click on: the arrow next to the **Line Color** button.

7   Select a colour that will show up against the plot area background.

8   Click on: **OK**.

Repeat the steps above for the other two text boxes.

3.9   Formatting the graph to house style

Exercise 7

Format the graph as follows:

• Typeface	sans serif
• Text size	
title	18 pt, bold
x/y axes titles	14 pt, bold
other text/numbering on *x/y* axes	12 pt, italic
legend	12 pt
• Text box	11 pt, border visible
• Headers and footers	add a footer with your name and centre number.

Method

Format in the normal way. Select the text box by selecting the box and dragging the mouse over its text. (You may want to zoom in to do this.) Format using the formatting toolbar buttons. *Note:* You may need to resize the text boxes so that the text fits inside. Use the toolbar buttons to centre the text (looks neat) within its box.

3.10   Save and print the graph still in portrait orientation

3.11   Close the file and exit Excel

In this section you will practise and learn how to:

- understand the purpose of XY scatter graphs
- create and use XY scatter graphs

    - apply a linear trendline
    - insert a trendline equation
    - join points of a scatter graph together to show *x/y* relationship

- apply superscript/subscript to labels
- insert special characters

Note: For the exercises in this section you will need to access the file **temperatures** on the CD-ROM.

4.1 What is an XY scatter graph?

An XY scatter graph shows if there is a relationship between two sets of data and identifies trends. Like a normal graph it has *x* and *y* axes. If the points plotted are scattered randomly, there is no correlation (link) between the two sets of data. For instance, you could plot a scatter graph to determine if there is a correlation between people who travel by bus and their shoe size. The data for the graph could look like the following table and the graph derived from this data like Figure 8.19. Since the points are randomly scattered there is no correlation between travel by bus and shoe size.

Person	A	B	C	D	E	F	G
Bus journeys/wk	2	20	10	0	4	15	22
Shoe size	12	5	3	10	8	4	7

Each point represents one person. This data point represents person G, ie Bus Journeys 22 (read from the x axis), Shoe Size 7 (read from the y axis)

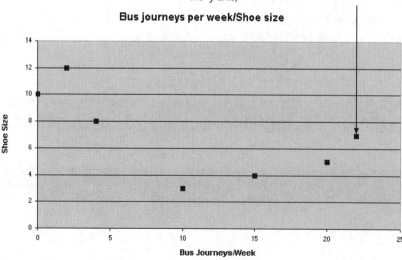

Figure 8.19 Scatter graph shows no correlation

As a second example, a scatter graph could be plotted to see if there is a correlation between the quantity of ice creams sold by a company and the daily temperature. The data for the graph could look like the following table and the graph derived from this data like Figure 8.20. If a trendline (this is a line that follows the trend, sometimes referred to as a line of best fit) is added and the points plotted are close to the line, this means that there is a correlation between the two sets of data. In this case, when the temperature increases so do the ice cream sales, showing a positive correlation.

Temperature	5	20	16	25	10	18
Ice cream sold	12	100	40	190	15	80

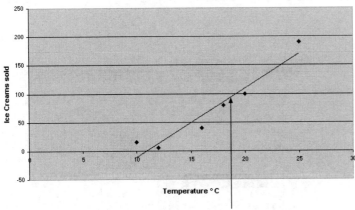

Trendline has a positive gradient (it goes up) indicating a positive correlation between the data

Figure 8.20 Scatter graph shows a positive correlation

A third example of a scatter graph plots the relationship between hours per week spent reading and hours per week spent watching TV. The data for the graph could look like the following table and the graph derived from this data like Figure 8.21. When a trendline is added, the points plotted are close to the line so this means that there is a correlation between the two sets of data. In this case the trendline has a negative gradient (it goes down) showing that the more hours spent reading, the less time is spent watching TV.

Reading	2	10	9	1	0	18
TV	12	3	4	15	18	0

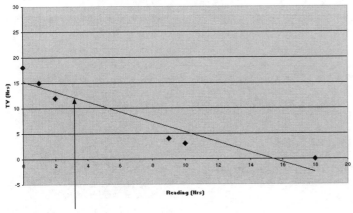

Trendline has a negative gradient (it goes down) indicating a negative correlation between the data

Figure 8.21 Scatter graph shows a negative correlation

4.2 Creating an XY scatter graph

Exercise 1

Open Excel and the generic file **temperatures**. Create an XY scatter graph to plot Maximum Temperature against Minimum Temperature for LONDON. Use the following titles:

Title: **LONDON MAXIMUM AND MINIMUM TEMPERATURES**
x axis: **MAX TEMPERATURE**
y axis: **MIN TEMPERATURE**
Do not display a legend.

Method

1   Load Excel and open the generic file **temperatures**.

2   Select the data to plot, ie C2 to N3.

3   Use **Chart Wizard** to create the graph, selecting: **XY (Scatter)** at Step 1 (Figure 8.22).

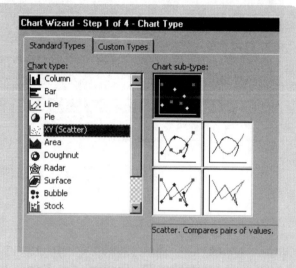

Figure 8.22 Selecting a scatter graph

4.3 Adding a trendline

Exercise 2

Add a linear trendline to the graph.

Method

1   Right-click on: one of the data points.

2   From the pop-up menu, select: **Add Trendline** (Figure 8.23).

3   The **Add Trendline** box is displayed (Figure 8.24).

4   With the **Type** tab selected, in the **Trend/Regression type** section, click on: the **Linear** option.

5   Click on: **OK**.

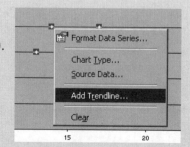

Figure 8.23 Adding a trendline

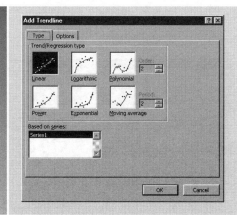

Figure 8.24 Selecting a Linear trendline

4.4 Formatting a trendline

Exercise 3

Format the trendline so that it appears as a solid line with a thick line weighting.

Method

1 Double-click on: the trendline.

2 The **Format Trendline** box is displayed (Figure 8.25).

3 With the **Patterns** tab selected, in the **Line** section, click in: the **Custom** option button.

4 Select the line style using the down arrow of the **Style** box.

5 Select the weighting using the down arrow of the **Weight** box.

6 Click on: **OK**.

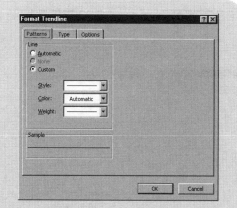

Figure 8.25 Selecting line style and weight

4.5 Adding a trendline equation

Exercise 4

Display the equation of the trendline at top left corner of the plot area.

 At this level you do not need to know the mathematics behind the equation, just how to display it. For information only, the equation is derived from: $y = mx + c$, where m is the slope and y is the interception.

Method

1   Access the **Format Trendline** box, as in Step 1 above.

2   Select the: **Options** tab.

3   Click in: the **Display equation on chart** box so that a tick is displayed (Figure 8.26).

4   Click on: **OK**.

5   The equation is displayed on the chart.

6   Click on it and drag it to the requested position.

Figure 8.26 Displaying a trendline equation

4.6 Formatting and resizing markers

Exercise 5

Format the markers as solid squares and size 10.

Method

1   Double-click on a marker.

2   The **Format Data Series** box is displayed (Figure 8.27).

3   With the **Patterns** tab selected, in the **Marker** section, click in: the **Custom** option button.

4   Select the style of marker using the down arrow in the **Style** box.

5   Select the size using the arrows in the **Size** box.

6   Click on: **OK**.

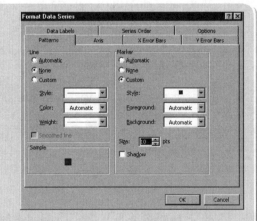

Figure 8.27 Setting marker style and size

4.7 Formatting the x axis

Exercise 6

Format the x axis as follows:

Scale: min 3, max 24, interval 3.

Method

These skills are covered in Sections 2 and 3.

4.8 Formatting the *y* axis

Exercise 7

Format the *y* axis as follows:

Scale: min 0, max 15, interval 3.

Method

As above.

4.9 Adding special characters

Exercise 8

In the title, at the end after the word TEMPERATURES, add the following: **°C**.

Method

1   Click on the title to select it and position the cursor where you want the additional text to appear.

2   From the **Start** menu, select: **Programs**, **Accessories**, **System Tools**, **Character Map**.

3   The **Character Map** box is displayed (Figure 8.28).

4   Click on: the degrees symbol °
    (if you hold the left mouse
    button down over the selection,
    the character will enlarge so that
    you can determine if it is the
    correct choice).

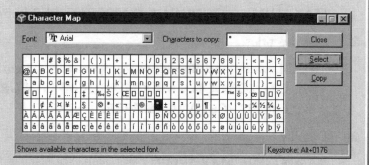

Figure 8.28 Character Map

5   Click on: the **Select** button.

6   Click on: **Copy**.

7   Click on: **Close**.

8   In the Excel window, click on: the **Paste** button.

9   Insert the rest of the additional text.

4.10 Formatting to house style

Exercise 9

Format the graph as follows:

- Typeface   serif
- Text size
  - title   20 pt, bold and italic
  - x/y axes titles   16 pt
  - other text/numbering on axes   14 pt
- Trendline equation   14 pt
- Add a header with your name and centre number.

Method

As in previous sections.

4.11 Save and print the file in landscape orientation

4.12 Close the file

4.13 Creating an XY scatter graph with three data series

Exercise 10

Create the following XY scatter graph using the file **temperatures**:

1 Plot the data for **LONDON MAXIMUM TEMPERATURES** against the **BARCELONA MAXIMUM** and **MINIMUM TEMPERATURES** from **JANUARY to JUNE** (inclusive) only.

2 Use the titles:

TITLE: **London and Barcelona Temperatures January to June**
x axis title: **LONDON – MAXIMUM TEMPERATURES**
y axis title: **BARCELONA TEMPERATURES**

3 Display a legend:

BARCELONA MAX TEMP
BARCELONA MIN TEMP

4 Display the graph in portrait orientation.

5 Join the data points on the line Barcelona Min Temp together using a solid line with a thick weighting. Retain the markers on this line.

6 Join the data points on the line Barcelona Max Temp together using a long dashed line with a thick line weighting. Ensure there are no markers on this line.

7 Add a texture fill to the plot area.

8 Format the *x* axis as follows:

Scale: min 5, max 25, interval 5

9 Format the *y* axis as follows:

Scale: min 5, max 30, interval 5

10 Add two text boxes:

Text box 1	Above maximum temperature Barcelona [2001]
Text box 2	Below minimum temperature Barcelona [2001]

Position text box 1 in the plot area above the Barcelona Max Temp line.
Position text box 2 in the plot area below the Barcelona Min Temp line.

11 Apply house style as follows:

- Typeface   sans serif
- Text size
  title   8 pt, bold
  x/y axes titles   14 pt, bold
  text/numbering on *x/y* axes   12 pt italic
  legend   10 pt
- Text box labels   14 pt, border visible

Headers and footers   add a header or footer including your name and centre number.

Method

Note: You have already learnt most of the skills to complete this graph so only new skills will be set out here.

1 Select the correct data, ie cells A2 to H2 and A4 to H5. This selection includes the three data series.

2 The legend is displayed automatically but you may need to resize the box by dragging the handles when selected so that it displays in full.

3 At Steps 5 and 6 you are joining the data points. (*Note:* Not adding trendlines.) To do this:

   a Double-click on: one of the data points.
   b The **Format Data Series** box is displayed.
   c With the **Patterns** tab selected, in the **Line** section, select: **Custom** then, style and weight.

   d In the **Marker** section, select: **Custom** or **None** (as appropriate). Select: style and size (as appropriate).

4 At Step 10, add superscript effects to font as follows:

    a   Key in the text including 2001.
    b   Select the text 2001 by dragging the mouse over it.
    c   From the **Format** menu, select: **Selected Object**.
    d   The **Format Text** box is displayed.
    e   In the **Effects** section, click in: the **Superscript** box so that there is a tick in it.

Superscript and subscript text effects can be achieved using the method above. Superscript text is text that appears slightly higher than other text on the line, as in the example above and in Source $^{©\ 2001}$

Subscript is text that appears slightly lower than other text on the line (eg as in chemical formulae: H_2O).

4.14 Save and print the graph retaining portrait orientation

4.15 Close the file and exit Excel

Graphs and Charts quick reference for CLAIT Plus (EXCEL)

Action	Keyboard	Mouse	Right-mouse menu	Menu
Access data in other formats				**File**, **Open**, **File of type** box, select: **All files**
Create a chart	Select the data to chart			
		Click: the ▥ **Chart Wizard** button		**Insert**, **Chart**
	STEP 1 Select: the chart type (including exploded pie, XY scatter graph) Click: **Next** **STEP 2** Check that the source data is correct, if not change it Click: **Next** **STEP 3** Select: the **Titles** tab Key in the title Select: the **Legend** tab Click: in the **Show legend** box to add/remove tick as appropriate Select: the **Data Labels** tab Click: **Show label** if appropriate Click: **Next** **STEP 4** Click: **As new sheet** or **As object in** Key in: the chart name Click: **Finish**			
Delete a chart	Select the chart. Press: **Delete**			
Edit a chart			Right-click on the chart. Select from options	
Emphasise a pie chart segment	Select the segment. Drag the segment outwards from the pie			
Font, type, size and style	Select object to format. Use the toolbar buttons to format			
Header and footer				**View**, **Header and Footer**, **Header/Footer** tab or **File**, Page **Setup**, **Header/Footer** tab
Labels, align	Double-click on the labels, **Alignment** tab			
Line weights and markers	*Setting line weights:* Double-click on the line, **Patterns** tab, **Custom**, **Weight** box *Setting markers:* As above, select from **Marker** section			
Number/Date format	Double-click on the axis values, Number tab			
Orientation landscape/portrait				**File**, **Page Setup**, **Page** tab
Plot area, background fill	Double-click on the plot area, **Fill Effects**. Select from **Gradient**, **Texture** or **Pattern**			

Action	Keyboard	Mouse	Right-mouse menu	Menu
Print a chart	With the chart displayed on screen			
	Ctrl + P Ensure **Active sheet** is selected. Click: **OK**	Click: the 🖨 **Print** button (This will automatically print the sheet)		**File**, **Print** Ensure **Active sheet** is selected Click: **OK**
Select data to chart	*Selecting adjacent data:* Hold down **Shift** whilst selecting *Selecting non-adjacent data:* Hold down **Ctrl** whilst selecting			
Set upper and lower limits and intermediate values on the x/y axes	*To set upper and lower limits for x (horizontal) axis (where applicable and the y (vertical) axis:* With the graph on screen Double-click: the **Axis** In the **Format Axis** dialogue box: Click: the **Scale** tab Key in: the new values in the **Maximum** and **Minimum** boxes Click: **OK** *To set intermediate values:* With the graph on screen Double-click: the **Axis** In the **Format Axis** dialogue box: Click: the **Scale** tab Change the **Major** unit to the required value Click: **Close**			
Shading in charts (to be distinguishable)	*Individual segments on pie charts:* Select the segment, right-click, **Format Data Point**, **Fill Effects** *Bars on bar charts:* Right-click on data bar, **Format Data Series**, **Fill Effects**			
Text box Visible border	**Drawing** toolbar, **Text Box** button **Drawing** toolbar, **Line Color** button			
Trendline	Right-click on one of the data points, **Add Trendline**, **Type** tab			
Trendline equation	Double-click on the trendline, **Options** tab, **Display equation on chart**			

Hints and tips

- Check your graphs and charts carefully. Are they displaying the data requested? Check that all labelling is correct.
- Check that pie segments, bars and lines are easy to distinguish on the printout.
- Do the printouts have the correct orientation?
- Have you included everything on the chart/graph?
- Have you formatted to the house style guidelines?

Graphs and charts: sample full practice assignment

Scenario

You have been conducting a survey and gathering information about a Country Park. You are now in a position to produce a report on your findings and will need to create some graphs and charts to illustrate some of the main points.

You will need the following files: **age**, **sightings**, **distances**, **shop profits** and **duration**.

You must prepare graphs and charts according to the following information:

- the House Style Guidelines (below)
- the specific information given within each task.

HOUSE STYLE GUIDELINES

Pie charts

• Typeface	serif (eg Times New Roman, Garamond)
• Text size	
title	font size 16, bold and italic
subtitle	font size 16, bold and italic
data labels	font size 14
legend	font size 14

Bar/column charts, line graphs and XY scatter graphs

• Typeface	serif (eg Times New Roman, Garamond)
• Text size	
title	font size 16, bold and italic
subtitle	font size 16, bold and italic
x/y axis title	font size 14, bold
other text/numbering on *x/y* axis	font size 12
legend	font size 12
• Text box labels	font size 12, border visible
• Trendline equation	font size 12

Headers and footers

All charts/graphs must include a header or footer including **your name** and **centre** number.

Task 1

You need to produce a chart, using the figures from the survey, to show the age range of visitors.

1 Using the appropriate software, open the file named **age**.

2 Create an **exploded pie chart** to display the **NO OF VISITORS** to the Country Park by **AGE RANGE**.

3 Title the chart: **VISITORS BY AGE**. Subtitle: **Sample of 1000**.

4 Ensure that each segment of the pie is distinctive in appearance. Use a legend for the age ranges.

5 Format the data labels on the pie chart so that a **PERCENTAGE VALUE** is displayed. Ensure that each of the data labels can be clearly read.

6 Emphasise the segment for the 16–24 age range by pulling it away from the rest of the pie chart.

7 Display the chart in portrait orientation. Format the chart according to the House Style Guidelines. Save and print the chart in portrait orientation.

Task 2

You need to produce a chart about bird sightings.

1 Using the appropriate software, open the file named **sightings**.

2 Create a **comparative vertical bar chart** to plot the number of sightings of birds from **Wednesday to Saturday** inclusive:

Use the title: **BIRD SIGHTINGS (Wednesday to Saturday)**
x axis title: **BIRD NAME**
y axis title: **NO OF SIGHTINGS**

3 Ensure the legend displays the days **WED, THU, FRI, SAT**.

4 Format the labels on the x axis so that they have an alignment of -90 degrees. Format the y axis as follows:

Scale: minimum value -3, maximum value 15, interval 3. Set numbers to 0 decimal places

5 Apply a different fill effect to each of the four series so that they are clearly distinguishable when printed.

6 Display the vertical bar chart in landscape orientation. Format the chart according to the House Style Guidelines. Save and print the chart retaining landscape orientation.

Task 3

You need to produce a graph, using the figures from the survey, to show the distances travelled compared with number of visits. It has been decided that January and August would be good months to plot so that you can see the differences between winter and summer visiting habits.

1   Using the appropriate software, open the file named **distances**.

2   Create an **XY scatter graph** to plot the data for the **No of visits (Jan and Aug)** against the **Distance travelled**. Use the following titles:

Title: **Distances travelled and number of visits**
Subtitle: **January and August**
x axis title: **Distance travelled**
y axis title: **No of visits**

Ensure a legend is produced which displays:

Jan
Aug

3   Format the x axis as follows:

Scale: minimum value 0, maximum value 28, interval 4

4   Format the y axis as follows:

Scale: minimum value 0, maximum value 32, interval 4

5   Join the points together that fall on the line Jan. Use a solid line with a thick weighting. Format the markers so that they appear as solid squares, size 8.

6   Join the points together that fall on the line Aug. Use a short dashed line with a thick weighting. Format the markers so that they appear as solid circles, size 8.

7   Remove the fill from the plot area of the chart so that the background appears white. (You may leave the gridlines displayed.)

8   Add two text boxes:

	Text	Position on chart
Text box 1	Fewer visits in January	Position above the Aug line
Text box 2	More visits in August	Position below the Jan line

9   Display the XY scatter graph in landscape orientation. Format the XY scatter graph according to the House Style Guidelines. Save and print in landscape orientation.

Task 4

You need to create a chart showing the profits made by the Café in the Park over a two-week period.

1   Using the appropriate software, open the file named **shop profits**.

2   Create a **line-column** graph to plot the **Café profit** (as columns) along with the **Average café profit** (as a line) against the **date**. Use the titles:

Title: **Café in the Park Profits**
x axis title: **Date**
y axis title: **Profits (£)**

Ensure a legend is produced that displays:

Profit
Average

3   Format the x axis as follows:

x axis labels: alignment of 90 degrees, date to appear as dd/mm/yy format

4   Format the y axis as follows:

Scale: minimum value -15, maximum value 195, interval 30

Numbers set to currency to display £ sign and two decimal places

Negative numbers to appear in red and with a minus sign

5   Apply a textured fill to the plot area of the chart. Ensure that the bars and line are still easy to distinguish with the new background.

6   Add the text **2002** in superscript font format, directly after the main title.

7   Display the graph in landscape orientation. Format the line-column graph according to the House Style Guidelines. Save and print the graph retaining landscape display.

Task 5

You want to produce a graph to display the relationship between distance travelled and length of stay in t\he park.

1 Using the appropriate software, open the file named **duration**.

2 Create an **XY scatter graph** to plot the **Distance Travelled** against **Duration** in the park. Use the titles:

Title: **DISTANCE TRAVELLED/DURATION OF STAY**
x axis label: **DISTANCE TRAVELLED (MILES)**
y axis label: **LENGTH OF STAY (HRS)**

3 Do not display a legend on the graph.

4 Add a linear trendline to the graph and display the equation of the trendline in the top left-hand corner of the plot area.

5 Format the trendline so that it appears as a long dashed line with a medium line weighting.

6 Display markers on the graph and format them so that they appear as solid squares and size 8.

7 Format the x axis as follows:

Scale: minimum value -2, maximum value 32, interval 2
Numbers set to integer format
Format negative numbers to display with a minus sign

8 Format the y axis as follows:

Scale: minimum value 0, maximum value 4.50, interval 0.5
Numbers set to two decimal places

9 Display the graph in portrait orientation. Format the XY scatter graph according to the House Style Guidelines but as an exception to the House Style use a sans serif font throughout this graph. Save and print the graph in portrait orientation.

Chapter 9

Databases (Unit 3)

1 Creating a database

In this section you will practise and learn how to:

- set up fields – name, data type, format and length
- enter relevant data
- save database design
- add/delete a field

Note: Before commencing on this chapter, it is recommended that you have worked through Chapter 5, or that you have achieved Unit 5, Databases, at CLAIT Level 1.

1.1 Creating a new database

Exercise 1

Create a new database of flats for rent using the following field headings. Use data from the **Flat details** information sheets. Select only those with **two bedrooms**.

FLAT NO	AutoNumber
LOCATION	Use codes given below
PRICE/WK	Currency, two decimal places
AVAILABLE	Date when flat will become vacant
DEPOSIT	Currency, no decimal places (see Deposit band look-up table)
REFS	References required. Use codes: **E** = Essential; **P** = Preferred
DURATION	Rental duration in months

Creating a database
When creating an Access database for the first time, it can be quite difficult to grasp but it will become clearer as you progress through this section.

About this database
There are seven fields for each record in this database, as follows:

FLAT NO is an AutoNumber field that Access will generate.

LOCATION and REFS are alphabetic fields (in Access known as **Text** fields). *Note:* These fields use codes instead of the full entries. Using codes saves time and storage space.

PRICE/WK, AVAILABLE, DEPOSIT and DURATION are all numeric fields (in Access known as **Number** fields). In Access **Date/Time** and **Currency** can be used as Number fields. In this case PRICE/WK and DEPOSIT will be set as Currency fields. AVAILABLE will be set as a Date/Time field. The format of such fields is determined when the database is designed. For example, a date format could be 10/02/03 or 10 February 2003 or 10-Feb-03 depending on the database design. It does not matter which format you use to enter the date since Access will always follow the format set. In CLAIT Plus assignments, unless specified, any layout of the date is acceptable. However, it must be in English format. In other formats, eg US, the month is placed before the day; displaying 10/02/03 (10 February 2003) as 02/10/03 (2 October 2003). Therefore the dates that you enter will be incorrect. To check that you will be displaying English date format and before starting on the database:

In the Windows desktop:

1   Click on: **Start**.

2   From the **Start** menu, select: **Settings**, **Control Panel**.

3   Double-click on: **Regional Settings**.

4   With the **Regional Settings** tab selected, check that: **English (United Kingdom)** is chosen. If not, select it from the drop-down list.

5   Use the **Date** tab to set specific date format for automatic insertions on Headers and Footers.

6   Click on: **Apply**.

Note: If you changed the setting, you will need to restart your computer for the new setting to apply.

Deposit band	Deposit (£)
A	200
B	260
C	290
D	320
E	400

LOCATION	CODE
CLIFTON	**C**
PORTISHEAD	**P**
REDLAND	**R**
COTHAM	**CM**
LONG ASHTON	**LA**

Flat details

LOCATION	Clifton		PRICE/WK		100.00	
AVAILABLE		1/10/02	**DEPOSIT**		E	
REFS	Essential		**DURATION**		6	
NO OF BEDROOMS		2		**GARDEN**		No

LOCATION	Portishead		PRICE/WK		50.00	
AVAILABLE		20/10/02	**DEPOSIT**		A	
REFS	Preferred		**DURATION**		6	
NO OF BEDROOMS		2		**GARDEN**		Yes

LOCATION	Redland	PRICE/WK	85.50
AVAILABLE	2/10/02	DEPOSIT	D
REFS	Essential	DURATION	3
NO OF BEDROOMS	2	GARDEN	No

LOCATION	Redland	PRICE/WK	100.00
AVAILABLE	1/11/02	DEPOSIT	E
REFS	Essential	DURATION	6
NO OF BEDROOMS	1	GARDEN	No

LOCATION	Cotham	PRICE/WK	75.50
AVAILABLE	28/10/02	DEPOSIT	C
REFS	Preferred	DURATION	12
NO OF BEDROOMS	2	GARDEN	No

LOCATION	Long Ashton	PRICE/WK	85.00
AVAILABLE	12/10/02	DEPOSIT	D
REFS	Essential	DURATION	3
NO OF BEDROOMS	1	GARDEN	Yes

LOCATION	Portishead	PRICE/WK	50.00
AVAILABLE	1/11/02	DEPOSIT	A
REFS	Preferred	DURATION	6
NO OF BEDROOMS	1	GARDEN	No

LOCATION	Portishead	PRICE/WK	65.00
AVAILABLE	1/11/02	DEPOSIT	B
REFS	Essential	DURATION	12
NO OF BEDROOMS	2	GARDEN	Yes

LOCATION	Clifton	PRICE/WK	85.00
AVAILABLE	1/12/02	DEPOSIT	D
REFS	Essential	DURATION	6
NO OF BEDROOMS	2	GARDEN	No

LOCATION	Portishead	PRICE/WK	75.50
AVAILABLE	16/11/02	DEPOSIT	C
REFS	Essential	DURATION	3
NO OF BEDROOMS	2	GARDEN	Yes

LOCATION	Cotham		PRICE/WK		85.00
AVAILABLE		12/12/02	DEPOSIT		D
REFS	Preferred		DURATION	12	
NO OF BEDROOMS		2		GARDEN	No

LOCATION	Clifton		PRICE/WK		85.00
AVAILABLE		1/12/02	DEPOSIT		D
REFS	Essential		DURATION	6	
NO OF BEDROOMS		2		GARDEN	No

LOCATION	Portishead		PRICE/WK		75.50
AVAILABLE		16/11/02	DEPOSIT		C
REFS	Preferred		DURATION	12	
NO OF BEDROOMS		2		GARDEN	Yes

LOCATION	Redland		PRICE/WK		100.00
AVAILABLE		14/11/02	DEPOSIT		E
REFS	Essential		DURATION	6	
NO OF BEDROOMS		1		GARDEN	No

Method

1 Load Access.

2 On loading Access, the **Microsoft Access** dialogue box is displayed.

3 In the **Create a new database using** section, click in the option button: **Blank Access database** (Figure 9.1).

4 Click on: **OK**.

Figure 9.1 Creating a new blank database

 When creating a new database you have the option of choosing a Wizard to help you, but they are not always suitable for CLAIT Plus purposes. Also it helps understanding of database design to set up a database without the help of a Wizard. Experiment with Wizards when you have time.

5 The **File New Database** dialogue box is displayed (Figure 9.2).

6 In the **Save in** box, click on: the down arrow to select the location for the database.

7 In the **File name** box, key in a suitable filename. In this example I have named the database **Flats**. *Note:* This will be the overall database name.

8 Click on: **Create**.

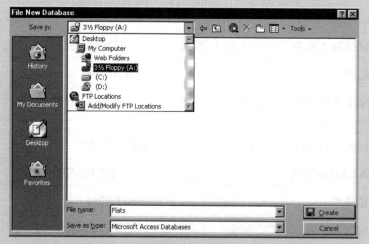

Figure 9.2 Naming and storing the database

9 The **Flats: Database** window is displayed (Figure 9.3).

Figure 9.3 Flats: Database window

1.2 Designing a table

Method

1 In the **Objects** section, the **Tables** button is selected by default (it looks as if it has been pressed in); if not, click it to choose it.

2 Double-click on: **Create table in Design view** (Figure 9.3).

3 The **Table** window in **Design** view is displayed (Figure 9.4).

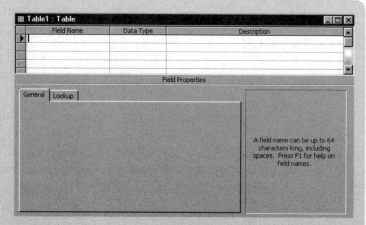

Figure 9.4 Table in Design view

Define the fields in a table.

 If you make a mistake when keying in, you can always go back and make corrections. If you miss out a field, see the quick reference at the end of this chapter for the method to insert it.

1   In the **Field Name** column and on the top row (where the cursor is flashing), with the **Caps Lock** on, key in the name of the first field, **FLAT NO**, and press: **Enter** to move to the next column.

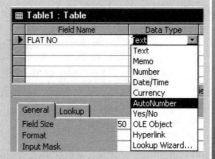

Figure 9.5 Selecting data type

2   In the **Data Type** column, click on the down arrow and click on: **AutoNumber** (Figure 9.5). Press: **Enter**.

3   In the **Description** column, you can enter a description of the information this field will contain. This is optional but can be useful for future reference. For data type AutoNumber this is self-explanatory, so leave the Description blank in this case. Press: **Enter**.

4   In the **Field Properties** section, with the **General** tab selected (Figure 9.6), options can be chosen from the drop-down lists.

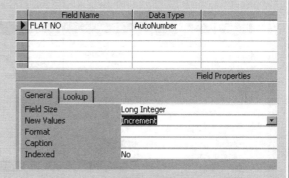

Figure 9.6 Setting field properties

Field Size: Click on: the down arrow, select: **Long Integer** so that it is displayed in the box. (*Long Integer:* Integer means a whole number, ie no decimal places.)

New Values: Click on: the down arrow, select: **Increment** so that it is displayed in the box.

(*Note:* In this case the options we require are the default options.)

5   Click in the next **Field Name** row.

Repeat steps 1 to 5 to set the Field Name, Data Type, Description and Field Properties for the other fields (refer to the information given in Exercise 1), except choose as follows and as shown in the screen shots below. *Note:* Other available options so you can make informed decisions when deciding on field properties for future databases that you design:

Text as the Data Type for **LOCATION** and **REFS**
Number as the Data Type for **DURATION**
Currency as the Data Type for **PRICE/WK** and **DEPOSIT**
Date/Time as the Data Type for **AVAILABLE**

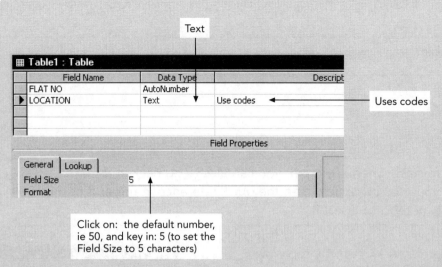

Text

Click on: the default number, ie 50, and key in: 5 (to set the Field Size to 5 characters)

Figure 9.7 Defining the LOCATION field

 The field size for text entries is set at 50 characters (the default). This will accommodate most entries and can be left as it is. Should you be very short of storage space (this is unlikely), then you could save some space by reducing the field sizes as appropriate.

I have set the field size to 5 characters because codes are to be used in this field. At present we have a maximum of 2 characters in the codes, but setting to 5 will allow for longer codes if required at a later date. *Remember:* Using codes instead of full entries saves time and storage space.

Currency

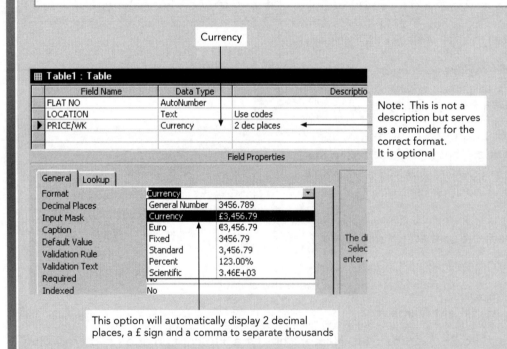

Note: This is not a description but serves as a reminder for the correct format. It is optional

This option will automatically display 2 decimal places, a £ sign and a comma to separate thousands

Figure 9.8 Defining the PRICE/WK field

 If you do not want to include a £ sign and comma, you can select either **General Number** in the **Format** box and **2** (after clicking on the down arrow) in the **Decimal Places** box. You can also select **Fixed** format. Fixed format will display any trailing zeros, eg 12.50 will display as 12.50 and not as 12.5.

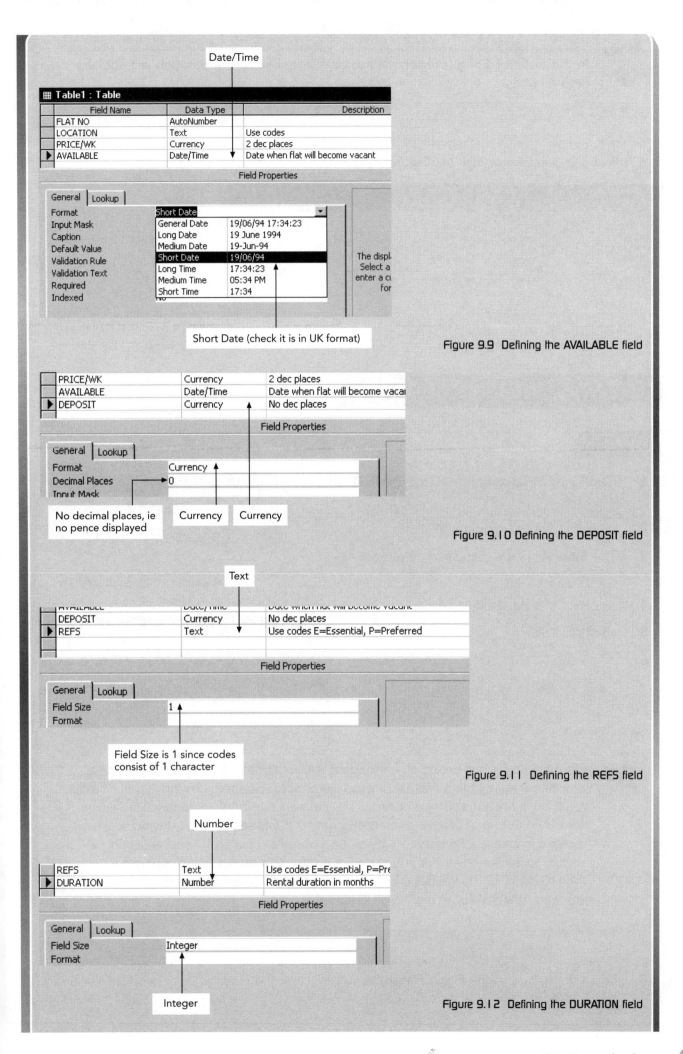

Date/Time

Short Date (check it is in UK format)

Figure 9.9 Defining the AVAILABLE field

No decimal places, ie no pence displayed

Currency   Currency

Figure 9.10 Defining the DEPOSIT field

Text

Field Size is 1 since codes consist of 1 character

Figure 9.11 Defining the REFS field

Number

Integer

Figure 9.12 Defining the DURATION field

In this instance **Long Integer** will not be relevant since the duration will not be a high number.

The Table design should now look like Figure 9.13.

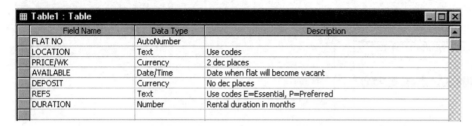

Figure 9.13 The Table design

1.3 Saving the table design

Method

1   Click on: the **Close** button of the **Table Design** window.

2   Click on: **Yes** to save changes.

3   The **Save As** box is displayed (Figure 9.14).

Figure 9.14 Saving the database

4   Key in a suitable table name.

5   Click on: **OK**.

6   A message is displayed (Figure 9.15).

7   Click on: **No**.

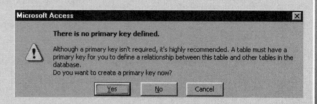

Figure 9.15 Primary Key options

A Primary Key is not essential, although it is usually desirable. It can be set as a field that uniquely identifies each record in a table. Examples of this type of field would be car registration numbers or unique part numbers. In some databases, there is no field that can be guaranteed not to duplicate an entry. In such cases, Access can create a Primary Key by setting up a field called ID and allocating a number to each record. Primary Keys speed up data retrieval and are useful when working with large databases or multiple databases. At this stage, we do not need to worry about having a Primary Key.

8   You are returned to the **Flats: Database** window and the new table is now displayed in the Tables list.

You cannot exit **Design** view without being reminded to save.

Should you need to make any changes to the design, click on: the table name to select it and then on: the **Design** button, make the changes, click on: the **Close** button and resave any changes.

1.4 Entering data

Exercise 3

Enter the relevant records into the database.

Method

1 In the **Flats: Database** window, double-click on: the table name.

2 The **Table** window is displayed (in **Datasheet** view) (Figure 9.16).

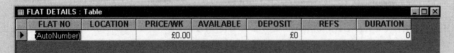

Figure 9.16 Table ready for input of records

Sometimes field names (and entries in fields) do not display in full. (The field names in this database do display in full.) When you need to widen a field column to display in full:

- Hover the mouse on the line between the field headings (the pointer changes to a double arrow).
- Hold down the left mouse and drag to the right until the entire field heading is displayed.
- Release the mouse.

You can also widen the column to fit the entry exactly by positioning the mouse as above and double-clicking.

3 From the FLAT DETAILS SHEETS, select the records that are relevant to enter in this database, ie they must have **2 bedrooms**. Key in the data in the appropriate fields as shown (Figure 9.17), pressing **Enter,** Tab **or arrow keys to move from field to field.**

Note: FLAT NO, ie an AutoNumber, does not need to be entered because it appears automatically.

FLAT NO	LOCATION	PRICE/WK	AVAILABLE	DEPOSIT	REFS	DURATION
1	C	£100.00	01/10/02	£400	E	6
2	P	£50.00	20/10/02	£200	P	6
3	R	£85.50	02/10/02	£320	E	3
4	CM	£75.50	28/10/02	£290	P	12
5	P	£65.00	01/11/02	£260	E	12
6	C	£85.00	01/12/02	£320	E	6
7	P	£75.50	16/11/02	£290	E	3
8	CM	£85.00	12/12/02	£320	P	12
9	C	£85.00	01/12/02	£320	E	6
10	P	£75.50	16/11/02	£290	P	12

Figure 9.17 Records entered into database

4 Proofread on screen against copy.

5 Correct any errors by clicking to position the cursor on the error, then correct as necessary.

 It is imperative that all data is entered correctly. If not, when interrogating the database, the results may be incorrect. Do not rush through the proofreading stage.

When there is a logic field (ie Yes/No) in the database, boxes appear in this field. Click in the box for **Yes**. Leave the box empty for **No**.

1.5 Saving and printing data

Exercise 4

Save the data and print one copy in table format. Ensure all data is displayed in full.

Method

1 Print the table in the normal way. (Use landscape orientation.)

2 Close the table by clicking on the: **Close** button.

3 The data is saved automatically.

4 If you have made any layout changes, you will be asked if you want to save these, click on: **Yes**.

1.6 Adding a field

Exercise 5

Add a new field to the database for the maximum guaranteed rental period renewals. Name the field **RENEWALS**. Enter the data as follows:

LOCATION	RENEWALS
C	3
P	2
R	3
CM	1
LA	4

Method

1 In the **Flats: Database** window, click on: the table name to select it.

2 Click on: the **Design** button.

3 The **Table** window is displayed in **Design** view (Figure 9.18).

4 Click the cursor in the row below the last field, ie DURATION.

5 Key in the field name, select the Data Type and define the Field Properties as appropriate.

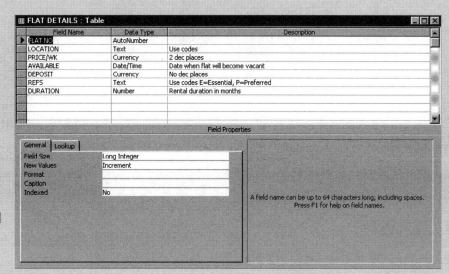

6 Close the table and save the changes.

7 Reopen the table in **Datasheet** view by double-clicking on it.

Figure 9.18 Table in Design view

8 Key in the data for the new field.

9 Proofread your new entries.

10 Close the table. The data is saved automatically.

> When adding a new field that is not to be positioned as the last field of the table, position the cursor in the field below where you want to insert the new field. Click on: the **Insert Rows** button. Enter the new field details as above.

1.7 Deleting a field

Exercise 6

It has been decided that references are required for all flats so this field is now unnecessary. Delete the **REFS** field.

Method

1 Access the table in **Design** view (as in 1 to 3 above).

2 Position the cursor in the field to delete, ie **REFS**.

3 Click on: the **Delete Rows** button.

4 You will be asked to confirm the delete. Click on: **Yes**.

5 Close the table, saving changes.

Exercise 7

Print the database in table format. It will look like Figure 9.19.

FLAT NO	LOCATION	PRICE/WK	AVAILABLE	DEPOSIT	DURATION	RENEWALS
1	C	£100.00	01/10/02	£400	6	3
2	P	£50.00	20/10/02	£200	6	2
3	R	£85.50	02/10/02	£320	3	3
4	CM	£75.50	28/10/02	£290	12	1
5	P	£65.00	01/11/02	£260	12	2
6	C	£85.00	01/12/02	£320	6	3
7	P	£75.50	16/11/02	£290	3	2
8	CM	£85.00	12/12/02	£320	12	1
9	C	£85.00	01/12/02	£320	6	3
10	P	£75.50	16/11/02	£290	12	2

Figure 9.19 Amended database

1.8 Saving and closing the database file

Exercise 8

Save and close the database file.

Method

From the File menu, select: **Close**.

 The database file and its components are automatically saved together. Each individual part, such as the table **CLASSES**, was saved as you progressed through the exercises. If, for any reason, any parts have not been not saved, you will be prompted to save before closing.

1.9 Exiting Access

Exercise 9

Exit Access.

Method

From the **File** menu, select: **Exit**.

Data types

Data type	Properties
Text (the default)	Field size default is 50 characters. Can be set to less if field is using coded data (Access will remind you to code the data because you will have restricted data entry!) Set if requested or short of storage space.
Number	*Field Size* Long Integer is the default – this is OK for whole numbers (an integer is a whole number). Integer is also OK for smaller numbers. Double – for numbers with decimal places. *Format* Choose: **Fixed** for two decimal places to show (even if the last is a zero). Choose: **Decimal Places** and enter the number required. (Leave the Format blank for other numbers.)
Date/Time	Choose the most appropriate format for the task. Check that the date is in English format, dd/mm/yy. (You can key in the date in any format and it will convert to the format you have set.)
Currency	Choose: **Format Fixed** to display two decimal places with no commas or £ symbol. Choose: **Format Currency** to display two decimal places, £ sign and comma between thousands. Choose: **Format Currency** and then **Decimal Places** 0 or 1 to display as above but with a different number of decimal places.
Yes/No	No need to set at this level.
AutoNumber	No need to set at this level.

Importing generic files and creating queries

In this section you will practise and learn how to:

- import generic files into Access
- create queries
  - use multiple search criteria
  - use range criteria
  - use AND and OR
  - use combined range and logical operators
  - use calculated fields
  - use wild cards

For this section you will need to access the datafile **agency** on the CD-ROM.

2.1 Importing generic files

Exercise 1

Import the datafile **agency** into Access. Save the datafile with the name **temps** in Access format. Check that all information is displayed in full.

 There are database applications other than Access. datafiles created in other applications can be saved in different formats. Some formats can be opened and read by applications other than the one the database was created and saved in. This is useful when transferring and sharing files. *CSV (Comma Separated Values)* is one of those formats. As its name implies, the data is separated by commas. In CLAIT Plus, datafiles to be imported into Access format are supplied in CSV format.

Method

1. Load Access.

2. In the opening dialogue box (Figure 9.20), click in: **Blank Access database** option button.

Figure 9.20 Access opening dialogue box

3. The **File New Database** box is displayed. Select a location for the file and key in the filename **temps**.

4 Click on: **Create**.

5 In the **temps:Database** window, click on: the 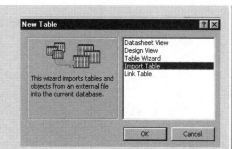 **New** button.

6 The **New Table** box is displayed (Figure 9.21).

7 Click on: **Import Table** and then on: **OK**.

Figure 9.21 Importing a table

8 The **Import** dialogue box is displayed (Figure 9.22).

9 In the **Look in** box, select the location of the file.

Note: Since this is a CSV format file, the file will not display in the window unless the **Files of type** option is changed.

10 In the **Files of type** box, select: **Text Files**.

11 Click once on: the file **agency** to select it.

Figure 9.22 Showing file types

12 Click on: **Import**.

13 The **Import Text Wizard** is activated. Ensure that **Delimited** is selected, click on: **Next**.

14 The next **Import Text Wizard** box is displayed (Figure 9.24).

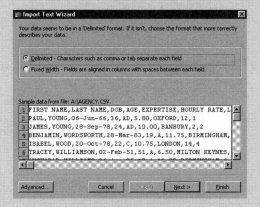

Figure 9.23 First Import Text Wizard

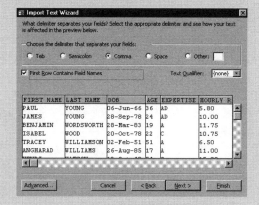

Figure 9.24 Second Import Text Wizard

15 In the **Choose the delimiter that separates your fields** section, ensure **Comma** is selected.

16 Click in: **First Row Contains Field Names** so that it has a tick in the box.

17 Click on: **Next**.

18 The third **Import Text Wizard** box is displayed (Figure 9.25).

19 Ensure **In a New Table** is selected.

20 Click on: **Next**.

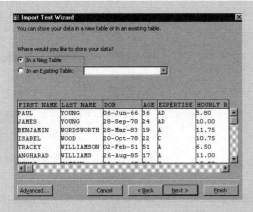

Figure 9.25 Third Import Text Wizard

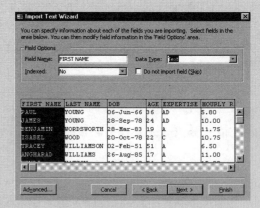

Figure 9.26 Fourth Import Text Wizard

21 The fourth **Import Text Wizard** is displayed (Figure 9.26).

Note: At this stage you can select Data Type and various other options but for CLAIT Plus this should not be necessary.

22 Click on: **Next**.

23 The fifth **Import Text Wizard** is displayed (Figure 9.27).

24 Click in: the **No primary key** option button.

25 Click on: **Next**.

26 The final **Import Text Wizard** box is displayed (Figure 9.28).

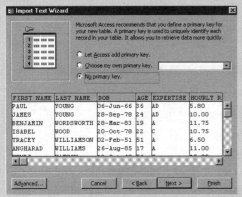

Figure 9.27 Fifth Import Text Wizard

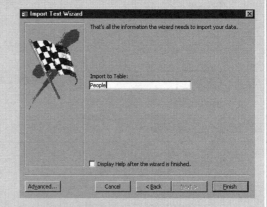

Figure 9.28 Final Import Text Wizard

27 In the **Import to table** box, key in a suitable name for the table.

28 Click on: **Finish**.

29 An **Import Text Wizard** information box is displayed (Figure 9.29).

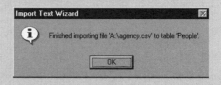

Figure 9.29 Information box about the Import

30 Click on: **OK**.

31 The table is now in Access format.

32 Open the table and scroll through it to ensure that all data is displayed in full. (*Note:* Remember to include field headings.)

33 Alter column widths as necessary (double-clicking on the field heading border is a good method because it autofits the contents to the column).

You have already created queries for CLAIT. This section builds on the skills that you have already learnt. Below is an overview of search criteria used at this level. Sample designs for the queries exercises are given but try to work them out for yourself before looking at the sample designs.

Working with queries

When setting up queries, use the following as a guide. In the Criteria row you can enter any of the following:

- Mathematical operators:

>	more than	>=	more than or equal to
<	less than	<=	less than or equal to
=	equal to	<>	not equal to

- An exact match, eg SMITHSON
- The wildcard * The * is a wildcard that stands for any number and type of character, eg if you were unsure how to spell the name you could enter SM*THSON or SM*SON. You can place the * wildcard before, after and between characters and you can use it more than once in a single field, eg SM*TH*
- The wildcard ? The ? wildcard acts as a placeholder for one character, eg SM?THSON
- LIKE This tells Access not to look for an exact match, eg LIKE SMYTHSON
- NOT If you want to find all the records but not SMITHSON you could enter NOT SMITHSON, or use <>SMITHSON
- AND You can use AND when you need restricted results, eg all events with a fee per guest of over £5.00 and under £10.00 use: >5.00 and <10.00
- OR You can use OR when looking for more than one match, eg SMITH or JONES or BROWN
- Fields containing YES/NO data. If Yes the data will show as a ticked box. Use **Yes** if you want to find the ticked box data and **No** if not.
- Working with dates:

  Before 10 February 2001: <10 February 2001 (*Note:* You can use an abbreviated version of the date and it will change to the set format, eg 10/02/01.)

  After 10 February 2001: >10 February 2001
  10 February 2001 or after: >=10 February 2001
  10 February 2001 or before: <=10 February 2001
  10 February 2001 to 20 February 2001 inclusive: >9 February 2001 and <21 February 2001
  or >=10 February 2001 and <=20 February
  or Between 10 February 2001 and 20 February 2001

  When looking for matches that do not work on one row such as SMITH >25 and JONES <25, ie you cannot have the criteria >25 and <25 on the same row, use the second row of the Criteria section as follows:

Show:	☐	☐
Criteria:	"SMITH"	>25
or:	"JONES"	<25

Note: You can use more than one 'or' row when necessary.

Exercise 2

Create a query to find names of people with **EXPERTISE** in **Administration** or **Accounting** (this field is coded AD = Administration, A = Accounting, C = Computing), earning **less than £6 HOURLY RATE** and **not** in the **MILTON KEYNES LOCATION**. Show the fields **FIRST NAME**, **LAST NAME** and **LOCATION**. Sort the query in alphabetical order of **LAST NAME**. Save the query as **EX2(your initials)** and print one copy.

Note: Access adds the quotation marks and # symbols to the query criteria. Remember you can use the **View** button to switch between **Design** and **Datasheet** view to check results of a query.

Method

Create the query in the normal way. Use the criteria given in Figure 9.30.

Field:	FIRST NAME	LAST NAME	EXPERTISE	HOURLY RATE	LOCATION
Table:	People	People	People	People	People
Sort:		Ascending			
Show:	☑	☑	☐	☐	☑
Criteria:			"A" Or "AD"	<6	<>"MILTON KEYNES"

Figure 9.30 Search criteria

Exercise 3

Create a query to find all records of **LAST NAME** beginning with **BE**. Sort in alphabetical order of **FIRST NAME**. Show only **FIRST NAME** and **LAST NAME**. Save the query as **Ex3(your initials)** and print.

Method

Create the query in the normal way. Use the search criteria given in Figure 9.31.

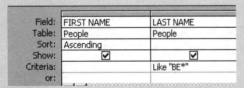

Field:	FIRST NAME	LAST NAME
Table:	People	People
Sort:	Ascending	
Show:	☑	☑
Criteria:		Like "BE*"
or:		

Figure 9.31 Using the wildcard *

Exercise 4

Create a query to find records with the **LAST NAME** of **THOMAS** or **YOUNG** or **HOYLE**. Show the fields **LAST NAME**, **DOB** and **AVAILABILITY**. Sort in chronological order of DOB. (*Note:* Chronological order means earliest date to most recent date. Reverse chronological order means most recent date to earliest date.) Save the query as **Ex4(your initials)** and print.

Create the query using the criteria given in Figure 9.32.

Field:	LAST NAME		DOB	AVAILABILITY
Table:	People		People	People
Sort:			Ascending	
Show:		☑	☑	☑
Criteria:	"THOMAS" Or "YOUNG" Or "HOYLE"			
or:				

Figure 9.32 Using OR

Exercise 5

Create a query to find all records with a **DOB after 1/1/80 and before 1/1/84 with EXPERTISE** in **COMPUTING**. Sort the query in numerical order of age and show all fields. Save the query as **Ex5(your initials)** and print.

Method

Create the query using the criteria given in Figure 9.33.

IAME	DOB		AGE	EXPERTISE
	People		People	People
			Ascending	
☑		☑	☑	☑
	>#01/01/80# And <#01/01/84#			"C"

Figure 9.33 Using range and logical operators

Exercise 6

Create a query to find all records with **NO OF PLACEMENTS more than 8** in **BIRMINGHAM** and **less than 2** in **OXFORD**. Show the fields **FIRST NAME**, **LAST NAME**, **LOCATION** and **NO OF PLACEMENTS**. Sort the query into descending numerical order of **AGE**. Save the query as **Ex6(your initials)** and print.

Method

Create the query using the criteria given in Figure 9.34.

Field:	LAST NAME	LOCATION	NO OF PLACEMENT:	AGE
Table:	People	People	People	People
Sort:				Descending
Show:	☑	☑	☑	☐
Criteria:		"BIRMINGHAM"	>8	
or:		"OXFORD"	<2	

Figure 9.34 Using the OR row

Access is able to perform calculations for you. This reduces the human error factor when calculating and also saves space by not storing this information in a separate field in a database table. Calculated fields can be created in queries using other field entries as the basis for the calculation, eg calculating and displaying how many items are in stock by subtracting the **NO SOLD** from the **NO IN STOCK**; calculating the number of tickets available for a concert by subtracting the **NO RESERVED** from the **MAX NUMBER**.

Calculations on individual fields can be performed, eg the average **AGE** for all records in the database; the total **NO OF PLACEMENTS** for all those located in **OXFORD**.

Exercise 7

Create a query with a new field heading **REMAINING** that calculates the number of placements left (**AVAILABILITY** minus **NO OF PLACEMENTS**) for all people with **Administration** expertise located in **BICESTER**. Sort the query in alphabetical order of **LAST NAME** and show the fields **FIRST NAME**, **LAST NAME** and **REMAINING**. Save the query as **Ex7(your initials)** and print.

Method

Create the query in the normal way, except:

Add the calculated field by keying in the new field name and the calculation as shown. *Note:* It is important that you key in the colon and the square brackets. Also check that you have keyed in the field names correctly.

Field:	LAST NAME	EXPERTISE	LOCATION	REMAINING: [AVAILABILITY]-[NO OF PLACEMENTS]
Table:	People	People	People	
Sort:	Ascending			
Show:	☑	☐	☐	☑
Criteria:		"AD"	"BICESTER"	
or:				

Figure 9.35 Query with a calculated field derived from other fields

Exercise 8

Create a query that calculates the total number of placements in **OXFORD**. Save the query as **Ex8(your initials)** and print.

1   In the Query design grid, display the fields **LOCATION** and **NO OF PLACEMENTS**.

2   In the **LOCATION Criteria** row, key in **OXFORD**.

3   Right-click in the **NO OF PLACEMENTS** Field row – a pop-up menu is displayed (Figure 9.36).

4   Select: **Totals**.

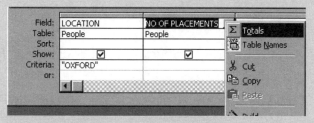

Figure 9.36 Accessing Totals

5   The **Totals** row is now displayed (Figure 9.37).

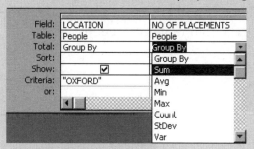

Figure 9.37 Displaying the Totals row

6   Click on: the **Group By** down arrow and select: **Sum** (Figure 9.37).

7   Check the query result (Figure 9.38) using the **View** button.

8   Save and print as normal.

LOCATION	SumOfNO OF
OXFORD	28

Figure 9.38 Using Sum in a calculated field

Exercise 9

Create a query that calculates the average **AGE** for all records in the database.
Save the query as **Ex9(your initials)** and print.

Method

1   In the Query design grid display the **AGE** field.

2   Right-click on the **AGE** field.

3   From the pop-up menu, select: **TOTALS**.

4   In the **Totals** row, click on: the **Group By** down arrow and select: **Avg**.

5   Check the query result (Figure 9.39) using the **View** button.

6   Save and print as normal.

AvgOfAGE
28.260416667

Figure 9.39 Using Average in a calculated field

2.4 Close the database file and exit Access

3 Creating reports

In this section you will practise and learn how to create reports:

- set orientation
- sort report data
- add group headers
- use different formats
- display summaries

- alter margins
- align data
- add headers and footers
- display fields in specified order
- label printing

For the exercises in this section you will need the Access databases **vacations** and **names** on the CD-ROM.

> At CLAIT Plus level most output from databases is required as reports. To date output has been directly from tables. Reports provide a more sophisticated and customised layout. Using the **Report Wizard** you can produce reports with different layouts and styles. Groupings and summaries can be included together with headers and footers and other useful items. Reports can be produced from tables or queries.

3.1 Creating a report from a query

Exercise 1

Using the database **vacations**, create and save the following query so that you can produce a report (detailed below) based on this query.

All properties BOOKED(A) 11 or less; PRICE CODE B; DATE BOOKED 20 Sept 2002 or later.

Produce a report in tabular format based on the query above. Sort the report in ascending alphabetical order of **PROPERTY NAME**. Display the fields **PROPERTY NAME**, **CODE**, **LOCATION** and **DATE BOOKED**. Give the report the title **LOW BOOKINGS PERIOD A**.

Method

1. Produce and save the query in the usual way. Ensure that it is in the sort order required for the report (this will save time later). *Note:* You can produce the query with all fields displayed so that you could use it again at a later date if required.

2. From the **Vacations: Database** window, in the **Objects** section, click on: the **Reports** button.

3. Double-click on: **Create report by using wizard** (Figure 9.40).

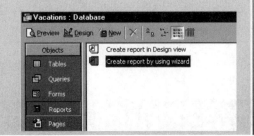

Figure 9.40 Creating a report

4   The **Report Wizard** box appears (Figure 9.41).

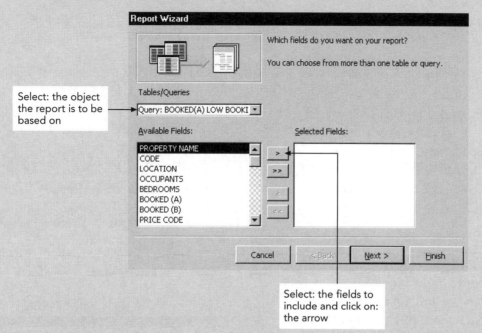

Select: the object the report is to be based on

Select: the fields to include and click on: the arrow

Figure 9.41 Report Wizard box

Creating reports without the aid of the Wizard is very advanced and time-consuming. You can create reports using the **AutoReport** options. This is accessed by clicking on the **New** button in Figure 9.40 and selecting one of the **AutoReport** options. Try these methods when you have time.

5   Choose the name of the object that the report's data is to come from in the **Tables/Queries** box.

6   Choose the fields by clicking on them in turn and then on: the > button, so the **Available Fields** move to the **Selected Fields** box. Select the fields in the order that you want them to appear on the report.

7   Click on: **Next**.

The >> button takes all the fields across at once in the original order. If you make a mistake and select the wrong fields, reverse the procedure by selecting and clicking on: the < or << button as appropriate.

8   The next **Report Wizard** box appears: Do not worry about groupings at this stage, click on: **Next** (Figure 9.42).

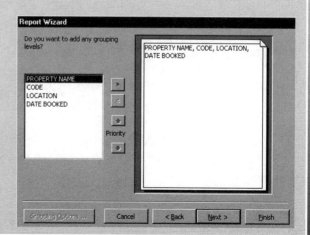

Figure 9.42 Selecting groupings

9 The next **Report Wizard** box appears (Figure 9.43). We have been asked to sort in order of **PROPERTY NAME**. This has been done in the query so will still be sorted in the report. If you choose to sort in the report, the sorted field automatically becomes the first field to be displayed on the report, so it would need to be moved at a later date. This is quite time-consuming to do so it is always best to remember to carry out the sort in the query. Click on: **Next**.

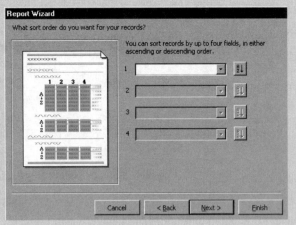

Figure 9.43 Selecting sort order

10 The next **Report Wizard** box appears (Figure 9.44). You have been asked to present the report in tabular format so ensure **Layout** is **Tabular**. Use your discretion for the best layout orientation. If a report is going to show numerous fields it will be wide; therefore it is best suited to a landscape display. Ensure the **Adjust the Field widths** box is ticked.

Ensure **Tabular** is chosen

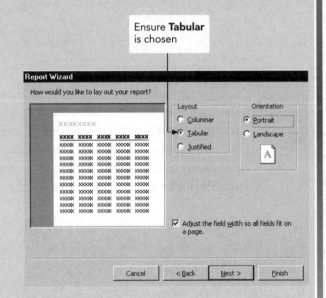

Figure 9.44 Choosing Layout and Orientation

11 Click on: **Next**.

12 The next **Report Wizard** box appears (Figure 9.45). Experiment with the styles. Each time you choose a style, example reports are displayed in the left box. **Corporate** or **Compact** are good styles to choose (for CLAIT Plus) because their layout is compact and the data will usually fit on one page.

13 Click on: **Next**.

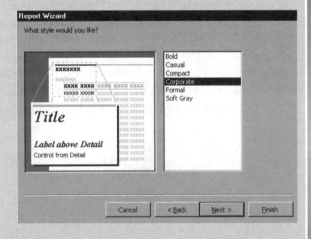

Figure 9.45 Choosing a style

14 The next **Report Wizard** appears (Figure 9.46). Key in the report title: **LOW BOOKINGS PERIOD A**. Ensure that the **Preview the report** button is selected.

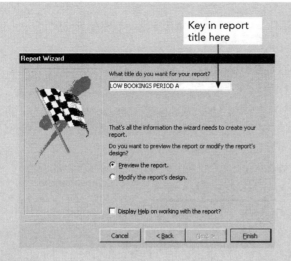

Key in report title here

Report Wizard

What title do you want for your report?

LOW BOOKINGS PERIOD A

That's all the information the wizard needs to create your report.

Do you want to preview the report or modify the report's design?

◉ Preview the report.

○ Modify the report's design.

☐ Display Help on working with the report?

Cancel   < Back   Next >   Finish

Figure 9.46 Adding a title

 The title may scroll out of view as you type. Do not worry. Always choose a descriptive title for you report. This will become the report name when it saves automatically.

15 Click on: **Finish**.

16 Check the report (zoom in and out by clicking the mouse over it) to make sure that all details are displayed in full. Access has a habit of cutting off the edges of some of the longer entries! This will not always happen.

If it does, remedy it by:

1 Proofreading and noting down where the problems are. (You may find it easier to work with a printed report at this stage. See Section 3.2 for instructions on printing reports.) In this example the report is OK as it is, but for practice the instructions below will demonstrate how to widen the **DATE BOOKED** heading.

2 With the **Report Preview** on screen, click on: the ![icon] **View** button.

3 **Report Design View** will now be displayed (Figure 9.47). The report is divided into panes.

Page Header pane: This sets out the field headings (in text boxes) as they will appear on the report

Report Header pane

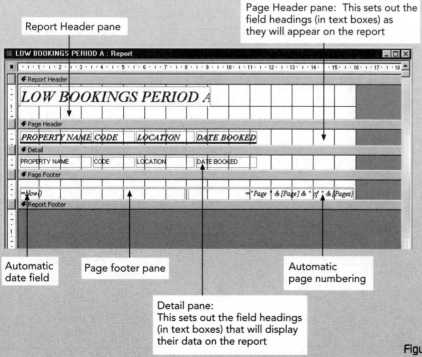

Automatic date field

Page footer pane

Automatic page numbering

Detail pane: This sets out the field headings (in text boxes) that will display their data on the report

Figure 9.47 Report Design View

4 Using the scroll bars, ensure that the item you want to alter is in view. In this case it should already be visible.

5 Click on: the box to select it, ie the **DATE BOOKED** heading in the **Header** pane. Drag the handle to the right to widen the box (Figure 9.48). (If you are altering an item in the Detail pane because an entry in that field does not fit, you will have to make a guess as to how wide to make it since the detail does not appear in **Report Design** view.)

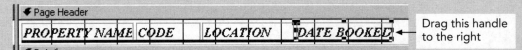

Figure 9.48 Widening the DATE BOOKED heading

6 Click on: the **View** button (this has now changed to a **Print Preview** icon) to return to **Report Preview**.

7 From the **File** menu, select: **Save**, to save the report design. (This is necessary even if your report is still not perfect because failure to save at this point will result in losing the changes that you have already made.)

8 Check the **Report Preview** and continue to fine tune and save the design as above until you are happy with it.

You may need to use the scroll bars to view different parts of the report, especially if it is in landscape display.

You can widen and narrow any of the items in **Design View** using the method above. You can move an item as follows:

1 Click on the item to select it.

2 Hover the mouse over the bottom of the selected item; the pointer turns into an open hand.

3 Drag the item to the required location.

When moving a field heading, you will need to move the detail so that it is still aligned with the heading.

- Select multiple items by holding down the **Shift** key when selecting.
- Right-click over selected item(s) to select from pop-up menu options.
- Instead of/as well as altering boxes to fit contents, you can change font/font size for the whole report.
- Be warned that perfecting reports can be a time-consuming and frustrating business.

If you have forgotten to sort as requested, you can do it in **Report Design View** using the ▓ **Sorting and Grouping** button.

3.2 Printing a report

Exercise 2

Print the report.

Method

From the **File** menu, select: **Print**, then click on: **OK** *or* click on: the **Print** button.

3.3 Changing margins

Exercise 3

Load the report that you have just created and change the margins to 20 mm on each side (Left and Right).

Method

1   With the report displayed, from the **File** menu, select: **Page Setup**.

2   The **Page Setup** dialogue box is displayed.

3   With the **Margins** tab selected, key in the new values in the **Margins** section.

4   Click on: **OK**.

Note: You can also change page orientation in this dialogue box.

3.4 Adding headers and footers, adding/deleting page numbers, date

Exercise 4

Working with the report created above:

Insert a left-aligned automatic field in the header for today's date.

Do not display page numbers.

Add a right-aligned footer to display your name.

1   Display the report in **Design View**. (Click on: the **View** button.)

2   The **Report Wizard** automatically generates today's date and page numbers and places them in the footer (Figure 9.49) so you are able to alter these to display/not display as requested.

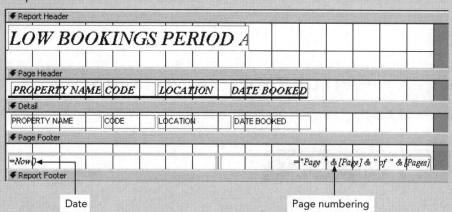

Figure 9.49 Date and page numbering

3   Move the report title in the report header down (by selecting and dragging it) to make room for the date.

4   Select the date and drag it to the left side of the **Page Header** pane above the title. (You can align it within its box using the toolbar buttons when this is requested.)

5   In the **Page Footer** pane, click on the page numbering box and press: **Delete**.

6   Click on: the [Aa] **Label** button on the **Toolbox**. (If the **Toolbox** is not displayed, display it using the **View** menu, **Toolbox**.)

7   Drag out a box on the right side of the footer section below the grey line.

8   Key your name in the box. Align using the toolbar buttons.

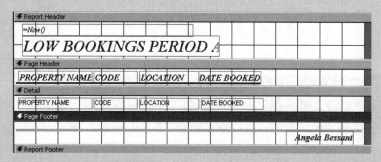

Figure 9.50 Report design with custom header and footer items

9   Review the report in **Report Preview** to check the layout.

Note: Always ensure that data is still displayed in full. In CLAIT Plus you will be penalised if data is truncated.

10 Save the changes when you are satisfied with the results.

11 Print the report.

 You can also add page numbers and date using the **Insert** menu.

Exercise 5

Create a report entitled **BOOKINGS PER LOCATION** for agent **PAUL**. Do not include locations **RIVERS** or **SEA**.

Group the report by **LOCATION**.

Display the totals in **BOOKED(A)** per location. Insert the description **Total number of days** next to the total figures.

Show the Average (in integer format) in **BOOKED(B)** per location. Insert the description **Average number of days** next to the average figures.

Display the field headings **LOCATION**, **PROPERTY NAME**, **BOOKED(A)** and **BOOKED(B)**.

Sort in alphabetical order of **PROPERTY NAME**.

Method

1   Create and save the query that the report is to be based on.

2   Produce the report using the **Report Wizard**, selecting grouping by **LOCATION** (Figure 9.51). Click on: **Next**.

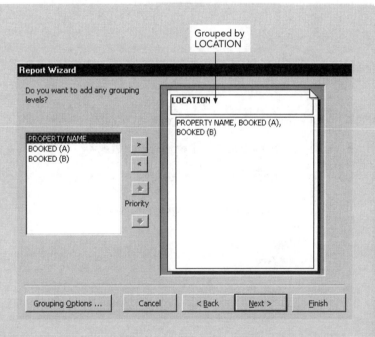

Figure 9.51 Selecting grouping levels

3   Click on: the **Summary Options** button (Figure 9.52).

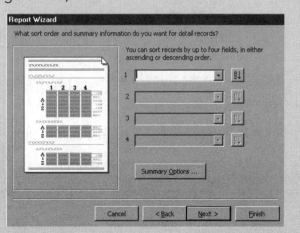

Figure 9.52 Adding summary options

4 The **Summary Options** dialogue box is displayed (Figure 9.53).

5 Click in: the **Sum** box for **BOOKED(A)** and the **Avg** box for **BOOKED(B)**.

6 In the **Show** section, ensure **Detail and Summary** is selected. This option displays the records as well as the results of the calculations.

7 Click on: **OK**.

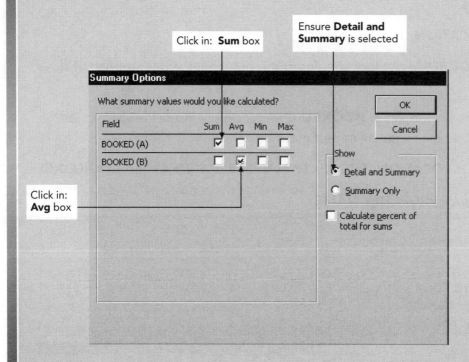

Figure 9.53 Selecting options

8 Continue to create the report in the normal way.

9 Check the report in **Report Preview**.

10 You will notice that the totals and text appear (Figure 9.54) on the report.

Figure 9.54 Summaries in Report Preview

11 Change to **Report Design View** and delete any unwanted content, eg the **Summary for...** text box and the **Grand Total** text and number boxes. (You will need to scroll down to see these in the **Report Footer** pane.)

12 Click in the **Sum** box and key in the requested text. Position as requested.

13 Click in the **Avg** box and key in the requested text. Position as requested.

14 To display the Avg figures as integers:

    a Right-click in the **Avg** figure box.

    b Select: **Properties** from the pop-up menu (Figure 9.55).

Figure 9.55 Selecting Properties

c In the **Text Box**, with the **Format** tab selected, select: **Format: Fixed** and **Decimal Places: 0** (Figure 9.56).

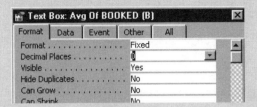

Figure 9.56 Setting Format/decimal places

d Click on: the **Close** button.

15 Insert a text box containing your name, right aligned, in the **Report Header** section.

16 Save and print the report.

17 Close the database.

When formatting numbers with decimal places, **Fixed** is a good format to use because it will display any trailing zeros.

Always check that you have completed everything asked. This could include some of the following: Have you grouped correctly? Is the report showing the correct records as specified? Are the fields in the correct order? Are the summaries correct and formatted as requested? Is the report in the correct sort order? Sometimes when grouping it will not keep its original sort order. You may find it easier to sort in the Wizard and then realign in Report Design View.

3.6 Creating labels

Exercise 6

Using the Access database **names**, create labels for the delegates to display information as follows:

FIRST NAME   **LAST NAME** (on one line)
LOCATION   **EXPERTISE**   (on one line)

Do not include field names on labels.

Sort the labels into alphabetical order of **LAST NAME** and print.

1 Open the database **names**.

2 In the **Names: Database** window, in the **Objects** section, click on: the **Reports** button.

3 Click on: the **New** button.

4 The **New Report** box is displayed (Figure 9.57).

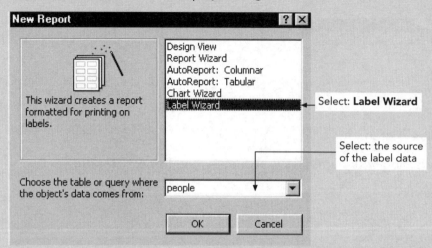

Figure 9.57 Creating labels

5 Select: **Label Wizard** and the table that the labels are derived from, ie people.

6 Click on: **OK**.

7 The next **Label Wizard** dialogue box is displayed (Figure 9.58).

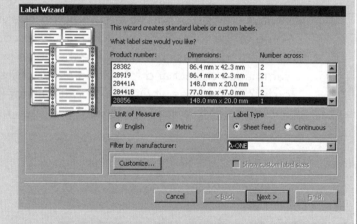

Figure 9.58 Selecting label type

8 Make selections as appropriate to the type of labels you are using (ask your tutor, or 28850 is a good choice as it fits on an A4 page).

9 Click on: **Next**.

10 The next **Label Wizard** dialogue box is displayed (Figure 9.59).

11 Make any formatting selections you want.

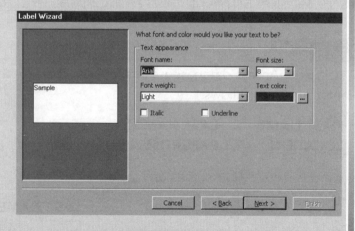

Figure 9.59 Selecting font and colours

12 Click on: **Next**.

13 The next **Label Wizard** dialogue box is displayed (Figure 9.60).

14 Add the label content by selecting a field and clicking on the arrow. Leave a space between fields. Move to the next row by pressing: **Enter** or by clicking the cursor on it.

15 Click on: **Next**.

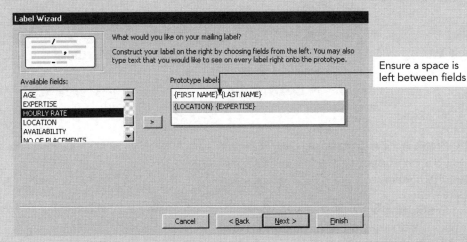

Figure 9.60 Adding content to labels

16 The next **Label Wizard** dialogue box is displayed (Figure 9.61).

17 Select the sort order.

18 Click on: **Next**.

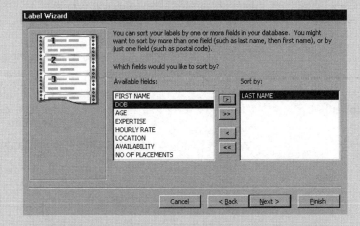

Figure 9.61 Sorting

19 The next **Label Wizard** dialogue box is displayed (Figure 9.62).

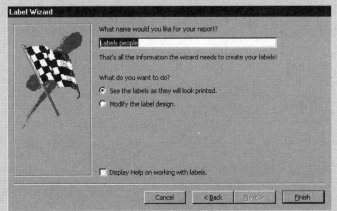

Figure 9.62 Adding the report name

20 Key in the report name.

21 Ensure that **See the labels as they will look printed** is chosen.

22 Click on: **Finish**.

23 Print the labels.

3.7 Close the database and exit Access

Databases quick reference for CLAIT Plus (Access)

Action	Keyboard	Mouse	Right-mouse menu	Menu
Close a database	**Ctrl + W**	Click: the ☒ **Close** icon on the database window		**F**ile, **C**lose
Close the Table window		Click: the ☒ **Close** Window icon		**F**ile, **Save As**
Create a database	Load Access Click: **Blank Access Database, OK** Select: the **location** Enter: the filename Click: Create Click: **Tables** button. Double-click: **Create table in Design view** Enter the field names. These will all appear (by default) as text entries under **Data Type**			
Data type, change	(see separate table for Data Types) Click: in the **Data Type** box next to the field name you wish to change Click: the arrow Click: the Data Type you require eg **Number** Select the Field properties (see separate table in Section 1 for a guide to Field Properties)			
Date format, overall	Start menu, Settings, Control Panel, Regional Settings, English (United Kingdom) (Use **Date** tab to set specific date format for automatic insertions on Headers and Footers)			
Primary key	Not required for CLAIT Plus (When required – select the field for the primary key and click: the 🔑 **Primary Key** button) Close the Table window by clicking: the ☒ **Close** button of that window Save the table design			
Enter data	In the Database window, double-click: the table name Enter the data required in the correct fields. Widen the field columns as necessary. Close the Table window as before. The data is saved automatically.			
Edit data	Open the table (if it is not already open)			
	Click: in the entry you want to edit Delete/overwrite the old data Key in the new data			
Field, add	In Design View: Click in the field below where you want to insert a new field			
		Click: the 🖳 **Insert Rows** button	**Insert Rows**	**I**nsert, **R**ows
	Add the field details. Re-save the table design			
Field, delete	In Table Design View Select the field to be deleted by clicking to the left of it			
	Delete	Click: the 🖳 **Delete Rows** button	**Delete Rows**	**E**dit, **Delete Rows**
	Click: **Yes**			
Find a record	With the Table displayed, position the cursor in the field you want to search			
	Ctrl + F	Click: the 🔍 **Find** button		**E**dit, **F**ind
	In the **Find What** box, key in what you want to find Click: **Find Next** Continue until all records have been found Note: You may need to choose a field that has a unique entry to ensure you find the correct record			

Action	Keyboard	Mouse	Right-mouse menu	Menu
Headers and footers in reports	From the **Toolbox**, select: **Label** In the Report header/footer section, click and drag out a box Key in your text			
Import generic file (CSV)	Load Access Select: **Blank Access database** Select: a location and key in filename Click on: **Create** In the database window within Access, click on: the **New** button Click on: **Import Table**, then on: **OK** Select: location of the file (change **Files of type** to **Text Files**) Click on: **Import** Import **Text Wizard** guides you through			
Labels, create	From the database window, within Access, click on: **Reports** Click on: the **New** button Select: **Label Wizard**			
delete	Set the **Indexed** field property to **No**			
Load Access	In the Windows 98 desktop			
		Double-click: the **Microsoft Access** shortcut icon		**Start**, **Programs**, **Microsoft Access**
Margins, alter				**File**, **Page Setup**, **Margins** tab
Open a table	In the Database window, make sure the **Tables** button is selected			
In Datasheet view		Double-click: the table name Change to Design view by clicking: the 🔽 **View** button		
In Design view		Click: the table name Click: the 🔽 Design **Design** button		
Print	Select the object you want to print			
	Ctrl + P			**File**, **Print**
	Make the necessary selections Choose Setup if you want to print Landscape Make the necessary selections from the **Setup** dialogue box Click: **OK, OK**			
Quick print		Click: the 🖨 **Print** button Access will automatically print the whole object		
Record, add		Click: the ▶* **New Record** button or Click: in the blank cell immediately after the last record	(Right-click to the left of any record) **New Record**	**Insert**, **New Record**
Record, delete	Select the record by clicking to the left of the first field of that record			
	Click: the ✗ **Delete Record** button	**Delete Record**	**Edit, Delete Record**	**Delete**
	Click: **Yes** to save the change			

Action	Keyboard	Mouse	Right-mouse menu	Menu
Replace field entries	**Ctrl + H**			**E**dit, **R**eplace
Report, create	Ensure the Database window is displayed and that the **Reports** button is selected Double-click: **Create report by using wizard** In the Tables/Queries box, select: the name of the object – eg query, table – that the report is to be generated from Click: **Next** Select the fields to include in the report using the ⏩ or ▶ buttons Click: **Next** (If you want to group the report – select the field(s) you want to group by here) Click: **Next** Sorting (Preferably ensure that the original object is sorted. However, if you want to change the sort order here select the field you want to sort by. Note: this could rearrange field positions in the final report) Click: **Summary Options** to include calculation results on the report Click: **Next** Select Layout Select the orientation you want – **Landscape** or **Portrait** Click: **Next** Select a style Click: **Next** Key in: the report title Click: **Finish**			
Sort records (quick sort)	Open the Table if it is not already open. Select the field that you want to sort by clicking on the Field Name at the top of the field column			
ascending order		Click: the 🔼 **Sort Ascending** button	**Sort A**scending	
descending order		Click the 🔽 **Sort Descending** button	**Sort De**scending	
Query, create in Design view	In the Database window ensure the **Queries** button is selected Double-click: **Create query in Design view** Select object query is based on Click: **Add, Close** The fields of the table are now displayed in a list box in the Query window Place the fields that you want to see in your query in the field row of the query grid by double-clicking or dragging them Note: Place the fields in the order that you want them to appear Then see *Specify Criteria*			
Query, calculations in fields	*Create a new field that calculates using other fields* With the query in Design view, key in a new field name in the field row Key in a colon then the calculation from other fields, eg NO IN STOCK: [NUMBER]-[NO SOLD] *Calculations within a field* In the query design grid, right-click on the field name Select: **Totals** The **Totals** row is displayed Click on: **Group By** down arrow Select calculation type required			
Query, create a simple query using the wizard	In the database window, ensure the **Queries** button is selected Click: **Create query by using Wizard** Follow the wizard's instructions			

Action	Keyboard	Mouse	Right-mouse menu	Menu
Query, sort	Click: in the **Sort** box of the appropriate field Click: the arrow Select: **Ascending** or **Descending**			
Specify criteria	Use the **Criteria** row in the grid to specify the conditions in a specific field – eg **RED** in the **Colour** field. (See Section 2.2)			
Print specific fields	Use the **Show** row in the grid to choose whether or not to display a particular field in the query A tick in the **Show** box means that the field will show, no tick means that it will not show Click to toggle between them.			
Save a query	**Ctrl + S**	Click: the 🖫 **Save** button		**File, Save as**
	To see the results of your query			
		Change to Datasheet view or Click: the ❗ **Run** button		**Query, Run**

Hints and tips

- *Important:* Always close the database file properly so that data is saved securely.
- Ensure that all data and field headings are displayed in full.
- Check that all data is sorted as requested.
- Check that reports show the data requested and are in the correct format.
- Check that summaries are displayed correctly when requested.
- Always enter and amend records carefully and proofread to minimise mistakes.

Databases: sample full practice assignment

Task 1

Scenario

You work for a voluntary organisation. The organisation has recently been arranging fund-raising marathons. You need to create a database and produce a printout of the details of sponsorship monies received so far from these events. You also need to produce labels for the runners to wear at a presentation evening. You will need application software that allows you to complete the task.

1   Open a database software application and create a new database using the following field headings. You should use field types (eg text, numeric, date) appropriate to the data.

Field heading
RUNNER NUMBER   use an Auto number
SURNAME
FIRST NAME
DOB   Date of birth
MARATHON   Marathon run, use the codes given below
TOTAL   Total sponsorship money, currency, two decimal places
FINISH   Completed the marathon, use a logic field type, ie Yes, No
MILES   Total miles per marathon (use table, integer format)

Marathon codes and miles per marathon

MARATHON	CODE	MILES
MINI	MI	5
SHORT	S	7
MEDIUM	ME	10
LONG	L	20
MEGA	MG	25

Enter only the relevant data for the runners where their sponsorship money has been received.

FIRST NAME	Hywel	SURNAME		Jones	
DATE OF BIRTH	19/6/49	MARATHON	MEDIUM	TOWN	OXFORD
SPONSORS	35	TOTAL		524.45	
FINISH	Yes	RECEIVED		Yes	

FIRST NAME	Angharad	SURNAME		Evans	
DATE OF BIRTH	16/3/59	MARATHON	SHORT	TOWN	CARDIFF
SPONSORS	10	TOTAL		25.75	
FINISH	No	RECEIVED		Yes	

FIRST NAME	Lois	SURNAME		Llewelyn	
DATE OF BIRTH	2/1/89	MARATHON	LONG	TOWN	EDINBURGH
SPONSORS	42	TOTAL		241.50	
FINISH	Yes	RECEIVED		No	

FIRST NAME	Richard	SURNAME		Benson	
DATE OF BIRTH	5/5/92	MARATHON	MEDIUM	TOWN	BRIGHTON
SPONSORS	15	TOTAL		55.00	
FINISH	Yes	RECEIVED		Yes	

FIRST NAME	Emily	SURNAME		Quinn	
DATE OF BIRTH	2/10/89	MARATHON	MEGA	TOWN	CARLISLE
SPONSORS	19	TOTAL		256.25	
FINISH	No	RECEIVED		No	

FIRST NAME	Andy	SURNAME		Davies	
DATE OF BIRTH	12/7/85	MARATHON	LONG	TOWN	BEDFORD
SPONSORS	10	TOTAL		160.20	
FINISH	Yes	RECEIVED		Yes	

FIRST NAME	Paul	SURNAME		Jones	
DATE OF BIRTH	2/7/55	MARATHON	MEDIUM	TOWN	YEOVIL
SPONSORS	29	TOTAL		421.98	
FINISH	No	RECEIVED		Yes	

FIRST NAME	Mark	SURNAME		Collins	
DATE OF BIRTH	4/10/88	MARATHON	MINI	TOWN	HULL
SPONSORS	10	TOTAL		25.50	
FINISH	Yes	RECEIVED		No	

FIRST NAME	Sharlene	SURNAME		Wells	
DATE OF BIRTH	27/2/95	MARATHON	MINI	TOWN	BATH
SPONSORS	20	TOTAL		21.00	
FINISH	No	RECEIVED		Yes	

FIRST NAME	Vicki	**SURNAME**		Logan	
DATE OF BIRTH	30/9/78	**MARATHON**	MEGA	**TOWN**	LONDON
SPONSORS	50	**TOTAL**		624.87	
FINISH	No	**RECEIVED**		Yes	

FIRST NAME	Jay	**SURNAME**		Kwan	
DATE OF BIRTH	29/3/42	**MARATHON**	SHORT	**TOWN**	LONDON
SPONSORS	43	**TOTAL**		678.10	
FINISH	Yes	**RECEIVED**		Yes	

FIRST NAME	Lorna	**SURNAME**		Campbell	
DATE OF BIRTH	18/6/77	**MARATHON**	MEDIUM	**TOWN**	OXFORD
SPONSORS	25	**TOTAL**		120.50	
FINISH	Yes	**RECEIVED**		Yes	

FIRST NAME	Ally	**SURNAME**		McDonald	
DATE OF BIRTH	21/12/88	**MARATHON**	SHORT	**TOWN**	LEEDS
SPONSORS	12	**TOTAL**		29.70	
FINISH	No	**RECEIVED**		Yes	

2   Save the database.

3   Produce a report in tabular format **SPONSORSHIP MONIES RECEIVED**.

Sort the data into ascending order of **SURNAME**.

Display all fields.

Ensure that the fields are presented in the field order given in step 1 and that all data is displayed in full.

Create a right-aligned header to display your name. Under your name, insert a right-aligned automatic field in the header for today's date.

Print the report in landscape orientation.

4   You need to add another field to display the town of each runner. You will need to update the database accordingly.

Add the field **TOWN** to the database. Use the RUNNER LIST FORMS for the data you need for the new field.

5   The runners require name labels to wear for a presentation evening. Create labels to display the information from the following fields:

SURNAME	**FIRST NAME** (on one line)
MARATHON	**TOWN** (on one line)

Note: Do not include field names on labels.

Sort the labels into alphabetical order of **FIRST NAME** and print labels for those whose sponsorship money has been received.

Task 2

You work as an Administrator at the central office for a group of small garden centres. One of your responsibilities is to maintain a database of plants in each of the centres and answer any enquiries.

(For information only, coding is A = Annual, BI = Biennial, HP = Hardy perennial, B = Bulbous, ES = Evergreen shrub, DS = Deciduous shrub, T = Tree, C = Conifer and CS = Climbing shrub.)

You will need the file **plants** for this task.

1   Import the datafile **plants** and save it in your software's normal file type. Save the database table as **centres**. Ensure that all information is fully visible.

2   Since the height is stated on the plant labels, it has been decided that the **HEIGHT** field is not required on the database. Remove the **HEIGHT** field from the database.

3   Some plants have arrived that are not already listed on the database so they need to be added. They are all of type **HP** (hardy perennials) and all need to be sited in **FULL SUN**. The delivery is 50 of each type. Update the database accordingly using the information below:

CENTRE	PLANT	COLOUR	NEXT DELIVERY
ACRES	AQUILEGIA	BLUE	30 AUGUST 2002
JILLY	SALVIA	VIOLET	30 AUGUST 2002
ACRES	ASTER	PINK	26 AUGUST 2002

4   In the database **PARTIAL SUN** should have been entered as **PARTIAL SHADE**. Change **PARTIAL SUN** to **PARTIAL SHADE** throughout.

5   At the **DANIELS** centre the **NO IN STOCK** of the plant **PHLOX** is **30 more** than showing on the database. Amend the details accordingly.

6   Some entries have been entered in error. Delete their records from the database. They are as follows:

ACRES centre the plants **ANEMONE** and **SEDUM**.

7   A delivery has arrived at the **DANIELS** centre. It is a delivery of **10 % HOSTAS** (TYPE **HP**). Update this record.

8   You need to produce a printout of all plants that need to be sited in the **SHADE** with a delivery **after the end of July 2002**. Include those that need **PARTIAL SHADE**. Print in chronological order of **NEXT DELIVERY** date. Print the query on one page in tabular format in portrait orientation. Ensure that all field headings and records are displayed in full. Ensure your name is clearly displayed on the printout.

9   You need to produce a list showing the number available at each centre for each **PLANT**. You will need to add a new field titled **NEW NO IN STOCK** that calculates the difference between the **NO IN STOCK** and the **NO SOLD** (NO IN STOCK minus NO SOLD).

Find the plants with **50 or more** in the **NEW IN STOCK** field of the type **HP** (hardy perennials). Use the results to produce a columnar report sorted by centre.

Display the following fields:

CENTRE, PLANT, NEW NO IN STOCK

Give the report the title:

UPDATED STOCK (HARDY PERENNIALS 50 OR MORE)

Print the report in portrait orientation. Ensure your name is clearly displayed on the printout.

10 You have been contacted to find out the number of PURPLE and RED plants sold at each centre. Find all these plants.

Use the results to produce a report grouped by **CENTRE**, sorted in alphabetical order of **PLANT**.

Display the total **NO SOLD** at each centre and the average of the **NO IN STOCK** (*not* **NEW NO IN STOCK**). Insert the description **Total number sold** alongside the total figure, and insert the description **Average number in stock** alongside the average figure. Display the totals in integer format and average figures to one decimal place.

Display the fields in the order specified:

CENTRE, PLANT, COLOUR, NO SOLD, NO IN STOCK

Give the report the title:

PURPLE AND RED PLANTS

Print the report in portrait orientation with a page number and date. Ensure that your name is clearly displayed on the printout.

Ensure that all field headings and records and your name are fully visible on the printout.

Appendix

Copying a file from the CD-ROM

1. Press the button on the CD-ROM drive to access the CD tray.

2. Place the CD in the tray with the label uppermost (ie showing).

3. Push the tray in to close it.

4. On the Windows 98 desktop, from the **Start** menu, select: **Run.** The **Run** dialogue box is displayed.

5. In the **Open** box, key in the name of the CD drive. *Note:* This is usually Drive D so key in **D:**

6. Click on: **OK.**

7. The contents of the CD-ROM are displayed.

8. Locate the relevant file. (If the file is contained in a folder, you will need to open the folder by double-clicking on it to display the filename.) See below if you want to select multiple files or the entire contents of the CD-ROM.

9. Right-click on the file.

10. Select: **Copy** from the pop-up menu.

11. Click on the down arrow of the Address box and click on the destination location.

12. Right-click in a white space in the destination window.

13. Select: **Paste** from the pop-up menu.

Copying more than one file from the CD-ROM

Follow the steps above except:

At step 8, select multiple files by holding down the **Shift** key (selects adjacent files) or the **Ctrl** key (selects non-adjacent files).

At step 9, right-click on the selection.

Copying entire contents

Follow the steps above except:

At step 8, from the **Edit** menu, select: **Select All.**

At step 9, right-click on the selection.

Adding your name and details to your documents

For assessment purposes, it is essential that your name, centre number, the date and the step number appear on your printouts. If you are working towards the qualifications, it is a good idea to get into the habit of labelling your printouts.

Most assignments ask you to do this as part of the tasks. In Access there is no obvious way to add your details to an Access printout on tables, queries or reports. The date will appear automatically on every printout (check that your computer's date is correctly set). You could add your initials to the end of every object that you create, eg if you are saving a query, save as 'price order sjm'. This will enable you to recognise your printout in a group situation. You would then need to write your name in full and the step no. directly onto your printout in pen.

Formatting a floppy disk

Most new floppy disks are already formatted for use on your computer. If not, you will need to format them before use. Formatting prepares the disk so that it is recognised by your computer and can quickly and easily store and access information on it. A floppy disk only needs to be formatted once. Formatting a disk will erase any information stored on that disk.

Formatting a disk in Drive A:

1   Load **Windows Explorer.**

2   Insert the disk into Drive A:

3   Select: $3^{1}/_{2}$ **Floppy (A:).**

4   Right-click: a menu appears (see below).

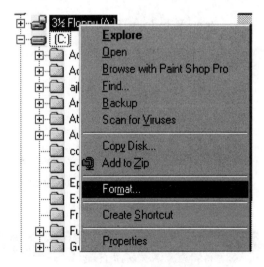

Formatting a disk

5   Click on: **Format.** The Format dialogue box appears.

6   Check the capacity of your disk:

High density – 1.44 Mb
Double density – 720 kb
Choose accordingly.
Note: High-density disks have two holes at the bottom.

7   Click on: the **Full** button.

8   Click on: **Start.**

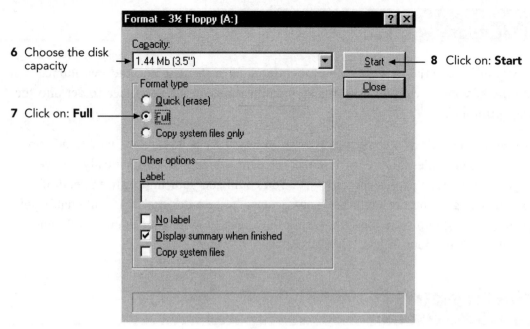

6 Choose the disk capacity

7 Click on: **Full**

8 Click on: **Start**

Format dialogue box

Backing up a disk

Backing up a disk means producing an exact copy of the contents of a disk. This is done as a security measure in case anything happens to the original disk.

To produce a backup of a floppy disk:

1   Open **Windows Explorer.**

2   Insert the disk to backup in Drive A.

3   Select: $3^1/_2$ **Floppy (A:).**

4   Right-click: a menu appears.

5   Click on: **Copy Disk.**

6   Follow the instructions on screen.

Checking spelling and grammar

There are many options available. Throughout the book, I have chosen to check spelling only (not spelling and grammar). I have also chosen not to check on an ongoing basis but after I have keyed in the entire document.

The above settings work well with my students. Should you wish to choose other options:

From the **Tools** menu, select: **Options.** Click on: the **Spelling & Grammar** tab. Select your preferences and click on: **OK.**

Changing the unit of measure

To change the unit of measure from inches to centimetres or vice versa:

1   From the **Tools** menu, select: **Options**, and then click: the **General** tab.

2   In the **Measurement units** box, click: the down arrow and then the option you want.

3   Click on: **OK**.

Autoformatting

By default Word will automatically format some input, eg lists, email addresses and so on. To turn autoformatting off:

1   From the **Format** menu, select: **AutoFormat**. The AutoFormat dialogue box is displayed.

2   Click on: **Options**. The AutoCorrect dialogue box is displayed.

3   Click on the tabs and customise settings you require.

4   Click on: **OK**, then on: **Close**.

Office Assistant

To hide the Office Assistant:

Right-click: over the Office assistant, select: **Options** and set them to your preferences, click on: **OK**.

To turn the Office Assistant on:

From the **Help** menu, select: **Show the Office Assistant**.

File maintenance within programs

In addition to using Explorer, you can carry out file maintenance within programs as follows. When opening or saving a file, you are able to gain access to your files within the window (shown below). This is common to all programs. This window was opened in Word and displays only Word documents (by default). If you want to see documents saved in other formats, click: the down arrow next to **Files of type** and make your selection.

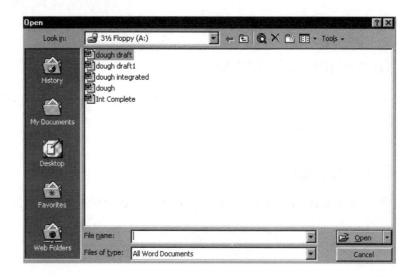

The main shortcut buttons that will be useful for New CLAIT and CLAIT Plus are shown below. Using these will enable you to find out details of your files.

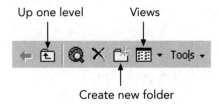

Clicking on the down arrow next to the **Views** button produces a menu where you can select what detail you want to see in the **Open** window. The choices are: List (the default), Details, Properties and Preview. The preview option is especially useful for integration assignments.

Right-clicking on a file/folder will bring up the pop-up menu shown. This allows you to carry out any of the tasks on the menu.

A guide to document layout

When you have edited text or moved text within an exercise, remember adjustment of line spacing is often necessary. When proofreading pay particular attention to line spacing between paragraphs.

When inserting a sentence within a paragraph, make sure the spacing after any punctuation marks remains consistent. Make the necessary adjustments if required.

Use the spellchecker but do realise its limitations.

Line spacing between paragraphs

Press: the **Enter** key twice to leave one clear line space between paragraphs.

Underlining/underscoring

Underlining should not extend beyond the word. For example:

<u>word</u> is correct   <u>word </u> is incorrect

Punctuation

Be consistent with your spacing after punctuation marks. Use the following as a guide:

Punctuation	Mark	Number of spaces before/after
Comma	,	No space before, 1 space after
Semicolon	;	No space before, 1 space after
Colon	:	No space before, 1 or 2 spaces after
Full stop	.	No space before, 1 or 2 spaces after
Exclamation mark	!	No space before, 1 or 2 spaces after
Question mark	?	No space before, 1 or 2 spaces after

Hyphen

No space is left before or after a hyphen, eg dry-clean.

Dash

One space precedes and follows a dash – never place a dash at the left-hand margin when it is in the middle of a word or a sentence, always place it at the end of the previous line.

Brackets

No spaces are left between brackets and the word enclosed within them. For example (solely for the purposes of assignments).

Views in Word

Normal View: This is the default and recommended view for CLAIT exercises. It allows for quick and easy text editing.

Print Layout View: This view allows you to see how objects will be positioned on the printed page. It shows margins, headers and footers and graphics. This is essential for the integrated assignments for CLAIT Plus.

Using indentation and tabs using the ruler

Indentation

Select the text you want to indent.

Drag the respective markers (shown below) on the ruler to the location you want.

First line indent

Left indent

Right indent

First line indents and hanging paragraphs using the Format menu

1 Select the text.

2 From the **Format** menu, select: **Paragraph**.

3 In the **Paragraph** dialogue box, ensure the **Indents and Spacing** tab is selected.

4 From the **Special** box, click on: the down arrow and select: **Hanging** or **First line**, as appropriate.

5 Check the **Preview** box below to see what the text will look like.

6 Click on: **OK**.

Tabs

Tabs are used to line up columns and Word offers four types of tab:

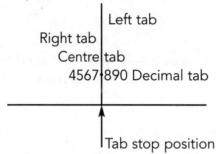

By default, tabs are set every 1.27 cm ($^1/_2$") from the left margin. When a new tab is set, Word clears any default tabs set to the left of the new tab stop. The type of tab stop can be chosen by clicking on the tab button at the left-hand edge of the ruler.

Tab button: Click to change between tab types ⟶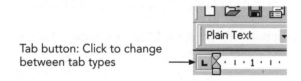

L Left tab

⅃ Right tab

⊥ Centre tab

⊥. Decimal tab

Note: In Office 2000, the following tabs:

I Bar tab. This draws a vertical line on a document.

▽ First line indent. This sets the first line of paragraphs.

⊔ Hanging indent. This defines the left margin of every line but the first line in a paragraph.